The Coloniality of Asylum

New Politics of Autonomy

Series Editors: Saul Newman and Martina Tazzioli

In recent years, we have witnessed an unprecedented emergence of new forms of radical politics—from Tahrir Square, Gezi Park and the global Occupy movement, to Wikileaks and hacktivism. What is striking about such movements is their rejection of leadership structures and the absence of political demands and agendas. Instead, their originality lies in the autonomous forms of political life they engender.

The *New Politics of Autonomy* book series is an attempt to make sense of this new terrain of anti-political politics, and to develop an alternative conceptual and theoretical arsenal for thinking the politics of autonomy. The series investigates political, economic and ethical questions raised by this new paradigm of autonomy. It brings together authors and researchers who are engaged, in various ways, with understanding contemporary radical political movements and who approach the theme of autonomy from different perspectives: political theory, philosophy, ethics, literature and art, psychoanalytic theory, political economy, and political history.

Titles in the Series

Spaces of Governmentality: Autonomous Migration and the Arab Uprisings
Martina Tazzioli

The Composition of Movements to Come: Aesthetics and Cultural Labour After the Avant-Garde
Stevphen Shukaitis

Foucault and the Making of Subjects
Edited by Laura Cremonesi, Orazio Irrera, Daniele Lorenzini and Martina Tazzioli

Italian Critical Thought: Genealogies and Categories
Edited by Dario Gentili, Elettra Stimilli and Glenda Garelli

In the Marxian Workshops: Producing Subjects
Sandro Mezzadra

Anarchisms, Postanarchisms and Ethics
Benjamin Franks

The Urban Enigma: Time, Autonomy, and Postcolonial Transformations in Latin America
Simone Vegliò

The Arab Spring Between Transformation and Capture: Autonomy, Media and Mobility in Tunisia
Oana Pârvan

The Coloniality of Asylum: Mobility, Autonomy and Solidarity in the Wake of Europe's Refugee Crisis
Fiorenza Picozza

The Coloniality of Asylum

Mobility, Autonomy and Solidarity in the Wake of Europe's Refugee Crisis

Fiorenza Picozza

ROWMAN & LITTLEFIELD
Lanham • Boulder • New York • London

Published by Rowman & Littlefield
An imprint of The Rowman & Littlefield Publishing Group, Inc.
4501 Forbes Boulevard, Suite 200, Lanham, Maryland 20706
www.rowman.com

Copyright © 2021 by Fiorenza Picozza

British Library Cataloguing in Publication Information Available

Library of Congress Cataloging-in-Publication Data

Library of Congress Control Number: 2020950801

ISBN: 978-1-5381-5009-2 (cloth)
ISBN: 978-1-5381-5011-5 (pbk)
ISBN: 978-1-5381-5010-8 (electronic)

Content

Acknowledgements

This book is a testament to a decade of involvement in migrant struggles, in praxis, and thought. It was written in different geographic locations and is woven of uncountable conversations and heated arguments, as well as affection, bitterness, rage, hope and even joy – what Audre Lorde would describe as 'the erotic'. Its second draft was elaborated during the COVID-19 pandemic in Mexico City, an ocean away from my native Italy, and from London and Hamburg – the northernmost ends of the geography of my heart. The predominance of online communication during the pandemic made space for retaking some old connections 'on the other side of the pond' while strengthening new ones, conspiring with a new elective Mexican family. In my darkest moments of that period, I was held by the virtual presence of Palestinian, Afghan, Syrian, Cuban, Mexican, Ethiopian and Iranian friends, who helped me cope with the ruptures, separations, uncertainties and fragilities of my own migration – having they, or their beloved ones, been migrants too. They all deeply suffered from the consequences of global coloniality and the unfairness of border regimes, yet they never derided my more privileged preoccupations. It is to them that this book is dedicated, for these mutual solidarity, complicity and tenderness are the most precious learnings and gifts that I have received from the last decade.

Intellectually, politically and affectively I owe an awful lot to the teachers, guides, comrades and students who have accompanied me in the course of my MA at the School of Oriental and African Studies and PhD at King's College London. Nicholas De Genova was the incredibly thorough and supporting supervisor of the dissertation that provided the foundations for this book. Danae Avgeri and Francesco Bosso were its most attentive readers, as well as dearest partners in crime and levity. Martina Tazzioli is the unwavering bastion that orients many of us, and I owe her the very publication of this book.

My PhD examiners, Shahram Khosravi and Bridget Anderson, allowed me to conclude that chapter of my life in the best possible way, encouraging me to continue writing far beyond what I could have expected. Alongside them, I am deeply grateful to Phil Hubbard, Paru Raman, Sami Everett, Hannah Schling, Simone Vegliò, Adam Elliott Cooper, Elena Fontanari, Bernd Kasparek, Mical Nelken, Gavriel Nelken, Simona Pagano, Maurizio Totaro, Yari Lanci, Samir Harb, Anna Grimaldi, Juan Grigera, Sam McLean and Sam Hayward – all of whom have accompanied me in unique ways through the journey of researching, writing and teaching.

Furthermore, the political and narrative imagination that animates this book was deeply nourished by Habib Zadran, Mahmoud Qudaih, Dagmawi Yimer, Rajaa Shamam, Aischa Abdirihman Dirir, Tanja van de Loo, Amarela Varela, Ángel Martínez 'Filosoflow', Annika Schnitzler, Ernesto Morales Bautista, Gabriel Brito Nunes, Chiara Mammarella, Diego Ferraris, Piero Consentino, Fabián Villegas, Ali Alizadeh and Marco Carsetti.

George Sidaoui drew the wonderful maps that visualise the places and trajectories I narrate and was one of the dearest companions at the time I wrote my thesis. Andrea Contenta read the last draft of this manuscript and thus had to fulfil the troublesome task of cheering me up against my continuous loss of meaning.

My father needs a special mention for convincing me to complete this book when I was only a step away from giving up. To my mum, I owe the scorching fury that animates the text; to my sister, the tenderness to soothe it, as well as the burdens she took to pave a smoother way for my coming into this world. To Carolina Purificati, I am bound through a deep-rooted friendship which keeps renewing itself as the waves roll onto the shore and back. And I thank Alan Moreno for his infinite patience in accompanying me through my shadows and for the bright days in Puebla looking for cave paintings.

To all the people in Hamburg, who in a way or another supported me in the course of fieldwork, I owe more than they could realise and more than I could convey here; this book would not exist without their generosity and companionship. For my London crew, I have infinite gratefulness and love; the years I spent there were among the most beautiful and dreadful experiences of my life and they all helped to enlarge my way of thinking and feeling. To my home – or idea thereof – in Italy, I have returned once more, to absorb and permeate the love of my summer companions while submitting the manuscript. Despite feeling I can never return permanently, it is one of the places that allow me to dream, bloom and feel through my skin the most – even during these dark times.

I haven't named you all, but you know who you are, and there are bits of you scattered throughout these pages.

Villastrada, July 2020

Introduction

Figure 0.1   Main Locations of Interest.

In October 2015, while I was planning to embark on a research project on the fragmented intra-European mobilities of refugees, I travelled to Germany to better grasp the events of 'the long summer of migration' (Kasparek and Speer 2015), which I had been witnessing vicariously from afar, in the media. The period between spring and early winter was marked by an unprecedented and spectacularised debordering and re-bordering of Europe, engendered by massive, unruly refugee movements. About a million people walked to and through Europe, physically and legally claiming the right to enter its territory and seeking asylum, with the material and political support of thousands of European citizens. At the end of my itinerary through several German cities, I arrived in Hamburg to visit Farhad, one of the main interlocutors of my previous research in Rome in 2014 (Picozza 2017a). Born and grown up in Afghanistan, Farhad had already spent several years on the move, crossing and inhabiting diverse locations scattered through Iran, Turkey, Greece, Norway, Italy and France, in the intent of cobbling together pieces of his rights and aspirations. In 2014, while trying to reach London from Calais, he mistakenly hid in a lorry with a different route and ended up in Hamburg, where he eventually found a job at a car dealership and decided to stay. He picked me up on a week evening after his work shift, and we caught up over dinner at an Afghan restaurant on Steindamm – a busy street next to the Central Station dominated by Turkish, Persian and Arab shops and restaurants. Before parting ways, Farhad suggested that I should visit the station on the next day because there were thousands of refugees transiting daily towards Scandinavia and hundreds of volunteers assisting them.

With Merkel's decision to keep the country's borders open both to incoming and transiting refugees, Hamburg Central Station had been radically transformed: every day there were hundreds of women, men, adolescents and children standing along the corridor of the Wandelhalle, the shopping mall above the platforms in the northern side of the station. Many sat on the floor outside the ticket hall, waiting for the next train to board, and the shopkeepers complained about the damage to their business created by the disorderly crowd. Volunteers in fluorescent vests ran up and down the escalators from the Wandelhalle to the platforms and back, picking up arriving refugees and guiding them to a makeshift infodesk, improvised out of a wooden board under the flight of stairs that took to the upper floor. With the aid of a laptop, a map of Scandinavia, one of Europe, and multi-language flyers on the asylum procedure in Germany, Sweden and Norway, they attempted to assess the needs, destinations and legal situations of the people in the queue, but accuracy was a virtually impossible task in the hectic mixture of voices and languages. Afterwards, the refugees were redirected to the ticket hall or the tents temporarily erected on Heidi Kabel Platz, on the eastern exit of the station,

Figure 0.2 Hamburg Central Station. *Source:* Fred Romero License: CC BY 2.0.

where they could get food and hot drinks, attend medical checks and warm up from the piercingly cold air. Passersby would stop by the tents to offer small amounts of money, food, clothing or simply a few hours of their time before or after heading to work. The refugees would try to leave on the same day but, for those who could not, the volunteers arranged temporary accommodation at the Deutsches Schauspielhaus Theatre, just across the street, or at the Central Mosque in the neighbouring St. Georg area; if they decided to stay in Hamburg, volunteers would accompany them to the Harburger Alte Post ZEA, the central registration centre in Harburg, a suburb south of the River Elbe.

The volunteers referred to each other as either 'helpers' or 'translators' – a division of labour premised on an unspoken racialised boundary that divided white Germans from a mixed group of people with so-called migration backgrounds,[1] including nonwhite German citizens, long-term refugee residents, and a conspicuous group of recently arrived refugees who rendered their days meaningful through volunteering at the station while waiting for the processing of their asylum applications. Some among the latter group had literally just arrived and, after having been themselves helped by the volunteers, would immediately return to the station to assist the newcomers. For a few months between summer and autumn 2015, the space of the station stopped being a mere commuting node and transformed into a hub of human connection and sociopolitical engagement.

Figure 0.3   The Central Station Helper Network.

Standing on the platforms of the station, one could observe the waves of a forceful tide renewing itself every hour, washing people in and out of the city of Hamburg, and in and out of the German borders, before the very eyes of the police, who did not intervene in the interactions between volunteers and refugees. It looked like Germany had adopted the same 'tacit alliance' with migrants that had long been deployed by southern European states (Kasparek 2015: 75), namely, by letting them transit through without fingerprinting them or registering their asylum applications.[2] The people in transit were mostly Afghans, Syrians and Iraqis; among them, there were spare groups of Iranians and Eritreans and, seldom, people of other nationalities. Most of them had travelled through the Balkan route, transformed at that time into a semiofficial corridor (Kasparek 2016), and were heading to Scandinavia. A few had landed in southern Italy and successfully crossed the heavily policed borders of Ventimiglia (Tazzioli 2017) or the Brenner Pass (Kasparek and Schmidt-Sembdner 2019). Some had no idea as of where exactly Hamburg was located: they had entered Germany from Austria, but instead wanted to reach Switzerland, France or the UK through Calais. Some spare groups considered Italy instead, as the European north they encountered in Hamburg looked so overcrowded that, in their eyes, it could no longer possibly be a 'safe' destination. In addition, in the chaos of the bus transfers from the southern borders,[3] many of those who had been officially registered never reached the camps to which they had been allocated, and headed to Hamburg in order to reach Scandinavia. At any chance, the refugee newcomers asked the volunteers for information about where it was best to apply for asylum: was Sweden better than Germany? Where was the asylum process faster? Which country was the least racist? Which one promised better job opportunities? Which one did not deport rejected asylum seekers? Such were the questions I heard uncountable times since my first day volunteering at the station as a Persian translator.[4] Rumours circulated about imminent deportations from Germany and, as the camps in Hamburg were full to their capacities, tents had been erected among containers, mostly lacking heating in the already-freezing temperatures. In the chaos of these unruly and unstructured movements, asylum migration seemed indeed to possess a certain 'autonomy', beyond any individual intentionality (De Genova et al. 2018; Papadopoulos et al. 2008).

Standing on the escalator while I guided a group of sixty people to the platforms, a twelve-year-old Afghan boy who was travelling on his own asked me whether I recommended Germany or Sweden. Refraining from giving direct advice on such delicate matters, I asked him if he had any family or language ties that would make one country more suitable than the other; in a rush to board their Lübeck-headed train, the queue pushed us along the platform, and I hastened to warn the boy that if he kept following that group, he would end up in Sweden. Then, an Afghan man in his twenties, who had

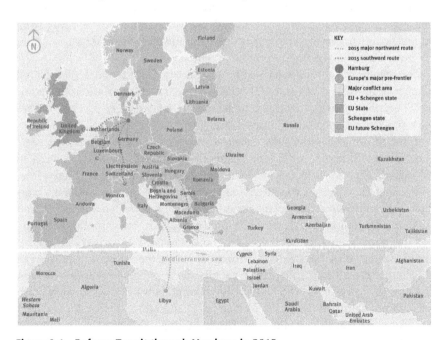

Figure 0.4   Refugee Transit through Hamburg in 2015.

been listening to the conversation all the while, took the boy by his arm and said with infinite tenderness: 'Come with me, I've got family in Sweden. We will take care of you.'

On the next day, I queued at the ticket hall with an Afghan man in a wheelchair who wanted to reach Brussels with a friend. When it was our turn, the railway employee behind the counter scolded me because we should have queued at the specific counter for people with disabilities. 'We're in Germany!' – he retorted sharply to my apologies for this oversight – and I could not tell whether his subtly xenophobic tone was directed to me, as an Italian supposedly oblivious to the observance of rules, or to the Afghan man, as a potential 'bogus' asylum seeker taking advantage of German kindness and welfare. Most likely, it targeted both of us, as the employees were often annoyed by the fact that I acted as translator from Persian into English but did not speak German, and nor did the refugees. According to the employee, it was not possible to book same-day tickets for passengers travelling in a wheelchair, to which I answered that the two men *needed* to travel immediately, because they were undocumented asylum seekers and had nowhere to sleep. The employee insisted that it was impossible, since the railway staff who supported disabled passengers were limited and needed to be booked in advance. As he stubbornly stood silent, staring at his computer monitor, the Afghan man lost his patience and shouted that he could fold the wheelchair himself, with his friend's help, and travel on the train seats like any other 'able' passenger. After all, he had reached Hamburg all the way from Afghanistan without the help of the German railway staff. After a little more arguing, the employee finally printed a train ticket.

The queues at the ticket hall could take hours, both because of the high number of transiting refugees and because, in-between translations and complex decisions over destinations, finances and safer routes, purchases were slow processes. Once, an employee straightforwardly refused to provide us with the information about the cheapest options to Copenhagen: 'We can't waste all this time on you!' – he snapped – 'Our customers are waiting in the queue. This is the Deutsche Bahn, not the United Nations!' I answered, testily, that the refugee I was attending to was also a customer, and not a marginal one, since same-day tickets for international routes amounted to around €200 for Denmark, and over €300 for Norway or Finland. Furthermore, because trains were often overbooked, those without a seat reservation were not allowed to board trains to Copenhagen. While the railway employees in Hamburg were aware of this issue, usually those at other stations were not, and thus the passengers who had already bought their tickets elsewhere were not allowed to board the trains in Hamburg, and had to wait until the next day. According to their policy, the Deutsche Bahn should have reimbursed them 50 per cent of the tickets and booked a hotel for the night, since the mistake was the company's and not the passengers' fault. However, they did not respect the policy with the refugees in transit because, more often than not, the latter could not provide bank account details for the reimbursement and, due to domestic regulations, those without passports could not have been hosted in hotels anyways. Mathias, one of the volunteers coordinating the infodesk, once demanded cash reimbursement for a family who was travelling with an ill baby. The employee stated that the policy was 'not valid for refugees' and added that 'after all, even in Syria there must be banks'; as the two of them got into a heated argument, the employee called the security to remove Mathias from the site.

Many other refugees were stuck in Hamburg for several days because the ferry connections to Scandinavia departing from the coastal cities of Kiel, Rostock and Lübeck, as well as the sleeping places organised by the local volunteer groups, had very limited capacities and thus the volunteers in Hamburg allowed only certain numbers of refugees to board the trains each day.

Despite these complicated routes, the word 'Sweden' echoed everywhere, generating the impression of a direct connection from Hamburg Central Station. The word 'Sweden' appeared on the cardboard placards in English and Arabic held by the volunteers coordinating imminent departures and echoed in the corridors through the voices of those leading groups to the trains. Despite the volunteers' efforts to contain the number of people

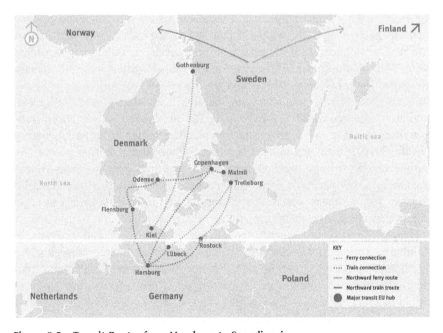

Figure 0.5   Transit Routes from Hamburg to Scandinavia.

boarding each train in an orderly fashion, large groups would start running along the platforms. Some of the 'translators' would run with them, shouting '*Yalla! Yalla!*' – 'let's go!' in Arabic. I myself would run among the others, worried that the people I was guiding may miss the train's departure. We ran as if there were no tomorrow, as if the borders were about to shut down, as if that train about to depart were the last one setting off to a better world. Mathias remarked to me once that running was 'inappropriate': that chaotic '*Yalla!* atmosphere' – as he used to call it – reproduced the experiences of stress and anxiety that the refugees had already protractedly suffered along their journey. But even if some volunteers did not acknowledge it, the refugees themselves knew only too well that the situation at the borders could have abruptly changed at any moment, from night to morning. Either caught in the flow or trying to navigate it against the current, both refugees and volunteers were part of a reconfiguration of the European space that was hardly foreseeable from the horizon of the station.

THE COLONIALITY OF ASYLUM AND THE SPECTACLE OF SOLIDARITY

This book offers an ethnographic critique of asylum from the standpoint of autonomous border struggles in Hamburg. It takes at its heart the quest for autonomy by both refugees and their supporters while it exposes how their struggles are caught within the meshes of coloniality – a structure of power, knowledge, and being that has long survived colonialism (Quijano 2000; Maldonado-Torres 2007) and that unevenly distributes wealth, health, life expectancy, resources, rights and freedoms. As I signalled in the above vignette about the division between 'helpers', 'translators' and 'refugees', crucial to the *coloniality of asylum* is the production of racialised subjectivities because, as a governmental practice rooted in colonial history (Wolfe 2016), 'race' naturalises the exercise of administrative power 'by Europeanized ("white") assemblages over non-Europeanized ("non-white") assemblages' (Hesse 2007: 656). This normalisation not only affects the relationship that 'refugees' entertain with the state but also with society at large and, in particular, with their 'supporters'.

Hence, the book documents the efforts of volunteers and activists in Hamburg, while it recounts collective and individual refugee struggles and fragmented trajectories, tying different locations, stories, dilemmas and conflicts within the tangle of the asylum regime. The latter is understood as a field of practices and discourses that, both at the imaginative and material levels, produce space, social relations and subjectivities which, in turn, are always in excess of the structures that determined them in the first place. This emphasis on the productivity of asylum aims to denaturalise and repoliticise this field, showing how processes of racialisation, illegalisation, objectification and 'refugification' partake in the mutual production of 'asylum' and 'Europe'. Keeping in mind that the *real* 'refugee crisis' was, and still is, occurring not in Europe, but rather in the Middle East and North Africa (New Keywords Collective 2016), this book does not provide a normative theory of asylum, nor does it universalise 'the refugee' as a disembodied global category. Rather, it follows Chakrabarty's plea to 'provincialise' Europe (2000), namely by interrogating the racialised hierarchies imbued within 'the right to asylum' and their reproduction of both Europe's 'Others' and its imagined 'self'.

As shown through the treatment of refugees by Deutsche Bahn employees, the *coloniality of asylum* informs the hierarchy of lives, rights and freedoms for which certain bodies are subjected to practices that are seldom experienced by others, in particular by white Western citizens and privileged non-Western people on the move, who are both placed at the higher end of the 'human' spectrum (Wynter 2003; Maldonado-Torres 2007). Coloniality renders refugee newcomers alternately objects of someone else's compassion, protection, management or political engagement and, in doing so, concomitantly reproduces their *exteriority* to Europe. However, as Farhad's story shows, beyond the rhetoric of recurring 'crises' and 'emergencies', refugees are in fact already very much a part of Europe, and an active one in reconfiguring and contesting its space, for they dwell, live, work, move through, socialise and participate in various ways in European urban and nonurban sites.

Importantly, as it will have already emerged through the interactions among refugees in transit, and between them and their supporters, colonial subordination is also always inhabited by practices of mutual care, autonomy, and resistance (Gopal 2019). To what extent grassroots practices of refugee support mostly led by white Europeans can be inspired by an anti-colonial spirit, committed to a horizon of full political, material and social equality with 'refugees' is one of the central questions of this book, and one that will not be normatively answered. Rather, throughout the following chapters the tensions between coloniality and autonomy will be explored in their spatial, legal and intersubjective dimensions.

The ethnography that informs this work was undertaken at a particular historical crossroad, one that gave unprecedented visibility not only to refugee autonomous movements but also to acts of solidarity under the slogan 'Refugees Welcome'. The 'obscene border spectacle' which, under restrictive policies, usually displays the securitarian exclusion from the 'West' of particularly racialised and classed migrants, while concealing their subordinate inclusion through illegalised labour (De Genova 2013), was momentarily reversed; as it had already happened in the case of the Italian rescue mission

Mare Nostrum (Tazzioli 2016), the German *Wilkommenskultur* was a 'good border spectacle', a *spectacle of solidarity*, which displayed the humanitarian inclusion of refugees, while it concealed their exclusion through illegalisation and deportation.

In that period, most EU and Balkan neighbouring states temporarily renounced to keeping refugees out, and rather channelled, filtered and regulated the speed of transit of their unruly mobilities. The Greek state directly ferried refugees to the mainland (Spathopoulou 2016), while most Balkan countries[5] allowed transit without registering asylum seekers (Cocco 2017; Kasparek 2016). The same happened in Germany and Sweden – both of which temporarily became 'transit countries' of sorts – and their de facto open-border policy backed up the massive involvement of self-organised volunteers, who provided both material donations and support to the logistics of transit virtually everywhere from the Balkan Corridor all the way up to Finland (Santer and Wriedt 2017). In contrast to other locations in south-eastern Europe, refugees had never been so visible in central and northern Europe; their arrivals had mainly been scattered and clandestine and, once they had submitted an asylum application, they were relegated to reception centres in remote areas (Fontanari 2015). Indeed, although for a limited space of time, 'the long summer of migration' radically transformed the geographies of transit throughout Europe, and thus also the appearance of its very urban centres.

However, other EU states, such as Hungary and Denmark, adopted a hard line from the onset and inaugurated a process of internal re-bordering, which engendered a series of contradictory measures.[6] The Dublin Regulation, which stipulates that undocumented asylum seekers should be fingerprinted and allocated to the first European country they entered, was repeatedly lifted and reinstated by different countries. The result was a chain of 'Schengen intermittences' (Garelli 2013), namely, temporary interruptions of the principle of free circulation through the reintroduction of internal border controls. Between 2016 and 2017, the Schengen Agreement was repeatedly suspended across eastern, central and northern Europe, and border checks were reintroduced both through razor wire and racial profiling (Schwarz 2016).

In this way, the main strategy of border externalisation (Bialasiewicz 2012) deployed in the previous decades – and reinstated from 2017 onwards – transformed into a temporary strategy of border re-internalisation.

What had been termed in political and media discourses a 'refugee crisis' was interpreted by some as rather a 'crisis of the border regime itself' (Bojadžijev and Mezzadra 2015; New Keywords Collective 2016; De Genova 2016c), as exclusionary policies were crumbling down under the pressure of a true 'autonomy of asylum' (De Genova et al. 2018). In the words of Jana, an anti-racist and no-border Hamburg activist, 'it was an empowering moment; we felt that something was really going on, that the border regime was

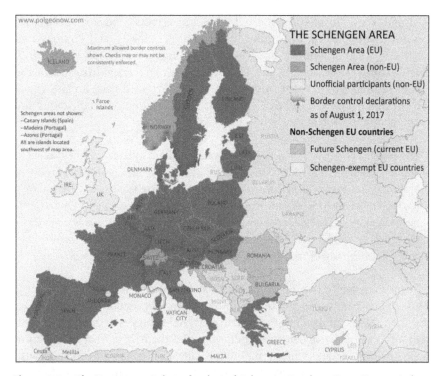

Figure 0.6   The Temporary Reintroduction of Schengen Borders. Evan Centanni, from blank map by Ssolbergj. License: CC BY-SA.

imploding. It was a chance that the people out there would realise the systematic structural failures of this city and this country.' German citizens were on the frontline of novel solidarity initiatives, articulated through different political frameworks pertaining to both political and humanitarian horizons. Overall, the 'Refugees Welcome' movement shared a principle of autonomy from both governments and NGOs: self-organised support groups were formed in virtually every neighbourhood in the proximity of refugee camps; caravans were organised with private cars to pick up refugees stranded in Hungary; and accommodation was improvised in private homes.

The radical potential of that historical moment mostly lay in the facilitation of irregular border crossings – an endeavour that before, as well as afterwards, could be cultivated only clandestinely, in an international regime that criminalised that kind of solidarity even in the case of rescuing people from certain death (Fekete 2009; Albahari 2015). And, yet, there they were, thousands of illegalised people moving around, with the support of thousands of European citizens. The European *spectacle of solidarity* opposed Merkel's democratic and humanitarian values to Orbán's authoritarian policies, and reinstated particular imaginaries of

East and West. It was imbued with specific affects, tied not necessarily to civil disobedience, but rather to hospitality, charity and compassion, and these were crucial in justifying the disjuncture between the hype of the *Wilkommenskultur* and the following dramatic restabilisation of the border regime. An excerpt from a later interview with Ella, an anti-racist activist in her thirties, makes clear how this disjuncture was conscious and even acceptable for many:

> The people coming were *those who were not supposed to come* and they would not have come before. In 2015 it was possible, because they heard it was open. I mean, it was always open to a certain extent. Maybe someone said: 'You know it's been quite open already for years. Maybe we should give it a try?' Or maybe the smugglers had bought more boats, who knows? But *we had been waiting for these people all the time*. How many people will get deported, how many will really be able to make their lives here, *that's another question*.

Were they really two different questions? Before travelling to Germany, I remember being gripped by profound discomfort while watching from afar the crowds applauding the recently arrived refugees at Munich Central Station. What did it mean to literally *applaud* them? To what extent were those seemingly autonomous mobilities and solidarities possible because the border regime itself was allowing them? Was donating material goods a gesture of solidarity or rather charity? Which historical memory was foreclosed by the notion of 'hospitality'? Whose presence was invisibilised by the emphasis on (white) European citizens in the media? And what relationship did it exist between those autonomous politics of 'helping' and the state interlinked practices of protection and deportation?

As an activist of the Karawane collective told me upon my arrival in Munich in early October 2015, it was precisely in that spectacularised moment of solidarity and hospitality that we had to pay attention to the *invisible* developments of the border regime. Indeed, behind the scene of the *spectacle of solidarity*, resumed in Angela Merkel's repeated claim '*Wir schaffen das*' ('we will cope'), both EU and local policies were developing at an extremely fast pace in unprecedented restrictive directions. Germany passed a new asylum bill in October 2015 (known as Asylpaket I), described by the country's Left Party as 'the worst attack on basic asylum right since the 1990s' (DW 2015); and subsequent restrictions were approved in February 2016 (known as Asylpaket II), part of which was the strengthening, acceleration and simplification of the deportation procedures concerning rejected asylum seekers.

At the EU level, from September 2015 onwards, the 'hotspot approach' was implemented in different locations of arrival by boat in Italy and Greece,[7] enforcing the fingerprinting of all incoming undocumented migrants, illegalising many of them already before they could access the asylum procedure, and immobilising those excluded from the new relocation system (Garelli and Tazzioli 2016). Sweden, which thus far had been the most relaxed country at the northern end of Europe, allowing both the irregular entry of those who wanted to stay and the irregular transit of those who headed to Norway and Finland, reintroduced border controls in early 2016. The 'Balkan corridor' itself was officially shut down in March 2016, clearing shortly afterwards the symbolic site of the self-organised refugee camp of Idomeni, at the Greek-Macedonian border (Santer and Wriedt 2017). Simultaneously, the EU signed a deal with Turkey (Heck and Hess 2017) concerning the readmission of undocumented migrants and stating a principle of exchangeability for which a Syrian refugee residing in the country would be enrolled in a process of resettlement to Europe, in exchange for each irregular migrant returned to Turkey. Finally, in October 2016, the EU signed an agreement with Afghanistan regarding the readmission of an unlimited number of Afghan rejected asylum seekers (Webber 2017), while Italy also resumed its infamous bilateral agreement with Libya, enforcing pushbacks at sea (Nakache and Losier 2017). In this way, the practice of border externalisation was re-instated both at the level of containment and exclusion at the border – dramatically curbing the northward influx of refugee newcomers – and at the level of the deportation arrangements concerning those who had already reached the inner European territory.

Questions about the role of refugee solidarity would become even more crucial in the wake of the restabilisation of the border regime (Hess and Kasparek 2017) but, in autumn 2015, the everyday horizon of the volunteers at Hamburg Central Station was completely caught in the material urgencies of *the blackmail of the crisis*; the primacy of material humanitarian urgencies did not allow time for considering and foreseeing the imminent political and legal developments, and implicitly sacrificed more long-term political intervention. Most of the volunteers had never before been involved in refugee support and, after the departures, left the platforms with a feeling of accomplishment, as people were supposed to have set towards their 'final' destinations. In fact, we knew nothing of what would happen next. We did not keep contact with the refugees in most cases, so we never knew what had actually happened to them. Had they been caught by the police along the way? Had they been deported, by virtue of the Dublin Regulation, to another European country after arriving at their supposed destinations? Had their asylum applications been eventually rejected? Had they been deported back to their countries of origin?

Refugee support, as well as academic and journalistic accounts, risk reproducing the border spectacle and reifying 'refugees' through snapshots of purportedly crisis-producing border crossings. Those crossings, however, are usually only the beginning of multiple struggles, among which also the *legal* struggle over recognition is but one aspect. Seeking asylum in Europe is inherently a *spatial* struggle, involving multiple transnational movements and, often, periods of settling in different locations than the one assigned by the Dublin Regulation (Kasparek 2015; Picozza 2017a). Yet, within this mobile spatiality, asylum is also a *temporal* struggle (Fontanari 2017; Khosravi 2014), a long and processual experience of *becoming* – and, possibly, *ceasing to be* – a 'refugee', a struggle over time lost on the move or in utter immobility, lost doing paperwork, lost being deported back somewhere. Ultimately, asylum is but a form of migration and thus a material *and* existential struggle over life itself, over subsistence, ambitions, desires and social relations. Asylum is thus a 'border struggle' (Mezzadra and Neilson 2013: 264; De Genova 2015), a key vector in the production of the world we inhabit, not only through organised political actions against border enforcement but also through mundane everyday practices which are often disregarded as 'pre-political' (Mezzadra and Neilson 2013: 265). It was precisely the long-term temporality and fragmented spatiality of the struggle for asylum that had brought me to Hamburg in the first place, but the very space in which refugee mobilities occurred was radically shaken up by the 'crisis', and this unavoidably required an adjustment of my research questions.

Moreover, the novel spectacle of solidarity reawakened important questions I had been pondering already for years, having engaged in refugee support way before starting to research asylum academically (see chapter 2). In particular, beyond the plethora of questions regarding the differences between humanitarian assistance and political solidarity, as well as the inherent limits of both, I distinctively remember often using the verb 'colonising' in the form of the question: *How can we avoid colonising the refugees we support with our own politics?* This is precisely one of the central quandaries that animated me to write this book, but with the important difference that, throughout the years, I have been building way more political community with some refugees, and thus the 'we' of the question is not necessarily directed to Europeans only. The kernel of this question is captured in the second main concept of the book: *solidarity as method*. Recognising that autonomous refugee solidarity was 'the pair of glasses' that prompted and enabled my research in the first place, I will explore the intersections between the *coloniality of asylum* – comprising both the state and other institutions – and the everyday social encounters between 'refugees' and the 'supporters' that supposedly contest that very regime. Intersecting the concepts of *the coloniality of asylum* and *solidarity as method* allows for a simultaneous focus on the political *production* of refugees, their legal *government* through diverse bordering practices hinging on their partitioning, confinement, containment and deportation, and the *socialisation* of refugees *as refugees*, through practices of support and solidarity that racialise, victimise and infantilise them.

THE MUTUAL PRODUCTION OF ASYLUM AND EUROPE

The book foregrounds two interrelated arguments: it shows how 'Europe' politically, legally and socially produces 'refugees' while, in turn, through their border struggles and autonomous movements, 'refugees' produce the space of 'Europe'. First, the following chapters will destabilise hegemonic narratives of asylum by showing how Europe actively *produces* refugees, rather than merely receiving them, through a differential, racialised and classed distribution of the freedom of movement, pertaining to the coloniality of power, the law and being. The exploration of different relational configurations between 'refugees', European states and European citizens will unveil how the *coloniality of asylum* objectifies, racialises and victimises 'refugees', while also normalising the experiences that they undergo. While asylum will be analysed as a socio-legal relationship to the state, 'refugeeness' will be understood as a sociopolitical and existential condition marked by thresholds of becoming and ceasing to be refugees. Concomitantly, the book will illuminate the close links between asylum, labour, (il)legalisation and deportability, thus expanding the scope of the *coloniality of asylum* through an analysis of the 'refugification' of a range of migratory experiences, themselves marked by legally enforced spatio-temporal suspension, in the form of waiting, deportability, immobility and/or hypermobility. Finally, through the prism of coloniality, the book will show how even those instances of solidarity that contest the border regime tend to unwittingly share its colonial premises – most notably in reproducing processes of socialisation of refugees *as refugees* and rendering their figure an emergent racial formation.

The second argument explores the reverse process: namely, how asylum itself, as a set of discourses and practices, produces Europe, as an imagined, material and legal space. Within this space, 'Europeanness' emerges as an identity rooted in specific postcolonial, postwar and postmodern spatio-temporalities, which render Europeans actors of hospitality and solidarity, in charge of rescuing refugees when the state abandons, or actively oppresses, them. In this sense, the figure of 'the refugee' also produces its counterpart, the 'refugee supporter', as an embodiment of a specifically European and postcolonial 'good' whiteness, premised on liberal, democratic and humanitarian discourses. Through the manifold examples pertaining to informal humanitarian 'helping' and self-organised anti-racist and no-border solidarity, I outline individual and collective conflicts arising in contexts of refugee support over the role of the state and of volunteering. The ethnography shows a complex web of practices whereby, at times, self-organised support is antagonistic to the state, while at other times, it operates in continuity with state discourses. Furthermore, I bring different examples through which European subjectivities are conceived of as three-dimensional and 'freely' mobile, while refugee subjectivities are flattened in racialised, gendered and classed terms that reduce them to objects of the management and support of others, in a move that mirrors the immobility and non-freedom to which the 'native' was condemned under colonial rule. Finally, by exploring refugee autonomous struggles for legalisation, mobility and belonging, the book shows that far from being subjects Other than, or external to, Europe, in fact they are very much *internal* to – and *producers* of – the European space where they live and through which they move and struggle.

Finally, this book foregrounds a problematisation of the tripartition of 'the refugees', 'civil society' and 'the state' which is widespread within most analyses of the 2015 'Refugees Welcome' movement (Funk 2016; Hamann and Karakayali 2016; Fontanari and Borri 2017). In policy, academic, media and societal mainstream discourses, 'refugees' are presented as *external* to Europe and irrupting in the scene, confined to the 'presentism' of a timeless 'crisis' and 'emergency' that suffers from historical amnesia over their presence in the European territory which, by now, amounts to several decades. In turn, 'the state' is alternately presented as a benevolent actor offering legal protection and material assistance or a malevolent and oppressive entity, driven by the will to exclude unwanted others and by a racist 'necropolitics' (Mbembe 2003; Davies et al. 2017). Even when presented as such, however, state racism seems a 'racism without race' (Lentin 2014; De Genova 2018) due to the colour blindness (El-Tayeb 2011) and 'political racelessness' of Europe (Goldberg 2006). In this sense, 'civil society', often considered as a 'European' whole (Crepaz 2017; Thiel 2017), implicitly coincides with citizenry in the form of citizenship (Chatterjee 2004; Mezzadra 2006) and is imagined, though not named, as *white* – as signalled in the example of the partitioning between 'helpers' and 'translators' through the unspoken racialised lines of the 'migration background'. This European 'civil society' seems then ultimately responsible for the protection of refugees, when the state fails them. However, this conceptualisation of 'civil society' as the realm of citizenry and the perennial counterpart to 'the state' re-perpetrates a historical erasure of nonwhite populations, displaced as permanent outsiders (El-Tayeb 2011), to be either welcomed and protected or excluded and deported. In this way, the concept of 'civil society' also erases the active participation of refugees themselves and other nonwhite people in the networks of solidarity that support refugee newcomers.

This critique poses important epistemological problems regarding the sociopolitical categories that denote subject positions in this book, such as 'refugees', 'migrants', 'supporters', 'volunteers' and 'activists'. They are all provisional and contested, and I am more interested in thinking about their productivity rather than reifying them in any way. In particular, while I widely use the term 'refugees' throughout the book, I do not mean any ontologisation of the category as one wholly different from the one of 'migrant' – nor do I uphold any self-evident meaning of the migrant category itself. Rather, in the following chapters, the racial, legal, social, temporal and spatial imaginaries that shape them will be fully interrogated. Furthermore, I enlarge the scope of the 'refugee' category politically, in order to signify the relationship that the people on the move who were part of my research entertained with the asylum regime, whether or not this occurred strictly in legal terms. Some of my interlocutors strategically appropriated this label in order to signal the global relationships of coloniality that determined their migrations in the first place; others rejected it altogether because of its Othering and racialising subtext, which is precisely born out of the same coloniality. Similarly, the category of 'supporter', widely used in Germany but closer to the English term 'ally', refers to non-refugee individuals who are in solidarity with refugees, but can alternately imply a humanitarian subtext, not far away from the categories of 'helper' or 'volunteer', or rather be closer to 'activist', implying the horizon of anti-racist and no-border politics. Importantly, these positions are often blurred and intertwined, meaning that, throughout the book, the reader will often encounter characters that occupy multiple positions simultaneously.

Thinking of these multiple meanings and contradictions invites the reader to think about which ideas of Europeanness, whiteness and coloniality are (re) produced through these divisions, both in the discourses and practices of refugee protection (at the state level) and refugee solidarity (at society's level). However, if during 'the crisis' power asymmetries pertaining to notions of Europeanness and non-Europeanness were all the while reproduced in initiatives of support and solidarity – often also by sharing state discourses of deservingness and differential access – this does not mean that the state and civil society are indeed *the same thing*; nor that charity-volunteering and no-border activism are *the same thing*. There are many discontinuities between these realms. Solidarity can occur from *within* the border regime, or rather radically *outside of*, and *against* it – and sometimes be enacted by actors that occupy both positions simultaneously. Rooted in the political left, as well as Christian morality and welfarism (Kelliher 2018), 'solidarity' was in my field a very contested term, appropriated and elaborated in different ways depending on the speaker and the context (see also Tazzioli and Walters 2019). Self-organised refugees used it in terms of standing in solidarity with each other and building political communities; anti-racist and no-border activists countered the rhetoric of asymmetric, charitable 'help' with ideas of political solidarity as a horizontal dialogue based on mutuality and learning, as well as the recognition of refugees as actors of their own struggles; finally, the (supposedly 'apolitical') 'helpers' also claimed to be moved from solidarity as a moral imperative. Internally to these different groups, claims of solidarity were also extremely varied in both conceptualisations and material practices. While I will move between these differences throughout the book, I look at solidarity as a fluid practice that does not necessarily happen in particular locations in which volunteering or activism are formalised: solidarity is rather an ethics and politics of care, one that, in the accounts that will follow, is practiced by many individuals, such as lawyers and social workers, as well as railway employees and, as already stated, refugees themselves, who are often 'supporters' of other refugees.

While all solidarity practices are imperfect and provisional, it is urgent to bring into full view their enmeshment within coloniality. Beyond the academic mandate to understanding the discourses we (re)produce, circulate and live by, this is a fundamental political task pertaining to mundane, daily involvement within the asylum regime, regardless of the position we occupy as refugees, supporters, activists, bureaucrats, humanitarians, researchers or policy-makers. The critical hope that prompts this book is thus to contribute to an anticolonial political imagination that can sustain daily struggles against the asylum regime. For a politics of autonomy to really challenge and undo coloniality, European middle-class white intellectual and activists need to grapple with the way colonially and racially-coded notions of *freedom* and *fugitivity* (Hesse 2014) percolate into their interventions, following an old historiographic habit that privileges white abolitionism over slave struggles (Gopal 2019); only this understanding can direct the envisioning of horizontal and radical practices of solidarity with refugees.

PLAN OF THE BOOK

The book is organised in eight chapters that revolve around key concepts and alternate between ethnographic accounts of volunteering and solidarity practices, refugee trajectories, self-organisation and legal struggles. It takes the reader on a wandering journey which departs and returns to Hamburg but dwells on stopovers in Rome, Oslo, Calais, Cairo, the Gaza strip, Idlib, Athens, Istanbul, Kabul, Tripoli and Lampedusa; it offers a polyphonic account of asylum struggles, including the voices of asylum seekers, recognised refugees, rejected illegalised refugees, migrants with different statuses, white and nonwhite volunteers, lawyers, social workers and no-border/anti-racist activists who are both from a refugee and a European background.[8]

That this book is ethnographic means essentially two different but interrelated things: that it is informed by personal engagement with particular places and people, and that it is also written descriptively and narratively in order to give a sense of place and convey the researcher's and her interlocutors' experiences during fieldwork. In other words, to say that the texture of this book is 'ethnographic' means that the theorisations developed within it always stem from, and return to, the specific places and people through which I have encountered the social, legal, political and existential world of asylum, 'refugeeness' and refugee support.

The first two chapters frame the main theoretical and methodological conundrum that underpins the book. Chapter 1 opens with the closure of the Scandinavian route, which engendered a transformation in the Central Station Helper Network, reducing its activities to providing humanitarian support in the institutional setting of the Bieberhaus building. Through an analysis of the power asymmetries between volunteers and refugees stranded in transit, the chapter discusses the main concept of *the coloniality of asylum* and situates the book's theoretical framework at the intersection of border studies and critical theories of colonialism and 'race'. It interrogates the racialised hierarchies imbued within 'the right to asylum' and their reproduction of both Europe's 'others' and its imagined 'self' along spatial, temporal and social lines. Finally, the chapter dwells on the legal production of 'refugees' as racialised and objectified Others subjected to Europeans' management, charity or, at best, political engagement.

Focusing on the concept of *solidarity as method*, chapter 2 seeks to unveil the enmeshment of refugee solidarity within the coloniality of asylum. Wrestling with the question of what it means to conduct a politically engaged ethnography within a context marked by coloniality, the chapter discusses solidarity as not merely a field of enquiry, but rather a true *method* which bears specific epistemological and political dilemmas. The chapter further dwells on the role of the 'margins' in both the contestation of and co-optation by the border regime, envisioning anti-colonial and anti-racist practices that can escape liberal, humanitarian and white understandings of the political. It sets the scene of the Hamburg's autonomist movement tracing its connection to both refugee struggles and the Refugees Welcome movement, and it presents the voices that will be louder in the rest of the book.

The central chapters delve into the intersections between asylum laws, refugees' mobilities and solidarity practices, tying together the question of 'the state' and the one of 'civil society' in the production of the coloniality of asylum. Chapter 3 departs from *the blackmail of the crisis*, which determines a primacy of material and humanitarian urgencies at the expense of more long-term political interventions. Through an analysis of the conflicts emerging both at the Central Station and the Messehallen – an exhibition hall turned temporary refugee camp – the chapter looks at the contested meanings and effects of solidarity practices, drawing on my interlocutors' conceptualisation of 'political' versus 'apolitical' support, that is to say between political *solidarity* – antagonistic to the state and conceived in terms of anti-racism and self-organisation – and humanitarian *charity* or *helping* – neutral to, or collaborative with, the state and driven by a more general humanism. Here, a critique of the concept of 'civil society' and its implicit whiteness is provided by emphasising the presence of refugees themselves within support networks.

Echoing the slogan of the protest group Lampedusa in Hamburg, *We're Here to Stay!*, chapter 4 looks at both collective and individual refugee disobedient mobilities that challenge the control imposed by the border regime. It illuminates the specific spatio-temporal dimensions of the coloniality of asylum law, which operate through the mutual workings of refugee *allocation* and *deportation*, and within a complex intersection of asylum, labour and illegality. It also offers an experiential critique of the imagined 'linearity' of the governmental category of 'transit', as well as the ambiguous equation of freedom with movement. Finally, it connects refugee mobilities to those of other 'non-Europeans' who are long-term European residents but are racialised and classed through similar patterns and undergo processes of 'refugification' which translate into the humanitarisation and precarisation of their everyday lives.

From the temporal perspective of the crisis' aftermath, chapter 5 returns to the relationship between volunteer-led refugee support and state-sanctioned refugee oppression – a relationship that is never univocal, but rather fluid and unstable, cutting across different lines of navigation, co-option and sabotage. It illuminates the *battleground of asylum* from the standpoint of refugee camps and the asylum procedure, analysing refugee support as a diffused activity that can be undertaken not only by volunteers but also social workers sabotaging deportations and lawyers providing free, independent legal consultation. Ultimately, the chapter questions both the expected 'stateship' of some actors and the expected 'allyship' of others, showing how contestation and co-optation are intimately interconnected and often overlapping, while also highlighting how some refugees who align with state discourses can imbricate themselves in the subordination of refugee newcomers.

The last two chapters dwell on the production of the racialised subjectivities of 'refugees' and 'supporters', highlighting fractures between the two groups and among each one. Chapter 6 offers manifold narratives of becoming, and eventually ceasing to be 'refugees', highlighting a series of *thresholds of asylum*. It delves into four main aspects of the formation of the subjectivity of my interlocutors, that is to say, the refugification produced by both the legal procedure of asylum and the subjection to other precarious legalisations that entail deportability; the racialised socialisation of refugees through assistance and support; their quest for existential mobility through physical mobility; and the engagement with self-organised political action intended as a form of resistance to the 'coloniality of being'. Finally, the chapter discusses the disjunction of 'protection' from autonomy and freedom, within both the law and the gaze of lawyers and volunteers, while also speaking to the limits of self-organisation in a context in which material conditions to properly transform one's life are lacking.

Departing from an analysis of the visual economy of the 'Refugees Welcome' movement, chapter 7 traces a genealogy of the racialised imaginary of refugee support to mainstream narratives of the abolition of slavery. It explores classed, gendered and racialised asymmetries between refugees and supporters, particularly looking at the production of a 'good', democratic and liberal whiteness within practices of solidarity. It dwells on how social relations between these two subject positions reproduce a purported incompatibility of Europeanness and refugeeness. Discussing conflicts arising around time disposability, ethical consumerism and gender relations, the chapter further blurs the line between humanitarian and political support, and it sheds light on how the figure of the 'refugee supporter' often ends up marginalising the role of refugees as both agents of their own struggles and actors of solidarity one with another.

Chapter 1

The Coloniality of Asylum

'Race', 'Refugeeness' and 'Europeanness'

By early 2016, the geographies of transit and solidarity that had radically transformed Hamburg Central Station had again shifted to a different configuration. With the introduction of the 'hotspots' in Italy and Greece (Garelli and Tazzioli 2016; Antonakaki et al. 2016), the progressive closure of the Balkan corridor (Kasparek 2016), and the EU–Turkey Deal in March 2016 (Heck and Hess 2017), illegalised transit towards northern Europe was severely curbed, and arrivals in Hamburg decreased dramatically. Neither Norway nor Finland allowed further transit of non-EU nationals without a valid visa, and Sweden only accepted ferry-borne asylum seekers in possession of national passports. Therefore, in January 2016, only a couple of hundred refugees would still transit through Hamburg each day and, in the months to follow, these movements would only concern spare numbers of scattered, invisible people. In turn, a great number of refugees were stuck in Hamburg: they had not registered with the local authorities, but they could not continue their journeys either. As the border regime had effectively restabilised its powers (Hess and Kasparek 2017), the *crisis of the border regime* had returned to being, primarily, a *crisis of the migrants themselves* (Tazzioli 2017: 13).

In January, both the tents on Heidi Kabel Platz, donated by the NGO Der Paritätische Wohlfahrtsverband, and the infodesk set up by the volunteers in the station's foyer were removed. Der Paritätische facilitated the relocation of the volunteers' activities to the second floor of the Bieberhaus, a privately owned building located in the same square where the tents had previously been, and employed three of them as project coordinators and mediators between the NGO and the self-organised group. Here, the radical support to the illegalised logistics of transit was replaced by mere humanitarian assistance to stranded refugees. The Bieberhaus retained nothing of the lively

'*Yalla*! atmosphere' of the station, the dynamic messiness of the departures, and their sense of hope and human connection.

It was rather a place of stillness, rigidity and strict rules, policed by Deutsche Bahn security at the building's entrance and accessible by volunteers only with registered cards, while 'refugees' had unrestricted access as long as they 'looked like refugees'. The rooms and the corridor had a bleak and suffocating atmosphere, resembling a soup kitchen where refugees queued and food was distributed by volunteers wearing gloves – a visual detail that resembled other instances of state or NGO-led aseptic humanitarian aid.

The volunteers who had previously coordinated the infodesk operated now from a *Beratung* ('consultation') office, but they were tired and burnt-out after months of organising sleeping places, spending their days in consultations and experiencing several encounters with people who did not fit any preconceived image of vulnerable and compliant refugees (see also Braun 2017).

The configuration of the space – composed of different rooms of which only the volunteers retained the keys – clearly divided 'helpers' from 'refugees', reflecting the unbalanced power relations between those at the *giving* and at the *receiving* end of support and advice. This was most striking in the communal hall, where the refugees lined up and the volunteers distributed food and drinks, as well as in the *Beratung* office, where volunteers and refugees were divided through the boundary of a desk. On my first day there,

Figure 1.1   The Bieberhaus' Façade. *Source*: Lars Slowak.

Figure 1.2   The Use of Gloves for Food Distribution. *Source*: Lars Slowak.

an Iranian young volunteer complained about refugee 'translators' who, she said, were just 'hanging out in the office, killing time and chatting'. During my shifts there – she remarked – I would have the *authority* to 'kick them out', because 'we' were busy with serious matters, while 'they' came only to socialise; in order to fulfil our tasks, it was imperative to decide who could legitimately stay in the *Beratung* room and who could not.

Moreover, many volunteers acted suspiciously towards the refugees they were attending to, behaving as if they had already comprehended their predicaments before actually listening to them: 'this person is lying!' – they would burst amidst a translation – 'It's impossible that they weren't identified and registered at the border!' In other instances, they repeated in an automated fashion to the stranded refugees that they were not allowed to cross into Sweden without papers, and they seldom seemed to question the wider structure of the sudden reimposition of mobility restrictions. This disjuncture between the refugees' own needs and aspirations, and the volunteers' inability to dialogue with them and devise alternative strategies particularly struck me in the case of split families, as parents were stranded in Hamburg with one of their children, while their spouses had already reached Scandinavia with another child, and family reunification processes took, at the very least, around six months. Although most volunteers recognised the injustice of those situations, their political imagination was choked by the widespread *normalisation* of the circumstances that permeate the life of someone labelled

as a 'refugee'. It was somewhat *obvious* that refugee families would be split
and parents separated from their children. Likewise, it was *obvious* that border crossings were not possible in the current political climate and that, in
the 'chaos' of around a million refugees entering Europe that year, the only
viable prospect for them was to be patient and wait. Refugees were implicitly
asked to abide by the rules of the very legal regime that was crushing them
into their predicament in the first place and, thus, to the codes of 'respectability' that are structured around citizenry, whiteness and nationalism (Mosse
1985).

On the side of the state, the main focus had also moved from the acceptance
and 'welcoming' of all asylum seekers to the deportation of those whose asylum claims would be deemed invalid. In the media, refugees were increasingly criminalised as 'bogus' asylum seekers, economic migrants, sexual
predators and terrorists (De Genova 2018). However, these transformations
in volunteers', state and media narratives were neither sudden nor unforesee-
able. Since its popularisation in 2015, the *Wilkommenskultur* had come to
indicate a heterogeneous set of state and non-state practices of hospitality and
solidarity that manifestly hinged on the imperative to separate the deserving
'refugees' who would be welcomed from the underserving 'migrants' who
would be deported. This bordering practice, pre-existent to the 2015 'crisis',
stems from a postcolonial reasoning for which those who are racialised and
(il)legalised as 'migrants' are partitioned through hierarchies of deservingness
and vulnerability (Picozza 2017a). Through these hierarchies, welfarism does
not only entail welcoming and assistance but also deportation (Walters 2002:
279; Khosravi 2016: 171), in order to balance the distribution of resources
that are unquestionably presented as scarce. The connections between welfare
and deportation, and between humanitarian inclusion and securitarian exclusion, are paramount to the *coloniality of asylum*, specifically because they
objectify 'refugees' and 'migrants' as subjects to be differentially adminis-
tered. Furthermore, as shown in the above vignette, these bordering practices
percolate into grassroots discourses and modes of operating.

When the volunteers supported the logistics of illegal transit through the
Central Station, there was in fact no shared consensus among them about
committing to supporting the freedom of movement of illegalised people.
Practical limitations, such as the availability of ferry tickets to Sweden, or the
accommodation capacity organised by volunteer groups in the coastal cities,
obliged us to organise travelling groups in certain set numbers. We thus had
to select and prioritise those we deemed the most 'vulnerable' – often families
and women travelling alone. One morning, I was sorting out a complex translation with a Roma family, of whom only the mother spoke some English.
Mathias, the volunteer leading the group, discouraged me from investing in
that case, since the Roma were, in his view, 'not our priority'; even if we

succeeded in helping their crossing, he explained, there was no way their asylum application would be recognised once on the other side. Another volunteer expressed his doubts over our work, because he felt that we were also 'helping many illegals' who were 'not real refugees'. Both volunteers were deploying the very state framework of deservingness, vulnerability and legal recognition. However, if one adopted the perspective of 'deportability' (De Genova 2002) in order to measure 'vulnerability', it was clear that those Roma were indeed very vulnerable to be detained and deported back to Balkan countries where their human rights are systematically violated.[1] The volunteers who expressed a judgement over the *legitimacy* of incoming asylum seekers in Germany, and thus in Europe, were oblivious of the immense violence that deportations exert on illegalised people (De Genova and Peutz 2010; Khosravi 2018). Most importantly, they did not question the fact that, being white EU citizens, they were unlikely to experience a deportation in their whole life, less so the agony of the asylum process, with its uncertainties and deprivations of freedoms at the mercy of state control and humanitarian relief; they had simply won a birth lottery.

This is why, I argue, neither a humanitarian nor a no-border frameworks suffice; solidarity becomes an empty word if one does not adopt an anticolonial framework, namely a commitment to a horizon of abolition of all (post) colonial relations (Mohanty 2003; Walia 2013), including the ones that produce borders and, accordingly, govern 'migrants', 'refugees' and any other category supposed to represent an aberration from emplaced citizenship and privileged, 'free' mobility. A great deal of pro-refugee politics seeks to renegotiate the terms and conditions of refugee 'protection' (Nyers 2010), disjoining it from freedom, and thus sharing the coloniality of the very regime they attempt to contest. Differently, an anticolonial framework first and foremost leads us to question white European authority to partition non-European and, for the wide majority, nonwhite or 'not white enough' foreigners between 'deserving' and 'undeserving'; the normalisation of this partitioning follows a colonial genealogy that will be discussed below, and is one of the main ways in which racial logics operate in contemporary Europe.

Furthermore, the ambiguity of the volunteers' practice of administering and partitioning lay in the fact that they were unwittingly 'helping' the German state itself, allowing it to withdraw from any direct management, control and channelling of refugee flows, as well as from the provision of material assistance (see chapter 3). Precisely because of this overlapping between state asylum politics and volunteers' solidarity, the context of the *Wilkommenskultur* was an enlightening laboratory for understanding *the coloniality of asylum*, that is to say, how colonial sedimentations, particularly regarding contemporary manifestations of the category of 'race', are rearticulated in the legal and social relations that refugees entertain with the 'host' society and its state.

Neither 'race' nor 'coloniality' are monolithic; they operate through multiple regimes of difference that are historically and geographically uneven (Wolfe 2016). Within the scope of this book, the main interest lies in understanding how the colonial heritage of 'race' is rearticulated in the practices of support, management and legal recognition of refugees.

Departing from the tensions between *the spectacle of solidarity* and the off-scene/obscene (De Genova 2013) 'culture of deportation' that underlay it, this chapter lays the main theoretical conundrum and analytical tools that underpin this book, drawing on both critical theories of colonialism and 'race', and border studies. This dialogue is as fundamental as still little explored. Thinking about the colonial genealogy of 'race' and its contemporary embodiments profoundly unsettles the governmental categories that are too often uncritically inherited by migration studies, destabilising both the construction of the 'migrant' and the 'refugee', and the Eurocentric whiteness that is pervasive of both the resulting conceptualisations and the positionality of most researchers who widely publish in this field (Aced and Schwab 2016).

The concept of *the coloniality of asylum* illuminates the racialising border-work of the 'refugee' category, which naturalises some people on the move as *objects* of European management, charity or, at best, political engagement. This fundamental objectification at the heart of *the coloniality of asylum* is predicated upon the purported incompatibility of 'Europeanness' and 'refugeeness' as conditions that, spatially, temporally and socially, are utterly Other. Because 'Europeanness' is ultimately constructed as a postcolonial racial formation of whiteness (De Genova 2016c) and 'refugeeness' as a postcolonial formation of non-whiteness, this irreducibility situates the 'refugee' as an increasingly racial category that rearticulates processes of racial formation trough the intertwining of victimhood, nationality, legal status, culture, religion and phenotypical attributes (De Genova 2018).

1.1. THE COLONIALITY OF ASYLUM

Among the different critical theories that attempt to make sense of the colonial past and present, sociologist Anibal Quijano's 'coloniality of power' (2000) is particularly useful for understanding the genealogies that produce the racialised imagination of 'Europeanness' and 'refugeeness'. As a structure that sustains hierarchies of power and knowledge, coloniality has proved more resistant than the political system of historical colonialism (Maldonado-Torres 2007; Mignolo 2011). Materially, it sustains a global political economy that hinges on uneven development, extractivism and a racialised international division of labour, capital and mobility. The modernity inaugurated with colonial capitalist expansion instituted 'race' as a *practice of governance* that, in order to control and divide labour power, produced legal, economic and social hierarchies between 'Europeans' and 'non-Europeans' (Quijano 2000). These racialised and classed hierarchies rooted in colonialism persist in the contemporary world, unevenly distributing life expectancy, access to resources, social mobility, political freedom and freedom of movement, structuring the very conditions of everyday life and lived experience (Maldonado-Torres 2007), and informing both mobility control (Gutiérrez Rodríguez 2018) and humanitarian relief (Braun 2017).

Within the specificities of contemporary asylum in Europe, the prism of coloniality conveys an analytical sensibility capable of drawing connections between colonial history and the supposedly 'post-colonial' present, particularly relating to the racialised *production, government* and *socialisation* of refugees. In fact, refugees are not the product of crises *external* to Europe; they are a product of 'Europe' itself – as both a project of global domination and a fragmented geopolitical assemblage. Refugees are first produced *politically* through neoliberal extractivism and warfare, including the direct involvement of EU countries in armed conflict, proxy wars, the arms trade, resource extraction and labour exploitation. Second, they are produced *legally*, through a visa regime that, since the 1990s, leaves little possibility for most nationals of African and Asian countries to access the EU beyond submitting an asylum claim, as well as their continuous re-displacement via the Dublin Regulation which, since 2003, obliges asylum seekers to seek protection in the first Member State they enter. Third, their 'refugeeness' is produced *socially* through practices of management and humanitarian assistance, variously led by the state, NGOs and self-organised support groups that inscribe refugees in repressive, instrumental or disempowering relationships.

Epistemologically, taking into account this threefold production of 'refugeeness' entails understanding 'refugees' not as preexistent subjects *received* by the European asylum regime, but rather as subjects *produced* through that very regime (Picozza 2017b), which turns people into (real albeit often unrecognised) refugees, or redoubles their refugee condition, by illegalising and rejecting them, through the 'differential inclusion' (Mezzadra and Neilson 2013: 157) of protection and deportation. In turn, refugees' belonging to Europe is also the product of their historical struggles (Picozza 2017a; Fontanari 2019; De Genova et al. 2018) which, in the face of countless efforts of expulsion, by now amount to several decades and should thus place them as part and parcel of the 'European civil society', regardless of their citizenship status.

In public discourse, the opacity of this productive process has led to the increasing fetishisation of the 'refugee' category', in the sense that Sara Ahmed (2000: 5) describes relating to 'the stranger' figure: refugees seem to take on a 'life of their own' because they are removed from the historical, social and material conditions of their existence, and asylum seeking is cut off from the workings of the border regime, the neocolonial engagements of European governments and capital flows, and the postcolonial relationship that tie European citizens to non-European 'refugees'. Therefore, 'the refugee' becomes a depoliticised, dehistoricised and humanitarised catchword, while Europe appears as a space of 'innocent hospitality' (Danewid 2017), whose 'admission' of refugees in its territories is not a matter of political obligations, but rather of ethical values of a democratic and 'innocent' whiteness (Wekker 2016).

Rejecting these historical and political displacements requires a critical framework that can fully illuminate contemporary asylum's colonial and racial dimensions. The *coloniality of asylum* provides a critical tool that can follow different lines of inquiry, some of which cannot be comprehensively discussed within the scope of this book and thus demand for further engagement. Importantly, although they can be separated analytically, these lines intersect and overlap in their material manifestations. First, as mentioned above, contemporary refugees flows are produced alternately – and at times simultaneously – by the legacy of the colonial past and the immediacy of the colonial present; second, there are particular continuities in practices of identification, management, containment, confinement and displacement between colonial rule and contemporary migration control (Walters 2015); third, there are resemblances between the colonial civilising mission and the postcolonial rescuing mission (Braun 2017); finally, the racialised, classed and gendered imaginaries that produce the citizen/refugee dichotomy are also the product of colonial genealogies, and they affect everyday social relations between these different subject positions.

Taking into consideration the important differences among manifold colonial contexts and their respective racial formations suggests that 'coloniality' cannot be understood as a linear succession between colonial rule and postcoloniality (Rigo 2005; Walters 2015), most importantly, because the nations that were the result of settler colonialism were never decolonised (Wolfe 2016), while virtually all countries that achieved formal decolonisation are now subjected to further neocolonial subordination and internal colonialism (Rivera Cusicanqui 2020). Therefore, any analytical engagement with the concept of *the coloniality of asylum* must account for contingent geopolitical and historical circumstances. Logics of colonial difference are neither fixed nor binary; they produce and operate through various spatio-temporalities, 'affirming some and forgetting others, while flexibly designating fitness for liberty, capacity for production, placement in historical development, contemporaneity or extinction' (Lowe 2015: 189). Specifically, the 'postcolonial Europe' (Bhambra 2009) which is the field of interest of this book, is in no way 'Manichean' (Fanon 1963: 41), but rather characterised by the proliferation of differential bordering practices (Mezzadra and Neilson 2013).

Despite the ostensibly nonracial language of border control (McKeown 2011: 9), at the core of the division between the European 'self' and the non-European 'Other' there is a matter of racialisation over the legal divide between citizen and migrant – for our purposes, the migrant *qua refugee*. As Nicholas De Genova (2018) argues, the racial formations that underpin contemporary migration control in Europe are never wholly reducible to phenotypical attributes (the black or brown migrant), but rather intersect with cultural and religious categories (the Muslim migrant/refugee), political signifiers (the 'terrorist' or 'sexual predator') and legal statuses (the putative 'illegal' status of asylum seekers attempting to reach Europe and their re-illegalisation through the very asylum regime).

Within this book, I will particularly dwell on how the coloniality of asylum racialises refugees *as refugees* in two main ways: via their (il)legalised or temporarily legalised status and their socialisation. It will emerge that these processes subject refugees to particular socio-spatial relations of racialised exclusion, segregation, assistance and charity, which unfold in formal and makeshift refugee camps, spaces of transit, detention centres, legal advice centres and also via socialising initiatives within the 'Refugees Welcome' framework – all of which represent experiences that would be unthinkable for most white European citizens, especially for the great majority of those who engage in refugee support.

Coloniality thus shapes both the legal *and* social relations articulating within Europe's geographies of asylum, particularly regarding the instances in which colonial reasoning translates into a predominant concern over policy, policing and management. That these social relations materialise in a naturalised distinction between a *subjectified* 'we' carrying out management or offering support, and an *objectified* 'them' at the receiving end of protection and solidarity – or policing and punishment – shows how coloniality shapes not only the subjectivity of refugees but also the one of European citizens, be they hostile to, or in solidarity with, refugees. As shown in the ethnographic vignette above, the 'we'/'them' distinction does not strictly adhere to nationality or preexistent racialisation patterns; the *coloniality of asylum* structures also the discourses of those refugees who, in different ways, collaborate with the border regime (chapter 5) or else adhere to the administering ethics of NGOs and volunteering groups. When this happens, volunteers themselves – be they 'refugees', 'Europeans', or any intermediate category – reimpose refugeeness on newly arrived refugees, relegating them to a 'coloniality of being' (Maldonado-Torres 2007) that deprives them of agency in the name of administration, and normalises oppressing, violent and often lethal experiences, such as illegal journeying, 'vulnerability to premature death' (Gilmore

2007: 28), arbitrary detainability and deportability, legal precariousness and spatial segregation. It is this *normalisation* that rearticulates the category of 'race' within the emergent racial formation of 'the refugee', who is *naturalised* and *objectified* as a body to be 'managed' or 'helped', and thus denied of subjectivity, agency and autonomy, particularly through humanitarian Othering, victimisation, anonymisation and infantilisation.

'Refugeeness' is often essentialised as a coherent condition characterised by trauma, wandering and destitution as primary and protracted experiences of life. This conceptualisation testifies to the testimonies of many asylum seekers, but simultaneously risks reproducing the epistemic violence that strips them of their subjectivity and agency (Jackson 2002), while also conflating them as a coherent social group (Malkki 1996), ignoring fractures along the lines of legal status, political ideologies, class, race, gender, sexual orientation and physical abilities (see chapter 6). This conflation is particularly visible in the recurring suspicion in the media over asylum seekers who display signs of purported material wealth, such as smartphones, or rather engage in self-organised protests against the regime that should, supposedly, 'protect' them. Seen through the lens of poverty, loss and passive victimhood, refugees are supposed to be in need of rescue and, thus, are not expected to show any autonomy, strength or dissent.

Opposing this reductionism, the prism of the *coloniality of asylum* ultimately suggests to take into account the coexistence of colonial subordination with colonial resistance (Gopal 2019) and thus understanding how coloniality is constantly resisted, negotiated, and redrawn by many refugees through their individual and collective struggles (Tazzioli 2017; Picozza 2017a; Fontanari 2019; De Genova et al. 2018), as well as by many supporters who seek strategies to escape the meshes of coloniality and envision horizontal practices of solidarity.

1.2. THE MORAL SPATIO-TEMPORALITIES OF 'EUROPEANNESS' AND 'REFUGEENESS'

At the inception of the global refugee system, it was Europe that produced massive asylum movements. In the wake of the Second World War, political violence, displacement, long-term dwelling in refugee camps, the intricate bureaucracy of asylum seeking, the infantilisation of humanitarian government and social marginalisation were common experiences for millions of Europeans (Arendt 1943). A spare number of historical studies detail in depth the reception of these refugees not only by other Western countries but also by Middle Eastern ones, articulating trajectories that were precisely the reverse of contemporary ones (Taparata and Ser 2016). How has this memory been lost? How did these 'refugees' and their children stop being such and became unnoticed 'minorities' in their new countries of residency? The answer to this question must be sought in the geopolitical and racial transformations that emerged in the postwar scenario. Insofar as it concerns migration to the United States or Northern Europe, the patterns of racialisation through naturalisation laws allowed for the progressive admission into whiteness of the most persecuted or impoverished Europeans, such as the Jews, the Irish and the southern Europeans (Jacobson 1999). Concomitantly, as Europe started homogenising the patchwork of its own whiteness, African decolonisation produced its own displacements to Europe, massively reversing previous colonial migrations and giving way to a public image of refugees as a non-European problem and product, marked by non-whiteness. The shift was completed with the end of the Cold War, by dissociating the active individuality of the anti-communist 'exiles' from the passive anonymity of the new 'refugee' masses. Significantly, with the dominion of Western Europe in the inception of the European Union, even the 1990s Balkan wars were displaced as not quite a 'European' problem (von Oppen 2006) and, consequently, the condition of 'Europeanness' and that of 'refugeeness' were rendered wholly incompatible, along a temporal, spatial, moral and racial projection.

This historical turn materialised in the introduction of the Schengen Agreement, which assigned EU citizens to the realm of *free mobility* and *post-nationality*, while it subjected illegalised migrants to increasing securitisation, imposing a visa regime on non-European citizens that were previously not bound to it and thus depriving them of most legal possibilities to migrate (Castles et al. 2014: 2); simultaneously, refugees became confined within the realm of *flight, forcedness* and *unfreedom*, subjecting their legitimacy to enter the European territory to the ethics of suspicion of an ever more draconian asylum process. The emphasis on migration and asylum was crucial to the production of the European space and identity, creating an 'inside' and an 'outside' through new bordering practices and narratives, homogenising the fractures of European identity and reinforcing narratives of democracy and liberalism through the prism of the right to asylum. Unsurprisingly, the Common European Asylum System has been an exceptional area of success regarding the integration and harmonisation of the otherwise fragmented geographies of the EU and Schengen (Guild 2006).

On the one hand the paradigm of 'forced migration' rightfully gestures to the global post- and neocolonial order, inasmuch as the overwhelming majority of current asylum seekers originate from countries that were formerly colonised by European powers, and that keep struggling under military occupation, war, neoliberal dispossession and capitalist expansion. Yet, on the other, it pathologises and homogenises refugees against both the paradigm of rooted national citizenship, and the one of free, privileged, cosmopolitanism.

This pathological dimension is one of the main tropes of the *coloniality of asylum*: it produces a patronising order of victims and saviours that is proper of humanitarian logics (Malkki 1996; Fassin 2012) and it creates a parallel between colonial subjects and forced migrants (Jackson 2002: 84). Even in the most sympathetic narratives, 'refugees' are relegated to a paradigm of 'fugitivity' (Hesse 2014) which can never aspire to the realm of 'freedom' ascribed to Europeans and other white Westerners alone.

So far, we have seen that the divide between the free mobility of 'Europeans' and the forced flight of 'refugees' has a legal and moral dimension. However, it also abides to particular spatialities, temporalities and racial logics. Europeans are assigned to the 'post-nationality' (El-Tayeb 2008) of the EU/Schengen assemblage, while refugees are tied to a double national belonging, which attaches their asylum claims – and the prospective denial or granting – both to their country of origin and to the country to which they are allocated through the Dublin Regulation (chapter 4).

First, the credibility of an application is legally judged on a territorial assumption of national belonging, framed within a spatio-temporal linearity that sees asylum seeking as a straightforward movement from a country of origin to a receiving one. Because of the erasure of migration from the official history of nation-states, which confines migrants and refugees to a continuous 'presentism' (Schmidt 2017; Lachenicht 2018), contemporary asylum movements seem sudden phenomena happening in a still world. This has a poor grasp of the multiple displacements evident both in the case of long-term conflicts and labour migrations precedent to the emergence of contemporary conflicts, such as the cases of migrant workers in Libya, Afghan refugees in Iran or Pakistan, and Palestinian or Iraqi refugees in Syria – many of whom will appear throughout the book, once arrived in Europe.

Second, in view of the Dublin Regulation, which establishes the criteria for the processing of an asylum application by only one signatory state, refugees are also tied to the European country that is responsible for their application and, although they can travel through the Schengen area, they cannot legally settle in a country other than the one assigned to them (Picozza 2017a, 2017b). This relegation to a national country within a supposedly 'post-national' Europe invests also third-country nationals on visas until they obtain long-term residency. In other words, regardless of their legal status, asylum seekers and non-Europeans racialised as nonwhite are relegated to a differential treatment and regulation of their mobilities.

Furthermore, there is a postwar, postmodern and postcolonial temporal framework in the imagination of the European space as opposed to the 'non-Europe' that produces refugees. Policies that portray Europe as an 'Area of Freedom, Security and Justice' (Juss 2013), understand it as a site of liberal democracy that has shaken off both its colonial and totalitarian past

(Bhambra 2009). Importantly, this construction affects a portion of invisibilised Europeans, the Roma (Yildiz and De Genova 2017), who are racialised and persecuted in particular ways, and yet disqualified from claiming asylum because of the 1999 Aznar Protocol, which establishes a presumption of safety within each Member State.

Through this temporal displacement of conflict and persecution, coupled with the geographic dislocation of EU military involvement outside of its territory, 'Europe' is imagined not only as a space of *safety* but also of actively sought *peace*. This is nowhere more evident than in the 2012 award of the Nobel Peace Prize to the EU (Hansen and Jonsson 2013), which invisibilised the direct involvement of several Member States in ongoing conflicts in Afghanistan, Iraq and Libya – all major producers of refugee flows. This produces a discursive order in which the conditional acceptance of illegalised migrants is ultimately presented as a matter of hospitality, benevolence and democracy – a conceptual framework that has wide currency also in academia, as testified by Alexander Betts and Paul Collier's (2017: 99) argument for a 'duty of rescue' based on compassion instead of colonial 'guilt'. Here, the authors reduce the Syrian war to a matter of interethnic conflict and anti-regime revolt, ignoring Euro-American (as well as Russian and Iranian) involvement in the conflict via military intervention and the arms trade. Dismissing colonial responsibilities as a matter of the past, forecloses any understanding of the 'colonial present' (Gregory 2004).

As Europe is inscribed within the *post-modernity* of liberal rule, refugees are confined to the persistent *modernity* (Tuitt 2013) of illiberal rule, hence reactivating the 'denial of coevalness' (Fabian 2002: 35) that was a central logic of colonial difference between the 'native' and the coloniser. Precisely this spatio-temporal framework of Othering reinforces Europe's liberal democratic values standing against totalitarianism, dictatorship and illiberal rule externalised as 'non-Western' aberrations. Importantly, this discourse is crucial not only to the crafting of state policies but also to the way European citizens perceive to have left behind the experience of sociopolitical suffering in the form of war, persecution and dictatorship, and can thus become agents of hospitality, solidarity and charity. In this process, the spectacle of suffering of refugees is offered to European citizens as a field of action and thought, producing a *spectacle of solidarity*, whereby the politics of suffering translates into an always already racialised politics of Othering.

The dominant understanding of EU citizenship – and thus citizenry – builds on the colonial heritage of the formation of 'whiteness' as a 'national identity' – one that is not merely understood as a biological trait, but rather as a commonality of 'disposition, culture, and habits' (Anderson 2013: 37). This conceptualisation renders all other noncitizen or nonwhite European 'natives' *impossible* subjects who, because of their racialisation, 'can never be at home in Europe' and thus never 'enough' European (El-Tayeb 2008; Yildiz and De Genova 2017; Cantat 2015). This is nowhere more stark than in the insistence to call many nonwhite Europeans 'second-generation migrants' (or third or fourth): while white 'migrants' become more easily naturalised within the 'native' majority, nonwhite individuals are still considered migrants even when they acquire citizenship (Anderson 2013: 7). As signalled in the introduction, in the context of Germany, the hidden racial subtext of the category of 'migration' is well expressed in the concept of 'people with a migration background', which has been adopted also in EU statistics (United Nations Economic Commission for Europe 2006). Despite the efforts to de-ethnicise and de-racialise this statistical category through the mere recourse to nationality or place of birth of the person concerned or their parents, its use has percolated in the wider society in a deeply racialised, classed and Othering fashion (Ebua 2012). What is crucial about the 'migration background' social category is thus how it produces not only an imagination of 'migration' but also an imagination of white citizenry as the 'core national group' (Elrick and Schwartzman 2015: 1546), defined as a 'community of value' (Anderson 2013: 2).

Fatima El-Tayeb (2008: 650) posits that debates around migration, 'the war on terror' and 'the clash of civilisations' all contribute to produce a 'European public', that is to say a 'common continental identity' concerned with particular sociopolitical debates, and hinging on narratives of what clearly *is* and what *is not* 'European'. Although 'race' is an unspeakable subject in the continent (Goldberg 2006; Lentin 2014), the hegemonic understanding of European identity is 'culturally, economically and politically marked white' (Hesse 2007: 659). Consequently, also citizen 'minorities' and stateless 'natives', are popularly conflated in the category of 'migrant', condemned to a racial, spatial and temporal *exteriority*. Even though they have physically inhabited 'Europe' for centuries, nonwhite bodies are portrayed as always 'just arrived' (El-Tayeb 2008: 653) and thus debated through a persistent 'presentism'.

This externalisation of the 'non-Europe within' is coupled with a colonial amnesia that displaces colonialism and imperialism both historically – through a dominant narration of Europe as the cradle of human rights, democracy and liberalism – and geographically, since the remnants of colonial expansion, such as the French Overseas Territories in the Caribbean and the Spanish enclaves of Ceuta and Melilla in Morocco, do not generally feature in official EU maps (Bhambra 2009: 69). The 'European Question' (De Genova 2016a) thus translates into the fundamentally critical dilemma of where the geographical, political, conceptual, cultural and racial borders of Europe are to be found. While its unstable spatial identity is clearly not best conceptualised through territoriality (Rigo 2005), this does not seem to shake a perceived stability of its cultural identity, in terms of a European 'self' and multiple non-European 'others'. Against the background of these reflections, it is imperative to remark that neither 'Europeanness' nor 'whiteness' are stable identities; at least not as stable as the grand narratives of the EU – and their invisibilised racial subtexts – would like. They are 'graduated' (Anderson 2013: 37), constructed via overlapping regimes that are legal, cultural and social, and perhaps newly fragile with the Covid-19 pandemic which, at the time of submitting this manuscript, is 'democratising' authoritarian border control and subjecting also many white European citizens to arbitrary policing and mobility restrictions – a topic to which I will return in the conclusions.

1.3. PROTECTION AND UNFREEDOM: HOW RACE BECOMES LAW

With Barnor Hesse (2007) and Patrick Wolfe (2016), I understand 'race' as a primarily *governmental* category that comes before any pseudo-biological ideology and *naturalises* 'regulatory, administrative power [. . .] exercised by Europeanised ("white") assemblages over non-Europeanised ("non-white") assemblages' as if it were a natural arrangement (Hesse 2007: 656). Colonial law played a specific role in this naturalisation of political subordination, constructing the subjectivity of the non-European 'Other' under paradigms of uncivilised inferiority and incapability of self-determination (Chatterjee 1993: 33). 'Race', as both a practice and an ideology, was not an aberration of liberal history; it was, and still is, a fundamental feature of the liberal ideologies inherent to the political economy of capitalist expansion (Quijano 2000; Hesse 2014). The same can be said for the origins of contemporary border control, rooted in the exclusion of Asians from white settler colonies, through the demarcation between 'free migrants' – originating in the liberal 'West' – and 'coolies' – originating in the authoritarian 'East' (McKeown 2011).

These histories of colonialism, 'race' and border control run deep through the workings of the contemporary asylum regime which, through its legal and material impositions, deprives refugees of self-determination and condemns them to the deliberations of state bureaucracies, as well as the humanitarian management of NGOs and para-state institutions. While the right to asylum is hypocritically upheld as one of the principles of modern liberal democracy, it is in fact a system of subjugation, objectification, racialisation and victimisation, dramatically resonant of colonial administrative practices which (dis) qualified admission to humanity and freedom. While the purported historical 'immaturity' of colonised populations justified their exclusion from the liberal framework of equality and rights, the current naturalisation of asylum seekers as victimised Others justifies their exclusion from the freedoms reserved to Europeans only, particularly not only the freedom of movement but also the access to other labour, civil and political rights.

In 2015, former German minister of the interior, Thomas de Maizière, stated that 'asylum seekers must understand that they cannot choose where they are seeking protection' (Harding 2015). This statement reflects the double bind of securitisation and controlled humanitarianism (Walters 2015), which *naturalises* asylum seekers as vulnerable subjects in need of state protection, so that their vulnerability forms, precisely, the grounds for alienating them of self-determination. This discourse lies at the core of EU policies of refugee allocation, which are the other side of the coin of migrant deportation (Picozza 2017b). While the denial of protection more clearly creates the conditions of refugee deportability, allocation policies themselves subject both asylum seekers in due process and recognised refugees to particular instances of displacement and containment. This is because these policies lie in constant tension with refugees' 'spatial disobediences' (Tazzioli 2017), and thus affect the spatio-temporality of their life prospects, simultaneously producing 'stuckness' and 'restlessness' (Picozza 2017a: 237).

Upon entering the territory of the EU, asylum seekers are assigned to a sole competent country, via the overlapping regimes of the Dublin Regulation and the Relocation System (Bačić Selanec 2015) which, respectively, allocate asylum seekers to their first country of transit, or to one chosen through a redistribution system that takes into account Member States' population size, total GDP, unemployment rates and average numbers of asylum applications over the previous four years. Although the two systems hinge on different logics of distribution, they both uphold a paradigm of 'protection' that disqualifies refugees from making autonomous decisions over where to settle. They share a core principle of *legislatively enforced allocation*, based on a conceptual framework for which refugees' autonomous mobilities are an 'abuse' of the EU's benevolence. Termed 'asylum shopping', this purported 'abuse' plainly refers to the fact that asylum seekers may dare to decide their place of residence and thus, potentially, also submit multiple applications in order to have a greater array of choices. The 'shopping' metaphor suggests a parallel with the distinction between 'asylum seekers' and 'economic migrants': while 'shopping' implies a calculating 'consumer', political asylum and humanitarian protection are framed as gratuitous state concessions, existing outside of capital/labour relationships, and nonnegotiable by asylum seekers.

German federal distribution policies peculiarly mirror the same principles as, after their first registration, asylum seekers are redistributed to different federal states through an algorithm[2] and subjected to the *Residenzpflicht*, a residency obligation introduced in 1982 and variously lifted and reinstated, which prohibits them to move without official permission from the federal state responsible for their application (Fontanari 2015). In 2016, this obligation was extended also to recognised refugees, under the rubric of facilitating 'integration',[3] and avoiding ghettoing. Importantly, the legal developments introduced between 2015 and 2016 produced a further partitioning of asylum seekers under the concept of the *Bleibeperspektive* ('Prospect to Stay'). Asylum claims were divided by nationality into different categories based on the previous year's acceptance rates, with the twofold goal of facilitating the quicker insertion in the labour market of some, while facilitating the deportation procedures of others. That the criterion was based on asylum seekers' nationality was in stark contradiction with the individual right to asylum described in the Geneva Convention, and upheld by both EU directives and the German Constitution itself. In its implementation, this partitioning produced the systematic differential treatment of different national groups of asylum seekers. A 'good prospect to stay' meant that the nationality of the applicant had had a positive recognition rate of more than 50 per cent in the previous year, and concerned only applicants from Syria, Iraq, Iran, Somalia and Eritrea, who were granted free language classes and access to the labour market while their applications were still pending. Conversely, at the lower end of the 'Bleibeperspektive' spectrum, the applications by nationals of 'safe countries of origin' were considered 'obviously unfounded', and this especially concerned Western Balkans' ethnic Romas, who were placed in fast-track detention centres pending deportation. In the middle ground, those whose 'prospect to stay' fell below 50 per cent but were not nationals of 'safe countries of origin', were categorised as 'complex cases' and faced longer waiting times for the assessment of their applications. In particular, the large group of Afghan asylum seekers present in Hamburg had their applications pending for over a year at the time of my research, and were meanwhile denied of the entitlement to the *Integrationskurs* (the official language classes), as well as mobility within Germany (under the *Residenzpflicht*), and access to the labour market while their asylum procedure was still pending.

This brief review of EU and German lawmaking regarding asylum shows that the refugee's relationship to the law is one of subjection, examination and precariousness (Behrman 2019) but, importantly, this is justified precisely in the name of human rights, safety and protection. Following a classical logic of 'colonial difference' (Chatterjee 1993: 18–34), authoritarian government is premised on the incapability of self-government by the 'natives' turned 'refugees', who are portrayed as 'radically different, and hence incorrigibly inferior' (Chatterjee 1993: 33). It is this *naturalisation* of legal subordination that inscribes 'race' in the body of 'refugees', whether by placing them under the restrictions of the asylum procedure and further laws imposed on recognised refugees, or rather by expelling them from the law, by labelling them as 'rejected' and thus 'illegal'.

As mentioned earlier, the legal geographies of allocation confine refugees to a twofold spatio-legal 'belonging': the one of a supposed place of origin and nationality, attested not only through their own declarations but also, in the absence of documents, through linguistic tests (chapters 4 and 5); and the one of a 'competent country', established through the application of the Dublin regulation or the Relocation Scheme. Refugees' national belonging is essential to their asylum application, for they can seek protection only if they face danger in their very country of origin. It is predicated upon a 'national order of things' (Malkki 1992) that implies an isomorphism of peoples, territories and cultures (Gupta and Ferguson 1992), and it reproduces 'refugees' as 'natives' condemned to immobility (Fanon 1963: 51; Appadurai 1988: 37). Yet, the national order of things is here complemented by a 'European order of asylum' which allocates asylum seekers to particular countries in which they are expected to stay put and, in the German case, even only to particular local regions through the *Residenzpflicht*.

The European order of asylum rests on the conceptualisation of the Dublin space as one deemed uniformly 'safe' so that refugees are expected to stop as soon as they enter it. This purported 'safety', however, is evidenced through the mere record of good governance, such as the ratification of treaties and norms (Juss 2013: 312) while, in fact, violations of human rights regarding asylum seekers have been testified in virtually all member states, and complaints filed to the European Court of Human Rights have variously pertained to violations of the Common European Asylum System, systemic deficiencies in reception, Dublin transfers, bilateral agreements with third countries, arbitrary detention, and collective expulsions (Gatta 2019). While, usually, anti-Dublin arguments reproduce a dichotomous imaginary of Europe which unevenly distributes human rights across north and south, and west and east (Hristova et al. 2015), oppressing policies at Europe's borders have been always premised on the interests of the whole of the EU, as it is testified by the continuous funding to Hungary and Greece to enhance border control.[4] Moreover, while human rights violations have always been more visible within the spectacle unfolding at the southern and south-eastern external borders, other types of institutional violence and human rights violations have always been present in northern and western Europe, though relatively more invisible; detaining asylum seekers is a common practice in many member states (Welch and Schuster 2005), most of which, such as the UK, Germany, Norway and Sweden, have repeatedly deported failed asylum seekers back to long-term conflict areas, such as Afghanistan and Somalia (Khosravi 2018).

Beyond the violation of particular directives or treaties, the discourse of 'safety' conceals that refugee safety is first of all put at risk by the necessity of embarking on illegalised, dangerous journeys by land or sea, and that this necessity is created by the visa and border regime that is in place in the whole territory of the EU. There is simply no European country granting asylum seekers safe access to its territory. Moreover, once they have reached the EU's territory, refugees' safety is again hindered through their potential dislocation under the Dublin procedure. Finally, ultimate safety depends on the outcome of one's asylum application, as rejection may well result in a deportation – potentially to a place that, despite being legally a 'home country', may retain no tie for those who have been on the move for years, or else have been born or grown up in neighbouring countries, as their parents were already refugees. To make this point clearer: it is not only that Italy or Greece may be unsafe for asylum seekers because of their lower standards of reception; Germany, the UK or Norway can be equally unsafe because they may subject asylum seekers to deportations to Italy or Greece, as well as to their countries of origin. Moreover, the countries that are deemed to be 'safer' for asylum seekers are often also those with the highest rates of deportation for those rejected, so that the 'systemic efficiency' in asylum procedure can also be mirrored by efficiency in detention and deportation.

The naturalisation of this order is evident in the language of policy, whereby the proper word 'deportation' – proper because of its Latin etymology of *de-portare* ('carrying away') – can seldom, if at all, be found. Instead, deportations are 'euphemistically' (see also De Genova 2014; Jansen 2015: 24) called 'transfers' in the Dublin Regulation; 'returns' in the CEAS directive[5] concerning rejected asylum seekers; 'readmissions' in bilateral agreements; and 'removals' in the UK, where 'deportation' only refers to the removal of criminal offenders. While the immense violence of deportations to EU Member States under Dublin, 'safe third countries' and 'safe countries of origins' has been widely testified, the right of European states and peoples to manage Others is still prioritised and thus the double bind of *protection* and *unfreedom* (De Genova et al. 2018) is naturalised and unquestioned.

Significantly, this naturalisation percolates also in policy-oriented scholarship: Alexander Betts and Paul Collier contend that 'there is nothing inherent to being a refugee that necessitates unrestricted global mobility or the ability to choose a destination country' (2017: 204). Positing 'refugeeness' as quintessentially about *protection*, and not about *migration, autonomy* and *freedom*, the authors uphold the equation between unruly movements and ungovernability (Tazzioli 2018a), privileging the interests of the state over those of refugees themselves. This emphasis on state governability completely lacks any self-reflexivity regarding the positionality of the writing subjects who, like the volunteers who opened this chapter, benefit from the globally racialised distribution of the freedom of movement; in fact, the mobility of Western, white-majority countries' nationals, such as the above-quoted scholars, or myself, is not considered as a threat to the spatial ordering of the world.

Betts and Collier's argument expresses well an idea of liberal freedom –
and of denial thereof – that is 'enunciated from the colonial site of the citizen,
an always already free white European or white American male, posited as the
subject of rights' (Hesse 2014: 299–300) and responsible for reflecting on the
application of liberty to other subjects. Traditional liberalism implicitly posited 'freedom as whiteness' and, while opposing it to 'non-white, non-citizen
unfreedom' (Hesse 2014: 299), ignored other notions of 'positive' freedom
such as those enacted by the struggles of slaves and colonised peoples, which
were relegated to the realm of 'fugitivity' (Hesse 2014; see also Gopal 2019).
Likewise, policy-oriented migration scholarship re-objectifies refugees as
bodies to be *conceptualised* and *managed* by others, thus denying them of
agency and freedom under the above-discussed paradigm of vulnerability,
inferiority and Othering. Differently, the literature on the fragmented border
struggles of refugees in Europe (Picozza 2017a; Kasparek 2015; Fontanari
2019; De Genova et al. 2018) shows that they are active agents in resisting
the coloniality of asylum and redrawing the European space.

Highlighting how colonial imaginaries reflect not only in state discourses
of 'refugees' but also in the conceptualisation of white European citizens,
takes us to the question of the contested relations between these two subject
positions; how to conceptualise solidarity in a setting marked by coloniality
will be the kernel of the following chapter.

Chapter 2

Solidarity as Method

On the Intractable Coloniality
of Asylum Ethnographies

On one of my first nights in Hamburg, my host brought me to a Refugees Welcome fundraising party at the Molotow Club – the last marker of leftist resistance on the Reeperbahn, otherwise dominated by sex shops, sex-clubs and mainstream nightlife. I was tired by a long shift at the Central Station but also curious to see something more of the anti-racist scene that seemed so active in the city. On our way to the club, I was approached by a white German activist in his thirties, who was a member of the Interventionistische Linke[1] and, in the summer, had co-organised a caravan to pick up refugees stranded in Hungary and bring them to Germany. Because I had been introduced by my host as an Italian activist researcher, he started detailing his connections to the Italian autonomous left and tried to figure out my possible location within those networks. Along the way, he remarked multiple times that the fundraising's proceeds would entirely go to 'the refugees'. I felt irritated by this disembodied catchword floating in our conversation, which seemed a mere marker of legitimacy and recognition between people who supposedly shared the identity of 'refugee supporters'. That day I had left the station with the many pressing doubts highlighted in the previous chapters and I was also particularly alarmed by the way some anti-racist activists seemed to revendicate a sort of moral superiority on apolitical volunteers (see chapter 3).

The Molotow Club resembled a leftist squat, with walls covered in anti-racist and anti fascist flyers and scribbles in the toilets. The main room, where loud techno music played, was filled with smoke pierced by green lasers and strobe lights. While we were already dancing, I noticed that the 'Refugees Welcome' logo,[2] so widespread back in 2015, was flashing on the wall. As I pointed at it and expressed my perplexities, my host, himself a white academic/activist, replied mentioning Gramsci: in times like those, he pointed out, 'we' needed to build hegemonic visual cultures that would sustain our political engagement. At the time, the logo was stencilled on the streets, hung on the walls of squats, spaces of refugee support and universities, and raised at football matches. At the Molotow Club, that flashing 'hegemonic' effort, coupled with the loud music, smoke and strobe lights, felt to me an empty slogan, with an aesthetic and ideological connotation, rather than a practical one. If the logo was meant to spread awareness around welcoming and co-habiting with refugees across mainstream society, here, it was rather flashing in a space already oriented towards anti-racism and no-border politics. However, the bodies occupying that space were all white and, for the vast majority, German. Was it this the 'we' meant by my interlocutor? Or did it encompass the refugees too, conflating any difference among them, and between the supposed 'them' and the supposed 'us'? It was certainly bizarre to seamlessly transit from the space of the Central Station, where I was immersed in embodied encounters with those people vaguely categorised as 'refugees', and who were caught in critical life decisions, and a techno party, where white German activists would enjoy themselves until morning.

Departing from these preliminary considerations on the collective subjectivity of refugee supporters, and my own discomfort with pro-refugee spaces that are either totally disconnected from refugee bodies (like the Molotow Club) or hierarchically organised around the division between 'refugees' and 'supporters' (like the Bieberhaus described in chapter 1), this chapter seeks to make sense of the enmeshment of refugee solidarity within the coloniality of asylum. A central question that moves the following pages is how practices of solidarity can be animated by an anti-colonial and anti-racist spirit, without falling neither in a liberal humanitarian paradigm, nor in the romanticised/heroised imaginary of migration that often underpins autonomist theories of 'the political', at the core of no-border frameworks. Particularly, the chapter discusses what it means to adopt 'solidarity' not merely as an object, but rather as a true method of research, bearing specific epistemological and political dilemmas that demand for appropriate, though provisional, strategies in terms of knowledge production, concerning both fieldwork relations and the writing process.

2.1. THE GERM OF THIS BOOK

The germ of this book was sown in 2010, when I started volunteering at Asinitas, a small organisation founded in Rome in 2005, and active in the fields of intercultural education, migrant reception and participatory art. I was twenty-two then and animated by both a spirit of political responsibility and one of human curiosity towards the people who, after almost a year of violent pushbacks at sea towards Libya[3] were so present in the news. My job consisted primarily in teaching Italian through a method based on storytelling and the body's involvement in the classroom through games and physical activities. Occasionally, I took care of other tasks, such as conducting narrative interviews for the organisation's Archive of Migrant Memories, and accompanying students in their bureaucratic vicissitudes – for instance renewing residency permits. The three years I spent at Asinitas were a quasi-ethnographic experience that provided me with an embodied and intersubjective understanding of asylum's political, legal and social dimensions – an understanding that has deeply informed my later academic engagement with the topic. To me, Asinitas was not only a space of work or sociopolitical engagement; it was in those years virtually the only horizon of my social life, and the cradle of affective and intellectual bonds that have subsequently endured the years and our multiple displacements, as it will often appear throughout this ethnography.

Primarily, those years informed my conception of the state in relationship to borders and asylum, as well as of asylum geographies as a multi-scalar matter, investing the spatiality of the state, borders, the urban, the bodies of refugees, and the initiatives of solidarity that produce the everyday social relations of most refugees throughout their first period of arrival. With my students, I occasionally visited transit nodes, makeshift tent camps, refugee shelters, self-organised squats and state offices. These different spaces, which constituted their everyday life, were extremely vivid in the classroom. Accommodation centres were narrated as military camps, especially the night-only ones which entailed a heavy regulation of the rhythms of everyday life, pacing the set times of sleeping, waking up and eating. These facilities were almost invariably located in remote areas with little transport connection, enforcing a heavy socio-spatial segregation of refugees. Those with the strongest motivation to start a new life in Rome travelled several hours a day in order to attend language classes; others who struggled with depression and trauma, just killed time in the accommodation centres, waiting for the outcome of their asylum application. State bureaucracy held overall a great influence on their everyday, their bodies, their mobilities and also their memory, as life histories had to be reshaped for the purposes of a successful asylum interview, with clearly established causes of flight, chronologies of events and trajectories of transit.

These narratives first drafted in my mind an image of asylum as a system of state oppression that deployed specific regulatory and disciplining practices, while also creating spatial, legal and social segregation. Even though I did not move out of Italy until mid-2012, it was already evident to me that those practices were not unique to the Italian state. My students' narratives were distinctively translocal and transnational: they moved through multiple displacements and journeys, connecting Rome to dispersed locations such as their families' homes in Afghanistan, Somalia, Eritrea or Kurdistan, nodes of transit in Turkey or Libya where they had dwelt for months or years, boat landings in Lampedusa or Ancona, and makeshifts camps during seasonal agricultural work in southern Italy. Most strikingly for what would later become my research interests, they spoke about several locations in northern Europe, such as Birmingham, Munich and Oslo, from which they had been deported under the Dublin procedure. The standpoint of the language school thus opened a window on the dreadful effects of European policies, which not only pre-emptively illegalised asylum seekers by denying them of any legal channel of access, but also re-illegalised them by way of intra-European deportations. After moving to London in 2013, the theme of refugee intra-European unruly mobilities and the state's attempts to hamper them became the subject of my MA dissertation, for which I returned to Asinitas to conduct fieldwork in 2014.

This critical gaze towards the state is, however, only one side of the story. From the standpoint of the school, I also started appreciating how refugee segregation was unwittingly reproduced at the grassroots level. The myriad of small organisations active in Rome, alternately concerned with material donations, language learning, legal support, medical care, or art therapy were indeed working in sympathy towards refugees, trying to break their isolation and cover the many lacks in state support. However, they were also reconstituting specifically asymmetrical relations between refugees and vol-unteers – those who *needed help* and those who *provided help*. I nurtured the impression that there was a particular way in which refugees were *socialised as refugees*: first, through their encounters with the EU asylum regime – and the relevant national practices of border control; second, through their encounters with the volunteers; and both had particular consequences for their perceptions of space, time, and the self (Picozza 2017a). I observed that refugees in Rome entertained social relations almost exclusively with Italian volunteers and social workers (apart from those with other refugees) and, even when they accessed the labour market, it was mostly in sectors where the employees were virtually all also refugees. Particularly in the prolonged periods of unemployment, they would sleep in accommodation centres *for refugees*, attend language classes *for refugees*, theatre workshops *for refugees* and soup kitchens *for refugees*. In other words, there was little scope for them to establish peer relationships with Italians or non-refugee foreigners; their encounters were generally emplaced within the asylum regime.

Asinitas was a particularly critical standpoint, because its founders had specifically envisioned the project as a pedagogical one focused on learn-ing, rather than material or legal assistance – a move that attempted a shift from relating to refugees qua victimised passive subjects, to relating to them as individuals, active learners and sociopolitical agents. Within the use of narration and storytelling in the classroom, we systematically avoided hinging on bureaucratic language, or asking students to recount their journeys and reasons for flight. Any pre-understanding of learners *qua refugees* was discouraged; our pedagogical and political framework rather encouraged us to dwell on biographical tropes that illuminated existential commonalities between refugees and non-refugees, between the students and the teachers. Nonetheless, this shift towards individuality risked an unwitting depoliticisation; beyond its pedagogical work, Asinitas sought to influence the broader Italian society through public initiatives, publications and documentaries, but it did not engage in any direct legal or political struggle. The language school offered the students a space of sociability and care that accompanied them in their first period in Italy, and it was frequent to hear them commenting on how, within our space, they felt at home, able to *be*, and to *be seen* for, who they truly were. However, those whose asylum applications were rejected remained undocumented, while those who were recognised remained jobless. Many attempted a move to the European north, but were then deported back to Italy, time and again – having, as a result, to reckon with years, or even decades, spent undocumented, unable to visit their families back home and secure any economic stability. Finally, and more strikingly, our group was completely oblivious to the question of racialised power asymmetries. After a few, more or less failed, attempts to integrate some students as cultural mediators, the team with which I worked was almost entirely white and feminised, and while this was never sufficiently problematised, it was also a pattern that I subsequently encountered elsewhere in Europe (see chapter 7).

2.2. SOLIDARITY AS METHOD AND THE ETHNOGRAPHIC ETHOS

Throughout the ten years following my first contact with Asinitas, I have been variously involved in the sociopolitical world of asylum as a spectator, an educator, a friend, a partner, a researcher, a detainee visitor, a no-border activist, a translator and a volunteer in different contexts in Rome, London, Hamburg and, more recently, Mexico City. These multiple levels of engagement have shaped my way of conducting ethnography and thinking about borders and asylum, especially relating to the imperative mutual necessity of research and direct solidarity. Accordingly, I have learnt to conduct ethnography affectively and politically, countering the opportunism and extractivism of social research and investing in social relations based on long-term understanding, trust, care and reciprocity, however provisional they may be.

Conducting ethnography within a regime in which I feel partisan and participative is in no way unique to my own biography; it resonates with the experience of many of the European researchers with whom I have shared my academic trajectory, who mainly got access to their research fields not through state institutions, but rather through solidarity and activism networks (see, among others, De Genova 2005; Kasparek and Speer 2013; Fontanari 2019; Gambino 2017; Heller et al. 2017). Whether framed explicitly in terms of 'militant research' (Garelli and Tazzioli 2013b) – that is to say a partisan project of knowledge production in support of migrant struggles – or implicitly, in terms of producing critical knowledge on the border regime (Papadopulous et al. 2008; Tsianos et al. 2009), a principle of solidarity with migrant struggles is, for us, 'like a pair of glasses on our nose through which we see whatever we look at. It never occurs to us to take them off' (Wittgenstein 1958: §103). Indeed, it is not possible to take these glasses off, because 'there is no outside; outside you cannot breathe' (Wittgenstein 1958: §103).

Yet, to recognise the particular kind of gaze that orients and structures our research is not merely a matter of shedding light on individual positionalities or political stances. Nor is it an uncritical celebration of refugee practical support as the ethical research process par excellence. It is rather a way of subjecting to critical inquiry that very principle of solidarity at the core of academic and political interventions put forward by (mostly) white Europeans; understanding solidarity as a *method* means adopting it as an 'epistemological viewpoint' (Mezzadra and Neilson 2013: 18), and asking what observing, and engaging in, practices of refugee support can tell us about the *coloniality of asylum*. Historian Joan Scott's suggests that one of the main tasks of critique is to look at the sources of our values, 'how they have come into being, what relationships they have constituted, what power they have secured' (2007: 34–35). In this sense, throughout the book, I maintain a critical analysis of the ambiguity of European refugee solidarity, whose search for autonomy is often caught within the meshes of coloniality, and which I render simultaneously an object *and* a method of research, one that illuminates multiple processes of production of spaces, subjectivities, social relations, knowledge and power. In this sense, I propose *solidarity as method* as a critical tool capable of interconnecting the border regime's oppressive practices to the colonial relations inherent to autonomous practices of solidarity.

Within 'solidarity', I encompass heterogenous practices enacted by refugees and non-refugees alike, either at grassroots level by noninstitutionalised groups (chapter 3) or clandestinely, by individuals emplaced within institutional settings (chapter 5). They include material, legal and political support, such as organising temporary sleeping places or long-term accommodation; facilitating the logistics of transit through in-loco support and the mobilisation of transnational networks; preparing asylum seekers for their official hearing; disrupting deportations; aiding refugee self-organisation inside and outside the camps; and organising political mobilisations, such as demonstrations and campaigns.

Although they may differ tremendously in terms of political frameworks – alternately rooted in the political left, Christian ethics, humanitarianism and welfarism (Kelliher 2018) – these practices are all interlinked by a search for autonomy from the state, and thus a self-organised structure, responding either to a total critique and rejection of the state as a direct oppressor of refugees or, at the very least, an acknowledgement of its failures in terms of protecting their rights. This search for autonomy is contested: self-organisation does not always escape the meshes of state governmentality, nor those of European coloniality. But it is precisely this contested nature that renders grassroots solidarity a site of struggle and production, and thus a suitable 'epistemic angle' (Mezzadra and Neilson 2013: 18) from which to explore the coloniality of asylum both in terms of the critical potential of these initiatives, and their reproduction of a politics of Othering.

The practices of solidarity that I narrate in the following chapters unfold 'in the margins of the state' (Das and Poole 2004); they include the Central Station Helper Network, the anti-racist legal consultation project Cafe Exil and the no-border alliance Never Mind the Papers, where I conducted participant observations between 2015 and 2017. Whenever it appears throughout the book, the 'centre' of the asylum regime – state offices, refugee camps and spectacularised border zones – is always evoked through the gaze of self-organised refugee and non-refugee activists, volunteers, social workers and lawyers or, alternatively, refugees contesting the institutions of the asylum regime through everyday embodied practices. These critical 'margins' show how colonial power operates in multiple ways, enmeshing also the places where the law does not reach, but they also harbour a potential for both autonomy and negotiation of recognition. Notwithstanding the local and national peculiarities of my fieldwork setting, my ethnographic material speaks to wider European processes for which 'the increasing coordination of anti-immigration policies at the supranational level' is concomitant to a 'crossborder restructuring of migration struggles' (Cantat 2015: 262).

Finally, and fully inhabiting the contradictions that shape this book, *solidarity as method* is simultaneously an epistemological device that allowed me to *see* – and later to *write* – in particular ways, and a political stance that allowed me to *do* certain things within and without the field. Methodology and epistemology are inherently political (Mezzadra and Neilson 2013: 17); they entail different ways of intervening in the world we are studying, producing knowledge and representations and relating to the interlocutors that render our research possible. In this sense, ethnography is not a mere method but also an ethos – and an intractably problematic one, which demands for a specifically politicised reflexivity, capable of accounting for its own conditions of possibility and inherent limits (De Genova 2005: 20). *Solidarity as method* is also thus indissolubly attached to the ethnographic tradition of prioritising *intersubjectivity* over any 'objective' fetishisation of categories (Jackson 1996: 9). My research subjects embody different legal, social and political approximations to the 'self' and the 'other'; none of them is constructed as an 'object of research', but rather as interlocutors within an ongoing dialogue that interrogates the politics of asylum in Europe.

2.3. HAMBURG'S GEOGRAPHIES OF ASYLUM

As it often happens with the unpredictability of ethnographic practice, my privileged field sites have been less the outcome of calculated scientific rigour and more of a sum of coincidences related to my own biography as a 'refugee supporter'. During my master's, I conducted participant observation at Asinitas in Rome and, during my PhD, I ended up in Hamburg with the purpose of seeing Farhad, a former Asinitas student and research interlocutor who had ended up there after a tortuous trajectory of legal uncertainties and fragmented displacements that lasted five years. Born and grown up in Afghanistan, Farhad arrived in Norway in 2011 as an unaccompanied minor but, upon turning eighteen, saw his asylum claim rejected. He thus moved to Italy and attempted a second asylum application, which had a positive outcome in 2014. However, due to the lack of job opportunities there, he again set northward, and spent a couple of months in Calais, trying to cross the Channel. Eventually, he unintentionally hid in a wrong lorry and ended up at the border between the Netherlands and Germany, where a Hamburg-based friend picked him up and brought him to the Hanseatic city.

In 2015, I had become particularly interested in the context of Germany, because the momentum of the *Wilkommenskultur* had brought the 'margins' of the 'EU border regime' to the centre of its public discourse. First, it had brought into view the 'north' of Europe, previously conceived as 'peripheral' to the more mediatised border struggles happening on the southern and south-eastern shores of Europe. Second, it had brought to the fore of public debate and everyday engagement the role of volunteers and supporters within and against the regime (Fontanari and Borri 2017: 12). The newly formed Central Station Helper Network and the overcrowdedness of camps had suddenly rendered Hamburg similar to southern-European transit nodes, but this was happening in an urban and national context marked by a particular history of refugee struggles and grassroots solidarity. Hamburg's geographies of asylum have been transforming through different historical stratifications depending on multiple factors and actors, most notably refugees' own mobilities and political struggles and the state efforts to contain them, including institutional arrangements over legal recognition, accommodation, residency obligations and deportation.

Although not mediatised in the European 'border spectacle' until 2015, Germany had long been a political centre of the asylum regime (Post and Niemann 2007). Most notably, the Dublin Regulation – which was precisely one of the factors that led to the complications and fragmentations of Farhad's mobilities (Picozza 2017a) – was modelled on two German innovations in lawmaking: the 1993 'safe third country' concept, which established that asylum seekers could be deported to some transit countries, and the 1982 *Residenzpflicht*, which imposed a 'residency obligation' within, and a prohibition of movement without, the federal state to which asylum seekers had been allocated.[4] More recently, Germany has been the leading actor in the centrality of the deportation debate in the EU, pushing forwards a reconfiguration of 'safe countries of origin' and including the effort to exclude some nationalities from the right to asylum, which has resulted, for instance, in the EU-Afghanistan deal (Webber 2017).

Throughout the decades, the German border regime has engendered a great number of migrant struggles and solidarity networks. With the closure of the guest worker regime, which had also facilitated the migrations of politically persecuted Turks, Greeks and Portuguese (Karakayali and Rigo 2010: 129), from the 1970s onwards, asylum became an increasingly sought-after legal channel for entry, also responding to the imposition of visas on nationals of several African and Asian countries (Nsoh 2008: 261). Until the 1990s, the largest incoming population of legally recognised refugees in Germany originated from the 'Eastern Bloc', and from Yugoslavia, but refugees from South Asia, the Middle East and Africa were also increasingly present. Among other examples, Hamburg became home to a relatively large group of Afghans escaping the 1979 Soviet invasion (Braakman 2005), as well as Iranians, after the 1978 Revolution.[5]

From the 1980s onwards, refugee newcomers have been segregated in accommodation camps at the outskirts of the city. However, the area of the Central Station connects them to the wider citizenry, both because of the spatial configuration of the migrant-owned small business in the neighbourhood of St. Georg, east of the station, and because of the state migration-related offices located south of the Central Station. Steindamm Street, with its majority of Turkish, Arabic and Persian groceries and restaurants, is a premier example of the stratifications of different migrations and how they reshaped the city. Steindamm has been at the core of research on 'linguistic superdiversity' (Scarvaglieri et al. 2013; Carson 2016) and could be an iconic postcard of 'postcolonial Hamburg', connecting the older generations of refugees and migrants to the newcomers, as well as to German citizens.

At the time of my fieldwork, the area south of the Central Station was a crucial node both at the level of state institutions and of grassroots support to refugees. The BAMF[6] quarters and the Ausländerbehörde were both located on Spaldingstraße, ten minutes away from each other. While the BAMF was responsible for asylum interviews and decisions, as well as for Dublin procedures, the Ausländerbehörde released or denied all residency permits, as well as deportation orders[7] – meaning that, at the time of my research, all asylum applicants in Hamburg became familiar with this area from their very arrival. For this reason, the anti-racist consultation project Cafe Exil was strategically located on Spaldingstraße, directly facing the Ausländerbehörde. Focusing on the provision of independent consultation, bureaucratic support and legal advice to migrants and refugees, the project was established in direct response to the 1993 *Asylkompromiss*, which revised article 16(a) of the Constitution of the Asylum Right and imposed unprecedented restrictions on German asylum laws, including the introduction of the 'safe country of origin' and 'safe third country' concepts. After the arrival of about 440,000 asylum seekers in 1992 – mostly fleeing ex-Yugoslavia – the topic of asylum became particularly heated in Germany, leading to both intra-parliamentary conflicts and anti-immigrant arson attacks (Kirchhoff and Lorenz 2018: 51). In this context, more and more anti-racist and pro-refugee networks started organising, including Karawane (Caravan for the Rights of Migrants and Refugees), Keine Mensch ist Illegal (No One is Illegal) and Kanak Attak (El-Tayeb 2008). Further networks emerged in the following decade and progressively introduced the question of transversal alliances between 'refugees' and 'supporters' within the autonomous left movement[8] (Ünsal 2015; Odugbesan and Schwiertz 2018).

The Hamburg autonomous movement has provided throughout the years a prime example of intersectional alliance between migration and urban struggles (Geronimo 2012; Borgstede 2016). Between the end of the 1980s and the beginning of the 1990s, a group of activist squatted a raw of buildings on the Hafenstraße, in the St. Pauli neighbourhood.[9] As they later reached an agreement with the city that allowed them to keep these buildings, these have remained a crucial site of support in recent years, especially during the peak of the Lampedusa in Hamburg protest (Borgstede 2016). Moreover, as the rents escalated throughout the 2000s, the Right to the City alliance provided a specific focus on gentrification, housing struggles and the reappropriation of public spaces (Birke 2016).

The period between the 1980s and the 1990s was also the theatre of the reformation of state-led programmes of refugee accommodation, culminated in the institution of Fördern und Wohnen, a state nonprofit company responsible for the accommodation of homeless people and refugees. Most refugee camps were located in industrial remote areas, away from the gaze of middle- and upper-class citizens (Riewe 2017). Simultaneously, refugees were subjected to the *Residenzpflicht*, which became one of the main focuses of the 2013 wave of refugee protests, culminated in the occupation of Oranien Platz in Berlin (Ünsal 2015; Meret and Diener 2019). In Hamburg, this new turning point was marked by the emergence of the 'Lampedusa in Hamburg' group (see chapter 4) who, after fleeing Libya, had transited through Italy and were thus excluded from the right to seek asylum in Germany, because of the Dublin Regulation. Their protest explicitly connected the wider realm of EU asylum policies with the plight of refugees in Germany. Backed by a massive support by the autonomous left, Lampedusa in Hamburg maintained visibility in the city through the erection of a protest tent on Steindamm, just outside the Central Station, which resisted multiple eviction attempts, until its removal in March 2020, enforced on the basis of public health during the COVID-19 pandemic.

In 2014, the alliance Never Mind the Papers was formed as a 'twin group' to the Right to the City, with the aim of offering a specifically no-border[10] perspective within the autonomous left. It included members of Lampedusa in Hamburg, their supporters, and other organisations, such as Cafe Exil. For this new alliance, the Hafenstraße squats were again crucial, as they hosted meetings and other activities. Never Mind the Papers became more and more visible in the city, both through demonstrations and mobi-tours to refugee camps, that is to say visits intended to get in touch with recently arrived refugees, breaking their isolation and offering them support to politically mobilise within and without the camps.

Until 2015, refugee support had been a prerogative of the state, the church[11] or the autonomous anti-racist/no-border left. However, the 2015 'refugee crisis' marked a shift in the popularity of grassroots refugee support and solidarity. As temporary refugee camps mushroomed in virtually every neighbourhood through containers, tents or the readaptation of empty hardware stores with camping beds and chemical toilets, local residents formed countless Refugees Welcome initiatives aimed at both providing material support and spaces of socialisation. The peculiarity of these initiatives was not only that the wider citizenry suddenly encountered the refugees that had so far been far away from their gaze; it was also that these often self-ascribed 'apolitical' citizens were suddenly connected to the anti-racist activists, who in many instances participated in the Refugees Welcome groups. Moreover, the new wave of refugees started organising politically in new configurations, especially relating to the deportation threats to Afghans and Roma. It is this specific context of encounter between different political frameworks, as well as the period of apparent state withdrawal and successive reinforcement of the border regime that shaped the background of my immersive fieldwork in Hamburg.

2.4. WHO ARE THE 'NATIVES' OF
THE ASYLUM REGIME?

In November 2016, while I approached the end of fieldwork and my return
to London, Farhad was about to leave Hamburg in order to renew his papers
in Italy and I asked if I could interview him in order to reflect on his long-
term trajectory. He sounded reluctant but, instead of plainly refusing, he
bounced the ethnographic gaze back to me: 'Fiorenza, how long has this
research been going on? Do you do anything else than your research?' As
I mumbled a tentative answer around the messy continuity between my
life and research, he pressed with another question: 'Why don't you write
about yourself? You also move a lot. You have become a *mohajer* yourself.' The ambiguity of this Persian word, meaning alternately 'traveller',
'migrant' and 'refugee', signalled the contested nature of our relationship
and is precious to introduce the question of the 'self' and the 'other' within
my ethnography. At the time, I occupied multiple positionalities: I was a
researcher, a white woman, a mobile EU citizen and a refugee supporter and
activist. These intersections highlight how researchers' identities are 'bor-
dered' (De Genova 2017b: 18), that is to say, how we are always already
enmeshed in the power relations that constitute our field. Yet, Farhad's
questions also interrogate how the very process of research constructs its
own 'field' (Gupta and Ferguson 1997), with its categories, distinctions and
demarcations. To start with, in my ethnography, there is no clear-cut boundary between the 'inside' and the 'outside', or between the 'field' and 'home'
(Gupta and Ferguson 1997: 112). Who is the 'native' of Europe's geographies of asylum? Is it the white 'European' who occupies public discourse
alternately welcoming or rejecting refugees? Or is it rather the *mohajer*, in
its alternative figures of 'migrant' and 'refugee', reproduced as a 'native out
of place' (De Genova 2005, 2016b)? Farhad and I are actually both native to
the asylum regime, albeit occupying different positions and, I suggest, we
should not be studied in isolation. Asylum ethnographies are dangerously
preceded by colonial ethnographies, if we think of their dual relationship to
colonial power (Asad 1973). While it is common to ask whether knowledge
production in this field can contribute to the border regime – for example,
by endangering migrants through the exposure of their illegal practices – it
is important to reverse the question: how does the coloniality of the border
regime always already shape the conditions of our knowledge production?
What are the circumstances under which a person like me can come to be
interested, sympathetic and committed to the experiences of migrants which
embody the European contemporary subalterns par excellence? Which
labels, questions and perspectives does coloniality push me to adopt and
which ones does it foreclose?

During colonialism, ethnographers were seen as mobile subjects enquiring into the lives of purportedly 'stuck', 'immobile' and 'timeless' natives (Fabian 2002; Appadurai 1988: 37; De Genova 2016b: 232). Conversely, most of contemporary engagements with refugees in Europe suppose emplaced, rooted and 'native' 'European' researchers conducting research with refugees who are seen as (hyper)mobile and uprooted. Even when researchers are mobile, as it is my case, their mobility is conceived of as 'free' and thus different from the 'coerced' movement of refugees. Farhad's questions precisely disrupted these assumptions, by addressing my own 'migrancy'.

In my past work, I had engaged with hypermobile Afghan refugees – including Farhad himself – looking at the impact of multidirectional mobilities on their subjectification as *unresolved 'selves-in-transit'* (Dobson 2004), a condition marked by fragmentation and temporariness, and always projected to an elsewhere and an 'elsewhen' (Picozza 2017a: 245). At the time of my fieldwork in Hamburg, however, this condition had very much become a marker of my own subjectivity, albeit under much more privileged conditions. At the time of writing, my social, emotional and professional life is effectively scattered across five countries, an ocean, three languages and a half, multiple bureaucratic and economic relationships to different states, and several sim-cards. International migration under global neoliberalism produces fragmentation and temporariness, shaping our experiences of movement, space, belonging and temporality in particular ways. These are issues that cut across Farhad's and my experiences, but they unite as much as they divide us.

That our lives, loves, aspirations and memories are scattered across different locations through which we move produces a commonality of existential, social, emotional and psychological experiences, and this is an empathic awareness that has often helped me supporting other people on the move on the personal level, especially during the first times of arrival in a new place and the relevant feelings of disorientation, loss of meaning and loneliness (chapter 6). However, it is precisely this commonality of experiences that increases the political divide between us, for the material conditions that allow us to act upon those existential conditions are dramatically differential. My legal status and my economic situation have so far allowed me to smoothly cross the different geographical locations of my life; Farhad's precarious legal status, conversely, implies that every transnational move is a potential impediment to going back to the previous location. While in the conversation above he called me a 'migrant', at other times, he challenged me on our differences, remarking that I had not been waiting for five years for the positive outcome of a Dublin procedure and an asylum application in order to be legally allowed to work. Moreover, he would point out that I did not have the urgency to support my family back home. Class privilege mostly

translates into disposability of time: being paid as a researcher means dispos-
ing of time for reflection, a time that may well be seen by others as 'leisure'
rather than 'work'. When Farhad asked me if I did *anything else than my
research*, he meant that studying was a luxury. This disposability of time renders not only academic work a 'truly intractable problem' (De Genova 2005:
29) but also activism itself, especially when it is asymmetrically constituted
through advocating for someone else's rights, rather than for one's own quest
(chapter 7). Farhad's questions thus clearly expressed the dialectics between
our commonalities *and* differences, a dialectics that I mobilise throughout the
book in the attempt to recognise political differences while simultaneously
dismantling them at the level of Othering. In other words, while I recognise 'refugees' as politically oppressed, and I specifically dwell on the their
racialisation, I also attempt not to essentialise them as a coherent group or as
coherent subjects.

The same anti-essentialist posture holds for the other pole of my research,
the refugee supporters, wherein I also lacked a straightforward 'insider' or
'outsider' position, but rather entertained multiple degrees of proximity and
distance, or approximation to self and Other. First, as signalled by Farhad, I was
myself a foreigner, but this had different meanings depending on the groups
and the individuals I interacted with. For the political activists, be they German
or refugees, I was mostly an 'insider' – due to the common internationalist and
anti-racist framework signalled in the opening vignette – and our easily established comradeship often translated into friendship. Particularly because of my
previous work in refugee support, I acted with care and patience and I was thus,
in their eyes, different from opportunistic researchers who, after obtaining their
interviews, disappear as suddenly as they had appeared.[12] I highlight this with
all the inherent ambiguity, because it was my supposed embeddedness that
granted me trust and thus access to the field. In multiple instances, I was told
that I could literally write what I wanted, that I was trusted, and that my writing
would be an occasion of reflection also for my interlocutors. Sometimes such
professions of trust were coupled with ironic mockeries of academic research:
'You're an activist first. We trust each other' – told me once Ella, a Never Mind
the Papers activist – 'If you need to write about this because that's how you
earn your money, it's fine. Write whatever you want. Anyhow, nobody's gonna
read it.' It was a provocative reminder of the fact that while researchers often
indulge in self-reflexivity ascribing excessive power to their position, in fact,
their interlocutors may be way more preoccupied of other urgencies and easily
'move on' after an interview.

The situation was quite different with the Central Station Helper
Network, especially regarding those 'apolitical' volunteers who were not
aligned with no-border and anti-racist politics. They also trusted me, for
we were volunteering together and they perceived me as a 'concerned

European'; however, because of my Italian nationality and the fact that I habitually resided in London, they saw me more as an outsider coming to research 'their' field. Both perceptions were true in different ways: I was not German, I did not speak German and I had not been living in Germany prior to my fieldwork – all factors which, effectively, made me an 'outsider'. However, I had entered their spaces with a set of previously gained skills that made me very much 'internal' to the realm of refugee support, particularly regarding language skills in Persian, Italian and Spanish; legal and bureaucratic knowledge of asylum; and sociocultural and interpersonal skills in relating to so-called 'vulnerable' people. These skills meant that I entered the field not as a wholly external 'participant observer' who needed to learn all the relevant codes and information, but rather as someone who already knew many of those codes and could make a direct contribution while also observing and learning.

Significantly, that I shared languages with refugees but not with 'the Germans' positioned me in a peculiar middle ground between the two groups, first and foremost because I did not fit the naturalised distinction between (white, German) 'helpers' and (racialised or migrantised) 'translators'. That the 'translators' were usually thought of as 'people with a migrant back-ground' was at odds with the fact that I spoke Persian while being white and European and lacking any family ties to that language. Most importantly, both Persian and Italian – and to a minor degree Spanish – created a complicity with many refugees, as 'the Germans' could not understand us. Many Never Mind the Papers' refugee activists, as well as migrants who attended Cafe Exil, had previously been living in Italy and this established a particular sociocultural recognition. My Italianness carried a wider meaning of 'southern-Europeanness' and 'Mediterraneanness', understood by both them and myself as a marker of a particular sociability, mental flexibility and inclination to overlooking strict rules, as well as a sociopolitical positioning at the bottom of hierarchies of Europeanness (Cantat 2015: 250). In particular, Cafe Exil's guests would often lament the 'cold' character of the Germans, as well as their obsession with rules and bureaucracy and would establish a particular complicity between us, premised on sociocultural stereotyping.

This complicity allowed me to grasp the extent of the frustration of many refugee activists regarding the way white privilege operates in the most radical circles of solidarity (chapter 7). Yet, as already signalled above, this complicity is a contested matter. If 'Mediterraneannes' can represent 'a counter-positioning to the official discourse on European identity' (Cantat 2015: 250), also because of its internal histories of racialisation and hierarchisation of whiteness, its meanings have also profoundly been redressed through the institution of the European Union and the Schengen Space. Italians have *become* 'white' (Gardaphé 2002) and they have been 'demigrantised', both in terms of internal and international south-north migrations. Nowadays, therefore, the fact that I am read as white by the police, and that my passport allows me to move more or less without restrictions, place me in a very different position from the refugees who participated in my research – be they activists or not. My de-migrantisation remains nonetheless provisional, as, in the wake of Brexit, EU citizens have been re-migrantised and, in a similar fashion, Germany has started imposing restrictions on their access to welfare (see Riedner et al. 2016; Tazzioli 2015b). The recognition of these historical dynamics establishes an important background against which one can recognise the material realities of white privilege while simultaneously not truly *believing to be white*. As James Baldwin (1998: 180) powerfully reminds us, being white is a 'lie' and believing it is a 'moral choice'.

The provisionality of whiteness notwithstanding, within leftist transnational activism and solidarity, the not-so-much-whiteness of Italians and other southern Europeans is too often mobilised as a claim of innocence, for instance by asserting that we are 'less racist than northern European or American societies' (Stanley 2015: 92). There are, however, two dimensions that establish a significant commonality between white Italians and white Germans: the collective amnesia over our colonial past (Triulzi 2006), popularly considered 'marginal' to the British and French empires, and the racial taboo that has followed the experience of Nazi-fascism. While both Italian and German colonialism were the theatre of some of the most atrocious crimes of the whole colonial experience (Bernhard 2012; Olusoga and Erichsen 2010), within the respective national collective memory these have been obscured by the crimes of Nazi-fascism (Schilling 2015). I highlight this displacement not with the intent of instituting yet another hierarchy between unquantifiable atrocities, but because there are specific connections between these distinct historical experiences which have been widely analysed elsewhere (DuBois 1947: 23; Arendt 1973; Fanon 1963: 101; Césaire 2000: 36). The most pressing result of this displacement, for the purposes of this book, is that the specific Italo-German colonial amnesia and racial taboo too easily externalise racism as a matter of right-wing politics, obscuring how colonial sedimentations impact on the racialisation of society at large (Goldberg 2006; Hesse 2007; Lentin 2014; Giuliani 2018), and thus also on the very spaces of refugee solidarity.

2.5. LISTENING, LABELLING, REPRESENTING

For the reasons highlighted so far, in the course of fieldwork, I usually conducted in-depth interviews only with people with whom I had established personal and political bonds over the course of time, be they refugees or supporters. There was, however, one episode in which I interviewed a Somali young man who I did not previously know. At the time, Abdullahi was waiting for the final outcome of his Dublin procedure, and we were introduced by Daud, a common friend who was a member of Never Mind the Papers and whom I had just interviewed. As Abdullahi could neither work, nor attend language classes, he was trying to contain his overthinking through endlessly watching TV at home. It thus did not surprise me that he eagerly agreed to the interview, seeing it as a potentially pleasant diversion from a suffocating everyday monotony. After all, that had also been a recurrent experience during my 2014 fieldwork in Rome. While I will discuss both Abdullahi and Daud's trajectories in chapter 4, here I reflect on that episode in order to discuss the modes of listening, labelling and representation that are ingrained in certain stereotypical fieldwork encounters, and to pave the way to the strategies I have sought in order to redress these dynamics.

Abdullahi's soft voice was difficult to grasp amidst the noises of the cafe in which we sat, yet his words seamlessly came out all at once, like a river. They flooded the table, my phone recording the interview, and his full cup of tea, left untouched within the incessant speech. It took about two hours to spell out all the geographical displacements and legal implications. Then, suddenly, he broke the fiction of the interview and threw us both into the awareness of our strange setting. He started explaining how he had learnt to trust strangers, particularly white women, and that thread unravelled painfully. A couple of years back, while waiting for the outcome of his asylum application in an accommodation facility in Sweden, he had fallen in love with an Albanian girl, but her family, who were also residents of the camp, disapproved of her relationship with a black man. They met secretly, backed-up by her younger sister, until their relationship was abruptly interrupted by the deportation of the girl and her family back to Albania. At this point of the story, Abdullahi paused, suddenly realising he did not even know why he was telling me those personal details, about which I had asked no questions. Yet, the conversation went on for another hour. The girl had been diagnosed with uterine cancer and her family wanted to marry her off so that she could give birth before her hysterectomy. She thought of escaping and reaching her beloved in Germany, but he rejected that prospect, thinking that his legal and material circumstances were too precarious to allow any stability for them. She would miss her family too much, he told her on the phone, but she heard no reason; she did not want to marry someone she did not love. He thus cut off the conversation and scolded her: 'at this point of your life, you don't have the chance to *love*'.

'You see, Fiorenza, I'm not worried about my Dublin case; I just think of her all the time' – he said to conclude the account. Only then was I struck by the fact that, throughout the whole interview, I had been insisting with the details of court hearings, making sure he was in contact with a lawyer in order to prepare for his asylum interview and suggesting he visited Cafe Exil. As a researcher, I could not escape the arena in which 'we' – whoever we are, journalists, researchers, documentarists, artists or supporters – deprive refugees of that tridimensionality of affection, liveliness and everydayness that is, after all, the fabric of the life of most people, regardless of their immigration status (Jackson 2013: 4). 'We' represent 'them' as victimised subjects or, in the best case, as carriers of some political value, almost invariably reproducing the landscape of the 'border spectacle'. However, refugee mobilities are not only waved of the structural constraints of war, poverty, persecution and legal precariousness; they are also made of affective relations, love, ruptures, rejoining beloved people or not being able to do so, as anybody else's stories. To highlight how this sense of one self and experience exceeds one's legal or political positioning does not mean to underestimate the latter, as I have already discussed above. That Abdullahi was giving more weight to the grief for an impossible love than to his legal precariousness did not change the fact that his possibilities of action were extremely constrained by the latter. What I aim to highlight here is rather the gap between how people understand their own experiences, perceptions and feelings, and how researchers and/or supporters interpret those subjective dimensions.

Before we parted ways, Abdullahi thanked me for listening. He felt lighter after telling his story and leaving it 'outside of himself'. This sense of relief after emotional interviews was not unique to my encounters with 'refugees'. In more than one occasion, white German supporters burst into tears or got otherwise emotional after recounting important episodes. Some specifically explained that they usually lacked such intersubjective spaces for reflection and that *being listened to* offered them a potential for healing. However, my interviews with German volunteers and activists had, from the onset, a balanced, dialogical quality, as we effectively shared both opinions *and* experiences of refugee support departing from similar positionalities. Differently, in my previous research experiences, as well as the one with Abdullahi, interviews with 'refugees' presented a specific imbalance: the interviewees shared painful experiences that, in their being political, were also very intimate. They offered this fragility to me as a material for reflection and, in turn, I adopted a quasi-therapeutic listening position, without necessarily sharing my own intimate information. But those labelled as 'refugees' are constantly interrogated by others enquiring about their 'experiences', they are literally *exposed* – whether in transit nodes, refugee camps, NGOs' premises or other volunteering spaces – to people coming and seeking their stories to tell, often asking questions that reproduce the discursive order of the asylum interview, as well as any other interaction with lawyers, social workers or medical professionals, whose role is to assess their 'vulnerability'. The result is not a counter-narration, but rather a mere reproduction of the tropes of the coloniality of asylum analysed in chapter 1.

2.6. THE VOICES THAT ARE LOUDER IN THIS BOOK

As I entered my research in Hamburg with the intention of developing a critical narration of asylum, this commitment translated not only in particular strategies of representation but also in the search for particular voices. I still collected data regarding the experiences of mobility of refugees within the Dublin space, but I attempted as much as possible to avoid any voyeuristic enquiry into their suffering and to rather subject this voyeurism to critical reflection. Compared to my 2014 fieldwork in Rome, which mostly focused on refugees waiting for their asylum procedure, in Hamburg, I engaged more with refugee activists, seeking to know not only about their *experiences* but, most importantly, about their *opinions* of both the asylum regime and European solidarity. As a result, the voices that have made their way into this book are mostly those of politically engaged refugees, who are for the vast majority men, and of politically engaged white Germans, of both genders, with the addition of some migrants who are not strictly 'refugees' in legal terms. This gendered imbalance, which represents a potential blind spot of the book, will be tackled in chapter 7, in order to show how, while this overwhelming majority of refugee men is symptomatic of my research field, it is often uncritically taken for granted by both researchers and activists, who do not sufficiently seek refugee women voices.

Prioritising refugee activist voices runs counter to the common ethical concerns of 're-humanising' and 'giving voice to' vulnerable, marginalised subjects. The commitment to 'give voice to the voiceless' perilously mimics the traditional anthropological imperative to uncover the 'native's point of view' (Geertz 1974). Feminist and postcolonial scholars have remarked how vision 'is always a question of the power to see' (Haraway 1988: 192), while speech is about the power to be heard (Spivak 1988). This book does not 'give voice' to others; it establishes an intersubjective dialogue, it learns from some refugee and non-refugee voices and it forgets, or sometimes even rejects, others. The voice of the oppressed is not necessarily 'innocent' (Haraway 1988), nor is it the one of the politically committed activists. I have attempted to avoid any romanticisation – as well as, hopefully, any appropriation – of both refugee and non-refugee activist voices. Instead of assuming any degree of moral or political 'purity' in their reflections and actions, I attempt to bring their engagements under critical scrutiny, while also including myself among them.

As the writer who somewhat fixes this dialogue in a provisional text, I occupy a simultaneously immanent and distant position. Being in the field as a researcher offered me a vantage point from which I could *see* in particular ways because I was not fully tied to the norms of activism and voluntarism. In the same time, this distance was provided by the financial capital of academia, which tied me to the commercialisation of knowledge and to an institution that is deeply enmeshed in the dynamics of contemporary racism, border control and capitalism (Mbembe 2016). I fully embrace this ambiguity and do not claim any particular 'legitimacy' to occupy the 'overcrowded' arena (Andersson 2014: 286) of asylum research, less so do I claim to have effectively 'decolonised' my research. My ethnography simply could not be 'decolonised', neither at the time of conducting fieldwork, nor at that of writing. 'Decolonisation is not a metaphor' (Tuck and Yang 2012); it can be achieved only through the material, legal and social liberation of refugees and other migrants, both by the conditions that push them to migrate in the first place and by the meshes of the draconian border regimes they are subjected to. It is to this horizon that the anti-colonial spirit that animates this book is oriented, instead of any decolonial claim at the level of representation that can sustain a further claim of innocence or legitimacy by the writer.

Tying back the conclusion of this chapter to the vignette that opened it, it is this anti-colonial spirit that has imbued me with an increasing frustration with, and alienation from, refugee support and left-wing, white anti-racist activism – especially when these political commitments establish a moral superiority through which people recognise their identities. While I have gained legitimacy in the field through my activist identity, I am far away from any simple reconciliation in terms of 'militant research'. At the time of writing, this alienation leaves me in a peculiarly suspended position, whereby I cannot find comfort neither in the academic, nor in the activist identity. Instead of resolving these contradictions, or relegating them to this chapter, I have chosen to make them the living texture of a book that offers no simple reconciliation, let alone normative answers, neither to the writer nor to the reader. The knowledge produced is open-ended and provisional and, as such, it demands 'further dialogue and engagement' (Jackson 2002: 262).

As Hannah Arendt (1958: 5) noted long ago, answers to political problems are a mundane and everyday matter, 'they can never lie in theoretical considerations or the opinion of one person, as though we dealt here with problems for which only one solution is possible'. It is to these political, mundane tensions that I now turn in chapter 3, which will focus on the conflicts arising among volunteers and activists in the context of *the blackmail of the crisis*.

Chapter 3

The Blackmail of the Crisis

Volunteering with Refugees in Transit and the Politics of 'Civil Society'

At the peak of the 'crisis', in August 2015, the central registration facility at the Harburger Alte Post[1] was so overcrowded that the very process of registration of asylum applications was decentralised and spread to other accommodation facilities – many of which were improvised through a hybrid management involving Fördern & Wohnen (henceforth F&W),[2] the German Red Cross and the military. Temporary camps mushroomed across the city, erected with tents and containers, as well as the readaptation of vacant DIY stores (Riewe 2017). Living conditions within these spaces were poor and overcrowded, as the city authorities were 'unable' – or rather *unwilling*, as we shall see – to provide for basic necessities. Despite the spike in arrivals and asylum applications, the Ministry of Interior did not proportionally increase the number of BAMF employees; therefore, the bureaucratic process was slow and confused, often leading to important mistakes regarding dates of registration and allocation to accommodation facilities. Many refugees protested the chaotic situation and concerned Hamburg residents formed 'Refugees Welcome' initiatives in virtually all neighbourhoods, supporting them with material donations and breaking their social isolation.

While most camps and the relative support initiatives were located on the outskirts of the city, two locations rendered the 'crisis' materially visible in the very centre of Hamburg: the Central Station, with the continuous transit of refugees and the tents erected by the helpers on Heidi Kabel Platz, and the Messehallen Convention Centre,[3] located in the Karolinenviertel, a five-minute underground trip away from the Station. Hall B6 of the Messehallen was rented by the city and converted in a temporary registration and accommodation camp for approximately seven weeks between August and September 2015. The hall hosted more than a thousand refugees, sleeping on foldable camping beds in areas portioned off through construction fences. When the first group of refugees was transferred to the Messehallen, the military were still organising the plastic fences that portioned the hall. There were only five chemical toilets, and the refugees were not allowed to use the hall's toilets. After just a few days, the refugees started gathering outside, protesting against their living conditions. Local residents called for a meeting on August 15 at the Millerntor-Stadion in St. Pauli, which was attended by about five hundred people. They formed a self-organised initiative under the name 'Refugees Welcome Karoviertel' (henceforth, RW-Karo), which would become one of the major voices within Hamburg's 'Refugees Welcome' movement.[4] The assembly formed working groups with different tasks including translation, psychological well-being, health, childcare and clothing donations. RW-Karo's volunteers collected the refugees' grievances and negotiated with the management the arrangement of certain issues, such as devising a separate area for women to wrap up their hijabs. They also distributed basic products that F&W was not providing, such as earplugs, toothbrushes, diapers and underwear. Finally, the working group responsible for political strategy and public outreach monitored the process of registration of asylum applications, which often led to mistakes, such as issuing transfer papers to other camps with a wrong release date, meaning that the refugees were then denied access to the allocated facilities.

After the first registration and photo-identification,[5] asylum seekers received a certificate called BÜMA, which represented a temporary permission to stay on the German territory. The paper contained personal data, a photograph of the applicant, and the name of the reception facility to which they had been allocated. It was theoretically valid only for six months, but with the delays in the processing of applications, many asylum seekers stayed in Germany for over a year with no other official papers. After the first registration, asylum seekers were distributed through the EASY system[6] to initial accommodation centres in Hamburg or other federal states. The BÜMA entitled them to travel for free to their allocated destination and could therefore be converted into a train ticket at the Central Station's Deutsche Bahn office. However, the refugees were given no specific indications over this process and it was thus RW-Karo that started organising transfers from the Messehallen, therefore, establishing a tight connection to the Central Station Helper Network. Moreover, the section of RW-Karo responsible for donations, the Kleiderkammer, became well-known across the country, attracting conspicuous financial donations, part of which were devolved to the Central Station Helper Network. Through these connections, many volunteers became involved in both initiatives, picking up arriving refugees, escorting to the platforms those who were heading somewhere else, and organising temporary sleeping places in Hamburg.

Originally, there were at least two distinct groups of concerned residents that spontaneously showed up at the Central Station with water and food: one of white Germans, and the other one of refugees who were already living in Hamburg. As they subsequently happened to help the refugees in transit to buy train tickets, the two groups soon merged and the network expanded, counting up to some four hundred volunteers, of which at least a hundred provided constant presence at the station. Beyond a majority of individuals with no previous affiliation, the network included members of Cafe Exil, the KoZe squat,[7] and, at a later stage, the NGO Paritätische. These different souls brought into the network different political horizons, practical skills, knowledge sets and material capacities. Members of Cafe Exil would offer bureaucratic and legal training to other volunteers; the KoZe provided sleeping places, as well as their kitchen for food preparation, while Paritätische donated the tents on Heidi Kabel Platz. In the words of Jana, who was involved in both RW-Karo and Never Mind the Papers, two coexisting spirits animated the Refugees Welcome movement in Hamburg: the one of 'I just want to help' and the one of 'I'm good at talking to the cops'. As a result, the Central Station Helper Network was a truly polyphonic enterprise, including volunteers who were very new to refugee support, long-term anti-racist and anti-fascist activists, and refugees themselves, many of whom had arrived just very recently. Some of the German volunteers were children of immigrant parents and contributed to translation in the foreign languages spoken by their families. Finally, even refugee newcomers who, upon arrival, had been helped by the volunteers would return to the station to volunteer themselves, as soon as they had taken care of the essential bureaucratic procedures and had been allocated to a camp.

Departing from this depiction of the heterogenous composition of volunteers, this chapter analyses the *politics of civil society* within the asylum regime, focusing on two interrelated aspects: first, it asks which *politics* is at stake in the very concept of 'civil society', which reproduces a discourse of the state, the nation and 'Europe'; second, it analyses the processes of *politicisation* that emerged from the actions and reflections of volunteers and activists involved in the 2015 'Refugees Welcome' movement. The chapter dwells on the conflicts emerging both at the Central Station and the Messehallen over the volunteers' contestation of, or co-optation by, the German state, and proposes a situated analysis of the meanings and effects of refugee support, drawing on my interlocutors' conceptualisation of 'political' versus 'apolitical' support, that is to say between political *solidarity* – antagonistic to the state and conceived in terms of anti-racism and self-organisation – and humanitarian *charity* or *helping* – neutral to, or collaborative with, the state and driven by a more general humanism.

It has been suggested that the 2015 'Refugees Welcome' movement was qualitatively distinct from the previous movement of political support to the 'refugee struggle' (Hamann and Karakayali 2016: 77–78), contending that the marker of difference lay in the 2015 volunteers' opinions of asylum policies, hinging on a 'conditional' acceptance of migrants, a moralised conception of 'forced migration' and an 'apolitical' attitude. This analysis certainly captures part of the composition of the movement, but it risks obscuring both the presence of long-term anti-racist activists and the processes of politicisation of volunteers, starting from the fact that they were de facto supporting the illegalised logistics of transit, and culminating in the support that some of them showed in the following year to anti-deportation demonstrations. Emphasising these tensions contradicts, in its own right, any simple understanding of the Refugees Welcome movement as a merely apolitical or humanitarian endeavour. However, I also argue that the simplistic distinction between 'helping' and 'solidarity' must be transcended as, in their material manifestations, they are placed along a continuum. In fact, regardless of the differences in reproducing or contesting certain bordering practices, refugee support occurs in a perennial mode of 'emergency' and 'exception', which I term here the 'blackmail of the crisis', in order to convey that the focus on material urgencies and immediate management almost invariably leads to sacrificing more long-term political interventions. This 'blackmail' contributes to a de-politicisation of asylum, as well as the inscription of the refugee question into a perennial 'presentism', which relegates refugees to the spatio-temporality of always 'just arrived' (El-Tayeb 2008: 653) outsiders.

3.1. WHERE WAS THE STATE? THE POLITICS OF 'CIVIL SOCIETY' AND THE 'EXTERIORITY' OF REFUGEES

The question of 'the refugee' is inherently linked to 'the state' and 'the nation' (Arendt 1973; Malkki 1995; Gill 2010; Behrman 2019) because without state borders and national citizenship there would not be any concept of 'asylum'. Yet, as I gestured in the above account, asylum is also very much connected to the question of society at large; particularly in 2015, citizen networks were the real agents of the *Willkommenskultur*, covering for the state's lack of administrative organisation and financial resources (Funk 2016: 292). Within my field, the German state, as well as supranational EU institutions and other Member States, exerted a great influence over refugees' legal status and mobilities, retaining a monopoly over legislation, legal implementation and policing. However, it was less clear in what ways the German state was *directly present* in refugees' daily lives, especially regarding basic rights and necessities, such as material assistance and educational support. These are rights that are legislatively granted by the state itself but delivered by either para-state or non-state actors – such as in the examples above of solidarity networks distributing tents, food and basic items. This case is in no way only true of Germany; everywhere in Europe the very process of asylum would be impossible without those organisations, actors and social relations that are in solidarity with asylum seekers and that not only provide support and material assistance but also often act as mediators in bureaucratic and legal processes (White 1999). Assuming a clear-cut distinction between 'the state' and 'civil society' obscures their overlapping, blurredness and enmeshment with each other (Gill 2010).

If we look closely at the geographies of solidarity emerging during the 'crisis', at the Central Station the state was *formally* absent at the level of policing and management, adopting the same 'tacit alliance' (2015: 75) with migrants that Bernd Kasparek has described in the case of Italy; asylum seekers were informally allowed to transit through the German territory, so that the state could avoid registering and assessing their applications. Even when asylum seekers were registered at the southern borders, in Passau or Rosenheim, they were put on buses with stopovers in Cologne – a trajectory that was not directly policed and allowed easy escape. Once in Hamburg, refugees in transit were assisted solely by self-organised solidarity networks. Nonetheless, the state was partially implicated financially in those networks. As Charles, a German volunteer involved both at the station and within RW-Karo, put it, 'The city founded organisations that helped us and the government supported them. That was the trick in order not to get involved directly.'

However, the city administration partly exerted its regulatory power through the Health Department (*Gesundheitsamt*), imposing food distribution regulations and medical checks. Yet, the responses to these impositions came, once again, from civil society. The volunteers stopped accepting food from the KoZe, and organised a specifically dedicated kitchen in the proximity of the station which could abide to health regulations. Medical checks, initially carried out by self-organised medical practitioners, were later taken over by the *Katastrophenschutz* (Civil Protection), financed both by state and Red Cross funds, whose team installed a container and brought in Red Cross paramedical volunteers and doctors of the *Kassenärztliche Vereinigung* (the regional Statutory Health Insurance Physicians Administration). Although the container was managed separately from the other areas of the Helper Network – the coordination of pick-ups and departures, the organisation of sleeping places and the distribution of donations – it was placed adjacently to the other tents, thus inserting the state, NGOs and individual volunteers in an interconnected spatial configuration.

It is thus imperative to interrogate and historicise the productivity of the naturalised distinction between 'the state' and 'civil society', and to do so precisely from within 'the elusiveness of the boundary' (Mitchell 2006: 170) itself. In the recent literature on the Refugees Welcome movement, there is little problematisation of the concept of 'civil society', as well as of the question of *who* exactly forms part of it. While it is beyond the scope of this book to unpack the complex genealogy of the concept – which has been thoroughly done elsewhere (Kaviraj and Khilnani 2001; Chatterjee 2004) – I am nonetheless interested in shedding light on its persistent presence and productivity both in my field and in the relevant academic analyses.

Some argue that 'civil society' was a progressive force against both right-wing protests (Hamann and Karakayali 2016: 83–84) and the state withdrawal (Funk 2016). Others contend that volunteering was part and parcel of a governmental strategy of 'anti-politics', channelling refugee flows through a simultaneously humanitarian and securitised management (Fleischmann and Steinhilper 2017). Despite their different conclusions, all these interventions lack a thematisation of the refugee presence within grassroots organising and, thus, end up reinforcing the tripartition of 'the state', 'civil society' and 'the refugees'. While this tripartition imagines 'civil society' as a (more or less benevolent) counterpart to 'the state', it reproduces the *externalisation* of refugees from both the 'nation' and 'Europe' as a whole, obscuring their presence within the arena of refugee solidarity, not only at the receiving but at the providing end of support. In fact, this imagination of 'civil society' rests on *citizenship* (Chatterjee 2004: 38), as both a legal and a sociocultural construct. Citizenry is alternately a national one – the 'German civil society' – or an international one – the 'European civil society' welcoming 'the refugees' (Thiel 2017; Crepaz 2017). The legal status of citizenship (national or EU) is enmeshed within a racialised imagination of 'civil society' as the realm of whiteness, namely, of white, concerned European citizens who act in support of refugee noncitizens, rescuing them from institutional state racism of far-right non-state violence.

Refugees' 'outsider' status is always posited on the basis of their actual presence which is deemed 'unnatural' within the space of the 'nation'. Refugees are thus 'external' not only to the state, to which they have to seek admission and recognition through an asylum application but also to society at large, which can alternately welcome or reject them, fostering a historical amnesia over their long-term presence in Europe, especially considering that many of them have legally become citizens in the past decades. This purported exteriority of refugees constructs them as objects of someone else's management and support, be it 'the state' and its institutions or rather self-organised groups of citizens. The result is that asymmetries in power relations and hierarchies of deservingness are reconstituted every time grassroots solidarity falls into humanitarian management and mimics the practices and discourses of the state.

3.2. WHO STOOD IN SOLIDARITY WITH THE REFUGEES? VOLUNTEERS' SOCIAL COMPOSITION AND ATTITUDES TOWARDS THE STATE

In March 2016, I interviewed Amir, a Syrian refugee and one of the key figures of the Central Station Helper Network. I was interested in hearing about his perspective on the division between 'helpers' and 'translators', especially because, at the time of the interview, he was employed by Paritätische as coordinator of the Bieberhaus project, and thus had reached a position of relative power within the network. To him, the volunteers with a 'refugee background' were absolutely crucial for the initiative, as 'the Germans' – regardless of their position as individual citizens or state officials – were unable to respond to the 'crisis' by themselves: 'We know better than them. We know our people and our people can trust us' – he remarked, referring to the fact that refugee volunteers were at the forefront of the relationships to the ones in transit. They had the required linguistic skills, as well as sociocultural knowledge and a specific sense of empathy and complicity, for they had themselves experienced the uncertainty of the illegal journey. Many German 'helpers' also had direct interactions with refugees in transit, but only with those who spoke English and, mostly, they rather took care of logistics and networking, such as seeking material donations and temporary sleeping places. Moreover, due to already established social connections, these white German volunteers collected information on the changing situation at the northern borders, in constant touch with other volunteer groups. They also negotiated with institutional actors, most notably the management of the Wandelhalle – the shopping mall corridor whereby the volunteers' infodesk was situated – and the Deutsche Bahn, which often granted free train-passage to the refugees heading to the coastal cities at the northern borders. These were tasks that could be undertaken only by people with German language proficiency and good knowledge of the local context. However, Amir ascribed this division of labour not only to a differentiation in skills, but also to an emotional disposition. In his view, some of 'the Germans' were not 'strong enough' to cope with the pressure of the arrivals, including minors travelling alone, people with disabilities and illnesses and, generally, a great amount of social and individual suffering.

In contrast to the station, RW-Karo was a more homogenous group, mostly composed of white German citizens. In the words of Jana, it was 'a professional inner circle of white German hard-core political people' – highlighting the class composition of many freelance professionals who had disposable time (see chapter 7). RW-Karo proposed to form a platform for fostering a *true* welcoming culture, combining practical aid with monitoring activities and political demands, particularly concerning the decentralisation of refugee housing instead of mass accommodation.

Jana's concern with the Messehallen was originally the temporary nature of the solution, as the city authorities had rented hall B6 with the agreement of clearing it before the beginning of a ship trade convention: 'They would bring in these people who had come in boats, and then they would move them out because some rich Germans would sell and buy boats' – she told me, underlying the bitter irony of the situation. While she originally planned a disruptive action targeting the publicity of the trade convention, she became more and more involved with different aspects of support, in particular relating to negotiations with the management of the Messehallen and the station's Wandelhalle. For months, she ran around from a location to another, while also participating in group meetings and giving interviews to the press. Like her, many others got involved with the idea of taking care of a given aspect of support but were soon dragged into many other urgent issues that demanded attention and response. Charles, a German man in his forties, had been watching the images of refugee arrivals on the TV and, while wondering about how he could get involved, had responded to a *Facebook* call by RW-Karo, offering to drive refugees to the station with his car. Soon, he got involved in the Central Station's *Abholung* ('pick-up') group, which was responsible for welcoming arriving refugees at the platforms, as well as organising imminent departures. He would spend at the station as much time as he could, before and after his work shifts. At the peak of the 'crisis', many volunteers barely slept, as it was essential to attend the many arrivals of the night trains. In Jana's words:

> The feeling of 2015 was that you couldn't sleep. You needed to do something, making tea, collecting money or clothes, informing people, empowering them. It was difficult to decide, but for sure you *had to* act. It was so visible. It was in my neighbourhood. All my friends were involved. The 'summer of migration' was an empowering moment. It was absolutely attractive how many people were working on the same goal and how many people experienced this for the first time.

This sense of urgency and belonging to a greater project was also my very own feeling. I got involved at the station upon my second day in Hamburg and I ended up staying there way longer than I had originally planned. Part of my fascination with the station was due to the boomerang effect that the volunteers' commitment had produced: the Deutsche Bahn's canteen would provide free meals to the volunteers wearing vests, while cafes and shops often gave us discounts, winking eyes and saying they knew that we were 'helping the refugees'. My fieldnotes featured recurring mentions of moments of unfiltered, human connection, particularly with the refugees in transit, in the shape of intense, albeit brief, conversations, glances, hugs, and other physical gestures, like holding hands, in the absence of words. Social barriers that are usually in place are often overthrown at times of 'crisis'. For instance, Charles recalled an episode in which he accompanied a family heading to Sweden who had just ten minutes to change trains; in that brief space of time, a volunteer gave them the money for the ferry, Charles asked the Deutsche Bahn staff to let them board the train for free, and then called the volunteers in Kiel to arrange someone to pick them up at the station, while someone else brought food for the trip. Later, the family texted him twice: from the ferry to thank him, and two months later, on New Year's Eve. Charles cried both times, as he did another time, together with other volunteers when a mother and son who had long been separated met again on a platform. Listening to these accounts in the course of our interviews reminded me of an episode in which I brought to the platforms a family who, for legal reasons relating to family reunifications, were splitting in different directions. They were all crying, I was alone, and we did not share any common language; not knowing what to do, I instinctively hugged them after leaving them to the respective platforms.

These emotional connections invested also the relationships among volunteers. Those who were still in the asylum procedure found at the station a political goal and social platform that drew them out of the emptiness of waiting in the camps. For one, Amir stated that he had truly found himself in Hamburg, thanks to the station (see chapter 6), which had given him not only a goal but also a job, a group of friends and a girlfriend. 'The Germans', like Jana, found a sense of connection to a wider community they had never met before. Lukas, a young law undergraduate student who had just moved to Hamburg felt that the station had completely changed his experience of the city: 'The people there were so different in any possible terms but they were still helping together on one thing. I've seen a lot more of Hamburg than I would have without the station' – he argued. For several months, he put his studies on hold and dedicated all his time to the station. When he did not do night shifts at the infodesk, instead of returning home, he would sleep at his university's library, which was located a short ride away from the station.

These positive feelings, however, did not prevent the emergence of many conflicts, in particular concerning the collaboration with, and arguable co-optation by, the state of these self-organised grassroots initiatives. In particular, the move to the Bieberhaus was a key contested issue. Although there had not been any direct intercession by the federal state of Hamburg – Paritätische had rented the building, owned by a private company, and Deutsche Bahn provided the security outside the building – the move implied an overall institutionalisation of the initiative. By that time, all the anti-racist activists had left the network.

Amir, who had instead embraced this institutionalisation through his employment by Paritätische, mocked them, highlighting how they disliked the government because 'they like self-organisation'. However, Amir himself, displayed contradictory feelings about the German state: 'They did nothing for us and we did everything for them' – he argued. 'Had we let all the refugees hanging at the Central Station, it would have been a big chaos here in Hamburg.' It was a matter of fact that part of the volunteers' job had been keeping the station orderly. At the ticket hall, without translators, the Deutsche Bahn employees would have been unable to communicate effectively with most refugees in transit; when the Wandelhalle managers complained about the refugees sitting on the floor and ruining the image of the upmarket shopping mall, the volunteers organised the tents outside the station so that the refugees could rest there instead; finally train chiefs would mostly let refugees board national trains for free, but first-class passengers complained if the refugees travelled for free in their carriage, so that it was, again, the volunteers' job to make sure that the refugees only sat in second-class.

All the volunteers I spoke to were ambivalent towards the state, ultimately seeing it as *the* (inefficient) interlocutor and imagined receptor of their demands. Some actually recognised it as the oppressor who was causing the refugee situation in the first place. And yet, if one is to accept that, at least partially, the volunteers were working *against* the state, the question emerges of whether the state would then actively punish or repress them. For Amir, volunteering at the station 'was like *playing*' because, back in Damascus, he had opened three hosting centres for refugees arriving from war zones and, as many of his friends had been arrested, he had eventually fled the country: 'The Syrian government wanted to control the refugees; it did not accept that we worked alone' – he explained – 'but here it's safe to do it, no one will arrest you because you're helping the refugees'. Other Syrians I spoke to also talked about self-organisation and activism in Europe as a 'joke' compared to the state repression they had faced back in Syria, and thus placed European anti-racist activists in a much less contested relationship to the state than what the latter claimed (see chapter 5). Hence, the question of state repression complicates any simple answer to the one of collaboration or antagonism between 'civil society' and 'the state', as there is a grey zone in which apparent withdrawal can be a strategy for the latter to avoid its responsibilities (Gill 2010: 636). For Mathias, a law graduate and one of the core members of the infodesk, the question of the state had no easy answer within the work undertaken at the station: 'The German state was lucky for any refugee they did not have to take in. It was clear that they wanted as many people as possible to leave Hamburg' – he argued. Despite this unwitting complicity with the state's aims, he was adamant of the primacy of assisting the refugees over any long-term political intervention. He admitted that 'there is always a political level wherever you work with refugees' but the volunteers' focus was, for him, to 'help the people in need', who were arriving 'exhausted after long journeys, caught in the uncertainty over reaching their final destinations. The station was no place for political work, it was just impossible.' These conclusions were very different from the ones of Lukas who, after the first month of euphoria, started harbouring many doubts over his own volunteering, and underwent a dramatic process of politicisation:

> Initially, I didn't think about the consequences of helping, about *who profits from your help*. It was kind of obvious that the refugees were profiting but, later on, I thought that's a task that the government should undertake. And I started having doubts. Many other people and institutions were profiting from our help, like the Deutsche Bahn and the Bahnhof Mission.[8] Were we not there, it would have been their task to coordinate support for people stranded at the station. And Paritätische also profited in terms of publicity and donations.

In the eyes of refugee newcomers, this chaotic continuum between 'the state' and 'the volunteers was most apparent. When I explained that I was studying in London and was in Hamburg only temporarily, they really struggled to understand *who 'sent' me there*. This mostly sprung from the fact that I wore one of the volunteers' fluorescent vests; we used them in order to recognise each other and be recognised by the refugees in transit but, in turn, the vests created an impression of formality, an immediately identifiable semblance of 'non-refugeeness' and thus, implicitly, of legitimacy and responsibility. Despite the fact that many volunteers were themselves refugees, the wearing of vests established a hierarchy between helpers and refugees in transit. During my time volunteering there, the latter would often ask if I worked for an independent NGO or for the German state.

Due to the tiring nature of political conflicts most anti-racist activists and Cafe Exil members soon left the Central Station Helper Network, and decided to dedicate their energies to other simultaneous struggles, such as the occupation of a church by the Romano Jekipe Ano group, threatened with deportations (Leko 2017). As refugee arrivals decreased and the momentum of the *Wilkommenskultur* started fading, the group became more homogenous. Upon their move to the Bieberhaus, it was mostly composed of young white Germans students and refugees who were either long-term residents or still in the asylum procedure. Ultimately, the network collapsed precisely over a conflict between the two groups. The 'translators' saw the initiative as a refugee-led one and criticised the late involvement and visibility of the Paritätische. Their critique culminated in some of them ripping off the NGO's sign at the Bieberhaus and substituting it with an 'Alkarama' banner – an Arabic word meaning 'dignity', which the dissenting group had chosen as

Figure 3.1   The Helpers' Vests. *Source*: Lars Slowak.

their name. In turn, the German 'helpers' who had dedicated so much time and energy to that project did not want to be relegated to the margins. The group did not survive this conflict. More and more people stopped being involved; the refugee man that was leading the 'Alkarama' subgroup was deemed a majorly conflictual individual, and thus kicked out. Eventually, the Bieberhaus allocated time expired, and the group dissolved.

3.3. THE BLACKMAIL OF THE 'CRISIS': CONFLICTS OVER THE POLITICS OF VOLUNTEERING AND THE 'ABSENCE' OF THE STATE

The Kleiderkammer's management of donations at the Messehallen became a state-praised 'good practice' and increased its presence in the media. As a result, it entered into increasing conflicts with the rest of RW-Karo, eventually forming a separated organisation, 'Hanseatic Help', under the slogan 'Simply helping where help is needed'. Jana was very critical of their humanitarian and purportedly 'neutral' rhetoric:

> They were giving interviews to the press, saying things like: *We help cause we're Germans and we give the good example*; or: *This is Hamburg!* We had heavy fights with them, because we could smell their paternalistic tone. They were not pointing the finger to the problem that the city was doing nothing,

while we were saying that it was a systemic problem. There are free houses. That people have to live under these circumstances is not just a drama; it's a political decision. It's a way to tell to the people beyond our borders and also back home: *Don't come here, the situation is bad in Hamburg.* The message from the state was absolutely clear: *We don't want to help you, that's why you have to live in bad circumstances here. Just don't come.* The Kleiderkammer was using the helping rhetoric, using the acceptance and respect that the city gave them. They were not demanding; they were not tacking the political issue. They were like: *Let's not talk about the problem; let's just solve it.*

In this excerpt, Jana positioned the state as the actor that was ultimately responsible for the theoretical protection – and practical abandonment and subjugation – of refugees, while simultaneously pointing to the fact that the state outsourced that responsibility to self-organised volunteers. But she also touched how this co-optation was not merely a top-down one; the very rhetoric deployed by the Kleiderkammer's volunteers established a community of values and responsibility between them and the state, and reproduced a symbiotic discourse of the 'nation' and the 'people' – in this case, within the particular displacement of the national scale to the idea of citizenry ('this is Hamburg'). Thus, the Kleiderkammer's discourse posited a distinction between 'the state' and 'civil society' that merely attained to legal authority, not to practical responsibilities over the reception of refugees. In this way, the *blackmail of the crisis* was reinforced, embedding the imperative to 'help' within a quasi-natural calamity, whose conditions of possibility, as well as strategies of solution, could never appear in the public discussion.

A discussion paper presented at the UN General Assembly in 2016 best exemplifies this naturalisation and co-optation. Adopting neoliberal discourses of 'flexibility' and 'creativity', the paper focuses on 'innovations' in Hamburg and Berlin's responses to the 'refugee crisis' and features a paragraph titled 'Deploying a Spontaneous Civil Society', whose main argument is that the citizens' 'creative' responses 'enhanced all phases of refugee reception and integration' (Katz et al. 2016: 18). At a first glance, the verb 'deploying' and the adjective 'spontaneous' seem an oxymoron but, actually (and unwittingly), this vocabulary resonates with the critique of state co-optation and outsourcing as strategies of migration governmentality (Fleischmann and Steinhilper 2017). The idea that solidarity networks 'enhanced' state policies erases any friction between the 'state' and 'civil society', and it does not come as a surprise that the paper mentions precisely Hanseatic Help as an exemplary initiative. The neoliberal logic of this discourse openly appropriates the volunteers' sense of *responsibility* (be that framed in political or humanitarian terms) into a question of 'enhancement' of *logistical management*. Unsurprisingly, civil society's players are here divided only into established NGOs and independent volunteers; there is no mention of anti-racist and no-border activists who were critical of the state and, like Jana, were present in the field before, during, and after the 'crisis'.

Against this reductionism, both the Central Station Helper Network and the RW-Karo group were truly spontaneous and heterogeneous. They were the theatre of recurring conflicts, not only relating to the relations between 'helpers' and 'translators', and between both and the refugees in transit, but particularly over their take on the putative *absence* of the state. Ultimately, the 'Refugees Welcome' arena, in Germany and beyond, was a field of struggle between those who believed in the strategic collaboration with the state and those who wanted to maintain an antagonistic autonomy from it.

Significantly, in the eyes of the refugees who were protesting their living conditions, the strategy of collaboration jeopardised their struggle. When the Messehallen was cleared, the refugees who had been hosted there were redistributed to empty DIY stores that had been converted into temporary accommodation facilities. The last group was picked up at night with a bus and transferred to a vacant hall in Bergerdorf, an industrial area 20 kilometres away from the city centre, which still lacked the very basics for accommodating the refugees. The latter organised a protest and refused to enter but, as they were planning a hunger strike, the *Kleiderkammer* volunteers were already setting up camp-beds in the new hall. While Jana was trying to mediate between the two groups, she saw her efforts liquidated by a protesting refugee who told her: 'Now you're decorating the *Lager*,[9] while we want no *Lager*!' Many months later, Jana highlighted this episode to me as a particularly representative one of the conflicts happening at the time. Despite the fact that she was not actively taking part of the 'decoration' of the *Lager*, the protester was contesting her mediation, making explicit that the polarisation between 'apolitical helpers' and 'political activists' was of little use in that particular predicament. Caught in the blackmail of the crisis, the 'supporters' were walking a fine line between *collaboration with*, and *contestation of*, the state. As I have also shown through the example of the fluorescent vests, in the eyes of the refugee newcomers, the German activists and volunteers could easily be perceived as just another branch of the state and the asylum regime. Particularly in the case of setting up temporary camps, the volunteers, animated by the desire to ameliorate refugees' reception conditions, were unwittingly participating in the coloniality of the asylum regime. In other words, they were emplaced in a neat division between those subjects who inhabited the *Lager* – non-citizens who were racialised as nonwhite and legalised as non-European – and those who participated in the management and 'decoration' of the *Lager* – citizens of the German state or migrants who had, to a certain extent, emancipated themselves from their own migrancy, and were thus emplaced in positions of relative power within the asylum regime (see chapter 5).

This colonial fracture was one of the main features of the blackmail of the crisis and, both at the Messehallen and at the Central Station, resulted in the prioritisation of practical assistance over political demands. While the 'crisis' was politically produced and was indeed a *crisis of the border regime* (New Keywords Collective 2016), it never stopped being a *crisis of the refugees themselves* (Tazzioli 2017: 13). If 'humanitarian crises' are always already political – both in their causes and consequences, as highlighted by Jana's comments on the deliberate abandonment operated by the state – the reverse is also true: political crises produce tangible humanitarian consequences and much of refugee support is dedicated to their relief.

The most evident symbol of this humanitarian management within the context of the station were the tents erected on Heidi Kabel Platz, where the refugees in transit could find shelter from the cold, as well as queuing for food and clothing distribution.

The anti-racist activists who were part of the network were very critical about these tents, as they deemed their function simultaneously an aid to the state's managerial agenda and a promotion of the visibility of the NGOs, whose logos were printed on the outer structures. Jacob, a German white activist of both Cafe Exil and Never Mind the Papers described to me their visual impact and how it capitalised on the suffering of the refugees in transit:

Figure 3.2   The Tents Erected Outside the Station. *Source*: Lars Slowak.

They were in one of the most prominent places of Hamburg. It was horrible. It was visible to everybody. The tents were like a museum or a zoo. People went to see 'the refugees' outside the station. It was something very new in Hamburg, because before tents and camps were only in the suburbs. So there was a huge visibility of everyone: the helpers, the refugees and Paritätische. The refugees had a long journey behind them and needed proper rest. There was a lot of space that could have been used around the station, like squats, and vacant buildings, but they just didn't use it.

I have already mentioned in chapter 2 that while refugee newcomers are physically concentrated in particular urban spaces or border zones, they are also constantly exposed to the gaze of non-refugees, be they simply passersby, journalists or researchers. However, Jacob's focus on the hyper-visibilisation of the refugees and the spectacularisation of the 'crisis' at the station is crucial to understand how the spatial segregation of refugees is reproduced at the grassroots level.

Many other conflicts arose over the network's mission and practices. Some blamed the state for its withdrawal and craved for more structuring and professionalism; others recognised that the state's intervention would have entailed greater control over the refugees in transit and were thus advocating for keeping the structure horizontal, nonhierarchical and self-organised. The anti-racist activists blamed the 'apolitical' helpers of being naive and patronising, as well as using the refugees for their own humanitarian satisfaction. In turn, the helpers blamed the activists of being aggressive during meetings, as well as using the refugees for their own political agenda. While the distinction between 'political' and 'apolitical' people was reiterated by most of my interlocutors, through my observations, I appreciated how virtually all initiatives of refugee support were characterised by a mixture of both humanitarian and political tendencies.

Furthermore, there were different conceptions of the political at stake, translating into contingent activities and approaches. To put it simply, the 'apolitical' people were often unwittingly participating in highly politicised actions; vice versa, the 'political' people often engaged in humanitarian assistance. Many of my interlocutors, like Jana and Lukas, crisscrossed the two poles of the 'Refugees Welcome' movement and anti-racist/no-border activism. Finally, while many of the new volunteers did not have any previous experience in refugee support, nor a particularly developed analysis of the border regime, they nevertheless were concerned with politics; others got politicised through their volunteering practice. Their knowledge developed through the direct encounter with refugees and grew both in relation to the geopolitical reasons that led refugees to flee, and to the effects of being subjected to the asylum process, including detention and deportation in the case of rejection. Throughout 2016 and 2017, I often saw some of the station's volunteers participating in anti-deportation demonstrations – even those who had initially commented that we were helping many 'illegals' who were not 'real' refugees.

Charles, who was involved both at the Central Station and the Messehallen, had been interested in politics since a very early age, since his parents had been helping refugee newcomers in the 1980s and 1990s, often hosting them at home. His feelings about the political dimension of refugee support changed since his first involvement with RW-Karo; in the beginning he felt a certain discomfort in dealing with political activists: 'I thought that first we had to help, and the political came second. Funnily, this has changed: now I feel that the political thing is much more important, especially in the long-term.'

Against any reification of 'political' versus 'apolitical' support, Jana argued that the two poles were actually complementary, suggesting that the new wave of volunteers needed a deeper understanding of structural racism and the working of the border regime but also noting that many among the long-term anti-racist activists were too isolated in their own theoretical politics and removed from refugee newcomers and the 'issues on the ground'.

3.4. HUMANITARIAN HIERARCHIES AND THE EXCEPTIONALITY OF REFUGEES

At the station, I was once asked to support the doctors at the medical container with translation from Persian. Differently from the chaotic dynamics occurring inside the station, with its incessant movements between the infodesk, the ticket hall and the platforms, the medical container had a specific hierarchical, professional and humanitarian socio-spatial arrangement. That day, a female doctor was in charge with the support of two paramedic volunteers, and I assisted them during the consultations of Afghan refugees, that day all men. Translating in that setting was a challenge: I lacked the specific medical vocabulary in Persian, and the gendered relationship between the men and me was a delicate matter in the case of sexual health complaints. Moreover, it was the first time in my life that I found myself implicated in such a distinctively humanitarian environment.

Most people came in with complaints linked to serious physical conditions or emotional distress. Because of the impermanence of the patients who were mostly still en route to Scandinavia or elsewhere, the doctors could visit them only once, and thus, in most cases, were unable to devise a proper therapy. I recall a young man who lamented back pain and burst into tears while recounting how Iranian soldiers had beaten him up at the border with

Afghanistan. Another one arrived in a very confused state and gave us a medical certificate that stated he had been found on the street with a dissociative disorder. Having been homeless for a prolonged time, with no access to shower facilities, the man brought into the small container a pungent smell. One of the paramedics promptly offered me a surgical mask, which I instinctively declined. Only then did I realise that I was the only one in the container not wearing one, apart from the refugee man. The use of gloves and surgical masks in non-pandemic times can be traced back to medicalised discourses around health, safety and bacteria and the association of migrant bodies with disease (Harper and Raman 2008). Yet, what struck me in that moment was that the mask had not been offered to me upon my entrance, thus hinging on that particular discourse, but rather upon the arrival of the man, arguably to 'protect' me from the mere annoyance of his smell. The paramedics' offer also struck me as a very impractical one for the purposes of my task: I was clearly struggling with translating, and it was essential that the patients could understand me as clearly as possible, without the mask further bordering our communication with its thick paper layer.

Later that day, a refugee teenager came to ask for a moisturiser. The doctor was puzzled by the request and it took her a couple of minutes to make sure she had understood well. She shrugged her shoulders and gave the boy a little plastic container. As the boy walked out and happily spread the moisturiser on his cheeks, one of his friends came in with the same request, and then some more people. Eventually, the doctor complained about these visits that took her time, while there were many people with very 'serious' complaints and urgent necessity to be treated. That at times of crisis and deprivation, taking care of one's body can be a very critical act of self-care – for the body is often the last resource one has got in order to keep a sense of normalcy and everydayness – did not seem a relevant issue for the doctor.

Hierarchies of deservingness are proper of both welfarism and humanitarianism (Yarris and Castañeda 2015) and are predicated upon paradigms of 'scarcity' of financial and material resources, as well as rights (Vacchiano 2011). These hierarchies reproduce the order of coloniality for which certain experiences are normalised in the case of refugees: in this case, it was obvious to the doctor that they should not expect to have proper care of their skin. That was not a legitimate need. Within hierarchical systems of assistance, requests that are not 'serious' or 'dramatic' are interpreted as whimsical, underserving and abusing of the 'benevolent' system, and refugees are thus constructed as mono-dimensional needy beings. In the words of Ella, a Cafe Exil's activist:

At the Central Station, you would see these volunteers screaming to a refugee: 'You've already had your sandwich!' They wanted to help, but they didn't want to think about what they were doing, why and how. Maybe you want to give an apple to someone, but they don't want it. Maybe they won't say 'thanks'. In *solidarity*, you have to *talk* to people and ask them: *What do you want to eat? Are you hungry? Maybe you're not; let's have a beer.*

Here, the difference between *solidarity* and *helping* does not lie in distinct practices, but rather in distinct frameworks of thought, especially relating to both a reflexive and relational modality which is the basis of horizontal relationships. Particularly, solidarity is premised on the awareness of *not knowing already* what the other person may want or need; solidarity is a dialogue, helping is a monologue. Ella's example of 'having a beer' is a provocative remark against the unidirectional institution of hierarchies of deservingness not only in terms of prejudging *who* may deserve assistance and support but also *which needs* are legitimate and deserving. Very much like the moisturiser was deemed 'unnecessary' or 'non-urgent' by the doctor, alcohol is deemed a recreational drink and, as such, does not fit assumptions of thirst, hunger, or other 'legitimate' bodily needs. Importantly, these hierarchies percolate also into the social relations that non-volunteers entertain with refugees, as I described in the introduction through the 'exceptional' treatment of refugees by the Deutsche Bahn employees.

3.5. SUPPORTING THE LOGISTICS OF TRANSIT AGAINST THE STATE OR FOR ITS BENEFIT?

During my second week volunteering at the station, Ismail, who had been an interlocutor of my previous research, came to Hamburg to visit our common friend Farhad. We had not seen each other in over a year and had a lot to catch up with. He had moved back to Greece, where his European journey had begun many years before but, in October 2015, went back to Italy to renew his residency permit; there he spontaneously decided to continue up north to see Farhad. On the first night we met, after a brief exchange regarding the station and the wider political context of the 'crisis', he started mocking me: 'So, now you make a living as a smuggler?' It was not a light joke. Among the Afghan community in Rome, there had often been arrests with the charge of human smuggling, involving also our acquaintances. Smuggling was a fine line (borderline-Europe 2017) which did not merely concern professional smugglers, but also relatives and acquaintances to which refugees en route asked for financial or practical help.

At the station that day I had attended to Tesfay, an Eritrean young man who was trying to reach Sweden together with his girlfriend. An uncle who resided in Frankfurt had agreed to send the money to continue the journey from

Hamburg, but, without an ID, Tesfay could not access any money transfer service. I asked the other volunteers for possible ways to get that money transferred, but no one was able to offer a solution. Tesfay waited at the infodesk the whole morning as I ran up and down between a train arriving and another one departing. At the station everything was so chaotic that it was almost impossible to follow one person in depth, and we were unwittingly reproducing the state politics of *waiting* (Khosravi 2014), asking the refugees to be patient until we were finally available. Eventually, I noted down my ID card's number on a piece of paper, so that he could send it to his uncle and I would myself collect the money. As I was heading to the Western Union branch on the second floor, Mohammad, a Syrian volunteer coordinating the infodesk, warned me that that was a risky business I should have stayed away from: we were helping people crossing borders illegally, he said, and if we had money personally transferred to us, the subtle line leading to smuggling would become thinner: 'at least take off your helper vest before going to Western Union', he urged me. After delivering the money to Tesfay as discretely as possible, I gave him my number and asked him to keep me updated about his journey. That way, I later learnt through a text that he had finally reached Norway and applied for asylum, after several days of bouncing back between the Danish land border and the coastal cities. However, I later refused to participate in any of these crucial intercessions, for I was concerned that the Western Union employees would become suspicious if I started withdrawing money every day.

The novelty of the 2015 Refugees Welcome movement lay precisely in the fact that, from Greece all the way up to Finland, volunteers were explicitly supporting the theoretically illegal, but practically allowed, logistics of transit across international borders. In the previous decades, this type of support could be cultivated only clandestinely, due to the introduction of carrier sanctions at the EU level in 2001, and extensions of responsibility around the crime of aiding and abetting illegal migration. Regarding external borders, the 'criminalisation of solidarity' (Fekete 2009) with illegalised migrants had made it increasingly difficult to follow the established 'law of the sea' that demands aid for boats in distress (Albahari 2015: 102) – at least until the political change introduced by the Italian operation 'Mare Nostrum' (Tazzioli 2016). At the level of internal Schengen borders, whereby illegalised refugees could always be targeted through ad hoc racial profiling, the logistics of transit had been organised by the illegalised migrants themselves, with the support of other migrants residing along the route and, of course, of smugglers. This would again become the case after 2015, but, in the particular moment of the long summer of migration, the illegal mobility of asylum seekers was de facto allowed by states and organised in a semi-formal international corridor (Kasparek 2016), producing spaces in which a particular kind of solidarity could emerge.

In chapter 7, I will return to the question of 'humanitarian smuggling' (*Fluchthilfe*), which can be seen as a subversive political act of civil disobedience, and which has been re-politicised as a number of volunteers were sued across Europe between 2017 and 2019. While this criminalisation of solidarity (Borri and Fontanari 2017; Tazzioli and Walters 2019) re-instates a separation between the institution of the state and its citizens, in 2015, there was a particular kind of convergence between (at least some) European states and self-organised volunteers. This convergence resulted in specific compromises, such as the fact that the volunteers at the Central Station, in helping the refugees to reach their destinations, also unwittingly helped the German state in at least two different ways: first, through the management of the logistics of national transfers, in the case of those who had been allocated to different federal states and secondly, through helping those who headed elsewhere – thus relieving Germany of the supposed 'burden' to register everyone transiting through and process their asylum applications.

All the volunteers I interviewed contended that if the state had got involved at the station, it would have been for worse. All refugees would have been registered in Germany, and many inserted in the Dublin procedure, which at the time already caused a clog in the BAMF's processing.[10] In this context, the German state performed differential and arbitrary practices at different borders and times. For much of summer 2015, refugees crossing from Austria could be registered as 'in transit' and would receive a paper stating that they intended to reach Sweden or Norway – which had absolutely no legal status, as Mathias explained to me. The same relaxed attitude was evident in Hamburg, whereby the police never intruded into the volunteers' interactions with refugees in transit, mostly because the majority were heading to Sweden, which did not oppose neither irregular entry, nor transit through its territory. At a second stage, however, both Germany and Sweden stopped allowing transit, and the police would often form cordons on the platforms of Munich station, checking potential asylum seekers through racial profiling. Moreover, in order to avoid diplomatic troubles with Denmark, which differently from Sweden had maintained a hard line with irregular transit, the German police would confiscate the passports of any asylum seeker found at the northern land border, so as to compel them to stay in Germany and register their application – upon the termination of which, their passports would be returned.

That multiple national states were involved in these geographies of transit complicates the picture of the relationship between volunteers and the state. Lukas highlighted how, for him, volunteering at the station was always political, even though some people may have not perceived it as such because 'getting people to cross borders is not something that everybody likes'. In the case of refugees wanting to transit to countries that did not maintain open-border policies, the volunteers would often show them the closest station to the border and advise them to walk through instead of travelling by international trains. So, in Lukas' eyes, the question was not just if the volunteers were working against the German state, but also if they were working *against* other nation-states. Thinking about refugee support in this transnational dimension thus opens up a further possibility, as not only there may be conflicts between refugees/supporters and one particular state but there are also conflicts between different states, and this was nowhere more evident than in the suspension of Schengen by ten Member States between 2015 and 2017 (Šeruga 2018). As with its historical precedent at the Italo-French border in 2011 (Garelli 2013), the poor application of Dublin by a number of states prompted in turn their neighbours to suspend the application of Schengen, and thus reintroduce internal border controls.

As discussed in the introduction, this international horizon was both present and absent at the station. Once refugees had boarded the trains, we would never know how many of those who left were really accepted in the countries where they had applied for asylum; how many were deported to their home countries; how many were deported under Dublin. With these questions in mind, I now turn to the next chapter, which looks at the intra-European convoluted mobilities and legal struggles of refugees, calling into question any supposed linearity of transit.

Chapter 4

'Here to Stay'

Autonomous Movements Across Europe between Incorrigibility and Refugification

Immediately after collecting his residency permit and travel document, Farhad packed his few things, hugged his roommate Ismail and left Rome with the intention to reach London, where a friend had offered him a job. However, after two months of unsuccessful attempts at crossing the Channel and strenuous nights in the Calais' 'jungle' (Reinisch 2015), he mistakenly hid in a lorry with a different route, and it took him some twenty-four hours to finally jump off without alerting the driver, only to find himself at the Dutch-German border. Mujeeb, an old friend who was struggling with his illegalised status in Germany after a rejection in Sweden, picked him up and brought him to Hamburg so that he could rest for a few days while deciding what to do next. Farhad returned to Calais but, this time, did not last much, too exhausted by the routine of tent-sleeping, food donations and the repeated humiliation of the police capture unfolding between the back of lorries and the port entrance. He thus gave up on London, returned to Hamburg and sought ways to settle there, first registering as an unaccompanied minor. After several months waiting in a youth accommodation centre, he found (illegal) employment in an Afghan car dealership, whose owner allowed him to sleep in the office and use the kitchen. Eventually, he decided to abandon the asylum process altogether, as his new life allowed for a 'normality' of sorts, away from refugee camps and transit informal settlements. Yet, this life was 'normal' only to the extent that the police did not stop-and-search him through racial profiling. If that happened, his travel document would have been stamped and, after three months from that date, he would have become potentially deportable to Italy.[1]

Farhad and Mujeeb used to pick me up at the Central Station after my volunteering shifts, and we would share walks, dinners, drinks and unending chats also with Omid, whose German asylum application had been rejected and was on a *Duldung* – a temporary residency permit for undeportable rejected asylum seekers – and Ismail, who had been recognised in Italy but resided in Greece and was in Hamburg for a short visit. The four of them had first arrived in Europe in 2011 and had undergone multiple detours, deportations and pushbacks, before they were even able to submit a first asylum application. Often, our conversations revolved around the refugee newcomers transiting through the Central Station, and culminated in comparisons between these 'new' straightforward journeys and their own convoluted 'old' ones. The four friends expressed a 'jealousy' of sorts: during the 'long summer of migration', it would take Afghans just about two weeks to reach Germany, while it had taken my friends years, relying solely on their own cunning and on mutual solidarity with other refugees along the route, because they could not afford the exorbitant prices of expert smugglers' fake passports. In their eyes, the newcomers had everything 'easy', with borders relatively open and hordes of volunteers helping them along the way. The purported willingness of the German state to accept them appeared in stark contrast to the plight of these four Afghan friends, who had been in Europe already for years but never achieved any stability, and continued inhabiting different precarious legal statuses.

Farhad and Ismail, who I met at Asinitas during my 2014 fieldwork, partook in larger transit currents through Rome. Already from 2010, when I used to teach Italian there, Rome was a hub for both northward and southward flows of asylum seekers. Notably, the main northward flows were from sub-Saharan Africa, transiting through Libya and Sicily, and from South Asia and the Middle East, transiting through Turkey, Greece and the Adriatic Italian coast ports. Their so-called secondary movements to Northern Europe unwittingly engendered further southward movements, as fingerprint records on the EU asylum database Eurodac – which sustains the application of the Dublin Regulation – resulted in deportations back to Rome Fiumicino Airport. Moreover, due to Italy's relative generosity in acceptance rates at the time, a number of asylum seekers autonomously relocated there after a rejection in another country. Such was the case not only for Farhad, who moved to Italy from Norway, but also for Ismail, who had been previously struggling with several Dublin transfers between Austria and Hungary. Finally, these southward mobilities often became again northward as, after receiving legal protection in Italy, many would set out for the European north which, despite confining them to a semi-illegal status that did not allow legal work or residency, promised more autonomy in terms of economic survival and social networks, at least within already established migrant communities.

The Ostiense Station, located in the same area of Asinitas' school, in the south of the city, became a well-established node of transit for Afghans to exchange information, get in touch with smugglers and be certain of food and clothing donations. The living map of their trajectories sketched complex postcolonial relations between Europe, Afghanistan, Pakistan and Iran, drawing not only on historical, linguistic and social legacies but also on contemporary military engagement of European and US powers (Gregory 2004). The Pashtuns were particularly connected to the UK, where their diaspora is well established; many were fluent in English and, following the 2001 US invasion, had been working as interpreters for NATO; others, raised at the border between Afghanistan and Pakistan, were fluent in Urdu and could thus more easily find work through the well-established Pakistani communities of London or Birmingham. Differently, Tajiks and Hazaras – many of whom had spent significant periods of their life in Iran – had stronger ties to German cities, particularly Hamburg, which they endearingly called 'the Kabul of Europe' (Braakman 2005: 29) since, from the 1980s, it has been home to the largest Afghan community in Europe, as well as to a significant Iranian one.

Yet, the colonial past and present were not the sole vectors shaping these convoluted northward *and* southward mobilities; these were also channelled by the geographies of the economic crisis disproportionately hitting the European south, and by the legal geographies of the Schengen Agreement and the Dublin Regulation, which acted simultaneously as deterrents *and* enablers of refugee intra-European mobilities. While the first abolishes internal border controls and guarantees freedom of movement also for subjects of international protection, the Dublin Regulation *allocates* – and thus *confines* – refugees to particular member states. Asylum seekers, however, continuously defy, individually and collectively, their allocation through their unruly mobilities, in the search for autonomy, recognition and survival (Schuster 2011; Kasparek 2015; Fontanari 2019). In my past work (Picozza 2017a, 2017b), I have sketched the figure of the 'Dubliner' to convey how mobile refugees entertain both a direct and *potential* socio-legal relationship with the Dublin Regulation; they experience fragmented temporalities, caught up in-between a simultaneous existential sense of 'stuckness' and 'restlessness'. From the different standpoints of Rome, London and Hamburg, I simultaneously witnessed the life-disruptive, damaging effects of Dublin transfers and asylum rejections, *and* the many possibilities for autonomy and legal interstices that refugees carve out of this restricted regime of mobility. In other words, while they constantly moved from a place to another, cobbling together pieces of their rights, desires and autonomy, the material and social conditions of their everyday life became increasingly fragmented: they might have had legal protection in one country, a black-market job in another, and friends or family in yet another one.

Drawing on this previous body of research, in this chapter, I explore the trajectories of refugees I met in Hamburg, with the purpose of illuminating the specific spatio-temporal dimensions of the coloniality of asylum law, which operates through the mutual workings of refugee *allocation* and *deportation*, and within a complex intersection of asylum, labour and illegality. These trajectories are simultaneously *biographically individual* and *historically collective*. They offer an experiential critique of the imagined 'linearity' of the governmental category of 'transit' (Hess 2012), and they nuance the ethnographic perspective of refugee movements offered in the previous chapters from the standpoint of the Central Station, both in terms of their multidirectional and long-term nature, and in terms of acts of solidarity that mostly come from other refugees along these journeys. While, in chapter 6, I will return to the subjective quandaries of mobile refugees who resist the coloniality implied in asylum's disjoining of protection from freedom, here I hint to the ambiguous equation of 'freedom' with 'movement' (Apostolova 2018): while refugees certainly exert a 'politics of incorrigibility (De Genova 2010) in the face of the asylum regime's constrictions, through those very autonomous mobilities, they are also reinserted in a process of 'containment through mobility' (Tazzioli 2017) – whose main characteristic is the constant reproduction of their deportability or 'Dublinability'. Geographic movement translates into legal movement between different statuses, and the overall result is a complex stratification of legality, illegality and semi-legality. Hence, the Dublin regime plays a pivotal role in the (re)production of migrant 'illegality' (De Genova 2002), while also (re)producing the commodification of refugees' labour power as disposable and deportable (Apostolova 2017: 209–2010). Finally, to further illustrate how asylum is embedded in a wider coloniality that also shapes migrant labour and illegality, I link refugee mobilities to those of other 'non-Europeans' who are long-term European residents but are racialised and classed through similar patterns. These mobilities produce a 'refugification' of other migrant statuses, which translates in the humanitarisation and precarisation of their everyday lives.

4.1. BECOMING REFUGEES: THE THREEFOLD BIND OF ASYLUM, LABOUR AND ILLEGALITY

Prior to 2015, refugees' unauthorised mobilities had already engendered several border struggles across Europe (Garelli 2013; Tazzioli 2015a). In Germany, different groups with variously precarious statuses started organising politically between 2013 and 2014, contesting both the national and international restrictions to their mobility exerted, respectively, by the Dublin Regulation and the German federal system of redistribution, both of which followed a principle of *enforced allocation*. In 2012, collective defiance of the *Residenzpflicht* – the residency obligation prohibiting asylum seekers to leave the area in which their application was being assessed – resulted in a march from Würzburg to Berlin, which culminated in the occupation of Oranien Platz (Fontanari 2019: 56). Simultaneously, protests against the Dublin regime were organised by the group Lampedusa in Hamburg, and rapidly inspired others who gathered around similar names, such as Lampedusa in Berlin and Lampedusa in Hannover (Borgstede 2016).

The men and women that formed the 'Lampedusa' groups were dragged to northern Germany by a specific current that sprung with the 2011 NATO intervention in Libya and the subsequent reconfiguration of the Italian transit space (Garelli and Tazzioli 2013a). For decades, Libya had been home to hundreds of thousands of migrant workers, mostly nationals of West African and South Asian countries. With the eruption of the war, and the increasing racist targeting of black foreigners, many of them fled the country and landed in Lampedusa, from where they were then redistributed to other regions under the 'North Africa Emergency Programme'. They all obtained humanitarian protection,[2] which granted them temporary residency permits but, upon the closure of the programme in 2013, they were offered a €500 one-off bonus, which compelled them to renounce, with their signature, to any entitlement to state assistance. Implicitly encouraged to leave Italy in search for a better future in the north, many of them ended up in northern Germany, only to find out that, due to the Dublin Regulation, their asylum applications would not be considered there.

That the protesters gathered around the names 'Lampedusa in . . . ' points to the geopolitical and social ties between apparently disconnected locations, such as Lampedusa, a small island in the Mediterranean closer to the African continent than to Europe, and Hamburg, the second largest city of one of the wealthiest Western countries. Their juxtaposition highlights how they are actually embedded in each other, hierarchically interconnected through the EU border regime and its mechanism of externalisation and internalisation of borders. The preposition 'in' that joins the two locations displaces the iconic EU external border into the putative 'interior' space of Europe (Fontanari 2019: 57), and it remarks that border struggles are inherently *transnational* (Cantat 2015: 253). Such connections are not merely theoretical; two of the most active members of the group often travelled to Italy for workshops and public talks, to Calais for demonstrations, to Greece for annual no-border camps, and to the camp of Idomeni during the 2015 'crisis'. They were also among the promoters of the 2014 'March for Freedom', a transnational protest of about four hundred refugees, who marched from Strasbourg to Brussels and demanded freedom of movement and residency permits, as well as the abolition of the Dublin regime, detention, deportation and policing (Nigg 2014).

The specific demands of Lampedusa in Hamburg spoke to the postcolonial and neocolonial historical stratification of multiple displacements, complicating any simple legal, spatial or temporal understanding of asylum seeking as a straightforward movement from a 'country of origin' to a 'hosting country'. One of the group's slogans, *Before being refugees we were migrant workers,* directly pointed to the instability of governmental categories, for migrant workers can *become* 'refugees' by crossing international borders *under certain conditions.* The trajectories of the members of the group showed that legal identities work as bordering practices, restricting people from the right to work, and subjecting them to deportability. It was first the neoliberal force of capitalism, unleashed in some of the most impoverished formerly colonised African nations, that drove these men and women out of the places where they had grown up, transforming them into 'migrant workers'. Differently, after their landing in Italy prompted by the incipient war in Libya, they became 'asylum seekers' and, at a later stage, 'subjects of humanitarian protection'. Finally, once in Germany, they morphed into semi-illegalised migrants, with no right to stay for longer than three months and no right to work, due to the clash between the Schengen and Dublin regimes.

These fragmented mobilities between physical spaces and legal regimes illuminate how the law subjugates refugees and colonises their subjectivity (Behrman 2014). The forcedness of their migration was primarily caused by poverty rather than war or persecution in a strict sense and, because poverty is not contemplated by the Geneva convention, they could not be recognised under the rubric of political asylum, but only obtain 'humanitarian protection'. Countering this framework, Lampedusa in Hamburg's narrative posited the legitimacy of their presence in Europe by referring to the coloniality of the global economy: 'at home, there are many ways of dying, war is one, but hunger is also an important one', used to say a spokesman of the group.

Another slogan, *All we need is Arbeitserlaubnis* (work permits), addressed the interdependency of asylum, illegality and labour in the opposite direction. This claim reversed normative restrictions of asylum that hinge on the perceived scarcity of state resources (Vacchiano 2011): it made clear that what those 'refugees' actually needed was not mere welfare *as refugees*, but rather the right to work as *migrant workers*. It was precisely the coloniality of the law, in the shape of the Dublin regime and the denial of access to regular employment, that re-illegalised them and pushed them towards the need for humanitarian assistance.

In a panel titled 'Moving Beyond Welcoming', held at the 2016 'Refugee Conference' (chapter 7), a Lampedusa in Hamburg spokesman illustrated the irreducible relation between legal and political struggles when these occur within legal regimes that illegalise and oppress people in the first place. The protest group had been fighting with the City of Hamburg already for three years, demanding their *right to stay*[3] and work. Ultimately, the response of the local government engendered divisions among the group: individual members were offered the *Duldung* status, but no collective solution was devised because it would have created a 'dangerous' precedent both locally and nationally for other illegalised groups to collectively demand their rights. The inherent 'politics of incorrigibility' (De Genova 2010) of Lampedusa in Hamburg was brought about with a third slogan: *We are here to stay!*, which testified to their awareness about their historical participation in the sociopolitical and spatial making of 'Europe'. Their political claims were not limited to seeking justice for the colonial legacies that created the conditions for their displacement (*We are here, because you were there*); they affirmed that their presence remade the European space they were already inhabiting, despite their putative unwanted status (*We are part of the history of Hamburg*). Carrying this awareness, the group organised guided city-tours, in which they showed the main locations of their struggle – a premiere example of what Nicholas De Genova (2015) calls 'the migrant metropolis', namely, a urban configuration that emerges, simultaneously, from the state's efforts to domesticate migrants' defiance, capital's co-optation of racialised labour *and* migrants' own subjectivity.

These simultaneous and contradictory tensions are significant because collective 'politics of incorrigibility' do not erase countless individual 'crises' and displacements, which remain invisible behind spectacularised mass 'crises'. In early 2016, two members of Lampedusa in Hamburg were deported to Italy under the Dublin procedure: one was apprehended by the police after a fire broke in the club next to which he was living, while the other was picked up from the hospital where he was receiving medical care, despite a health certificate that advised against his forced removal. Their legal predicaments were particularly precarious, because they had not renewed their Italian permits for a long time, their asylum applications had been rejected in Germany, and their German *Duldung* had also expired. In Italy, they lived on the streets, barely relying on solidarity networks, exposed to police harassment, and one of them was given an expulsion order, which subjected him to potential detainability in the case of further police checks.

4.2. BECOMING (UN)DEPORTABLE: THE SPATIO-TEMPORAL ORDER OF ASYLUM

Simultaneously to Lampedusa in Hamburg, two more groups of rejected asylum seekers threatened with deportations organised collective struggles for their right to stay in Hamburg: *Romano Jekipe Ano*, formed in 2014 by a group of Balkan ethnic Romas (Leko 2017), and *Afghanistan ist kein sicheres Land* ('Afghanistan is not a safe country'), emerging in 2016 under the leadership of Hazara Volks-und Kulturverein, an association of ethnic Hazaras, whose main focus had thus far been their persecution in Afghanistan. In 2017, the three groups joined forces with Never Mind the Papers, and co-organised anti-deportation demonstrations under the slogan 'Migration is a Right, Deportation is a Crime!'

The *Duldung* legal arrangement was crucial to all of them. It represented a middle ground between recognition and deportation, literally a 'toleration' of undeportable asylum seekers, either because of lack of cooperation by the authorities of the countries to which they were to be deported, or the persistence of humanitarian crises that rendered their deportations unfeasible or unlawful under international treaties. Meant to be only temporary, a *Duldung* permit was limited to the duration of an individual's 'undeportable' status; yet, it was indefinitely renewable and thus left rejected asylum seekers in a perennial state of waiting, precariousness and uncertainty (Fontanari 2015). While regulations have been changing through time, usually the *Duldung* status does not entail the right to work or either severely restricts it; moreover, it doubly confines its holders by subjecting them to the *Residenzpflicht* and not entitling them to travel documents, and thus to travel outside of Germany.

According to the Federal Statics Office's figures, by the end of 2015, there were already more than 150,000 rejected asylum seekers on *Duldung*, of which 14,000 were Afghans. As my Afghan friends rightly prefigured in their analysis of the 'crisis', the German discourse of 'welcoming' was utterly dissonant with the reality of many who were already residing in the territory. Moreover, while Syrians rapidly rose to the symbolic status of 'genuine', suffering and deserving refugees, Afghans were increasingly constructed as 'economic migrants' and thus 'bogus' asylum seekers, who had no real *Bleibeperspektive* ('prospect to stay'). At the level of the state, the whole *Wilkommenskultur* was based on the partitioning between those with a good *Bleibeperspektive* – based on the rates of acceptance of the previous year – and those who fell below that threshold. For a minimal statistical difference, the Afghans did not enjoy a 'good' *Bleibepersvektive* and were thus subjected to differential treatment, access to rights and speed in procedures. Significantly, however, the Afghans that were deported in 2016 were not those who had arrived in 2015 – whose asylum applications were still pending in the clog of the 'crisis' – but rather those who already resided in Germany and were 'tolerated' under the *Duldung*. In other words, while the state's narrative posited migration as a self-evident 'problem' and deportation as a self-evident 'solution' (De Genova and Peutz 2010), there was no linearity between the two, but rather a temporal disjuncture between the arrival of the newcomers and the deportation of the old illegalised residents.

Beyond this temporal disjuncture, there is also a spatial one in the legal conceptualisation of asylum, hinging on a supposed but unrealistic *linearity* of transit. This narrative ascribes asylum seekers to a 'home country', ignoring prolonged histories of past displacements, like the ones of Lampedusa in Hamburg's members. Its paradoxical result is that national identities end up holding a differential, almost inverse currency in the distinct contexts of applying for asylum and avoiding a deportation after rejection. For instance, contemporary Afghan asylum migration builds on over forty years of conflict and military occupation which have led to different sedimentations of previous mobilities: many of those who now seek asylum in Europe have already been displaced long ago to Pakistan or Iran. This is usually a disadvantage when they apply for asylum, as the violent and exclusionary treatment that they suffer in those countries is not considered a sufficient reason for persecution. Asylum seekers thus have to construct their narratives as belonging to Afghanistan and fleeing either foreign occupation or Taliban persecution; this construction, in turn, is often jeopardised by translators deeming their Persian accent Iranian or, their Pashto accent Pakistani. Conversely, when they are threatened with deportations to Kabul, the reverse mechanism holds: it can be more strategic to signal that they have never been in, and thus have no social connection to, Afghanistan. This is in no way unique to the Central Asian country; it rather testifies to the double-edged nature of nationality, which can speed up asylum procedures as much as it can speed up deportation ones, thus holding an inverse currency depending on the specific legal predicament of an individual.

By erasing these historical sedimentations, the legal and 'spatial fix' (Garelli and Tazzioli 2013: 1010) of national identities subjects asylum seekers to arbitrary and uneven disbelief, particularly tested against their accents. I often came across Syrians who had previously lived in Gulf Countries, due either to family ties or work opportunities, but had no difficulties with their asylum interviews in Germany because they had retained the local accent developed during childhood and adolescence. Conversely, I once attended to a middle-age Syrian man at Cafe Exil who had grown up in Libya, where his father used to work, and had thus developed a mixed Libyan/Syrian accent and dialectal vocabulary. After the eruption of the war in Libya he had returned to Syria, only to find there an equally unsafe and deteriorating situation, and had thus travelled along the Balkan route in 2015. In Germany, his asylum application was rejected because the Syrian translator deemed his accent Libyan and, thus, the applicant, a liar. Similar predicaments concerned Palestinian-Syrian asylum seekers, because Syria used to be home to many Iraqi and Palestinian refugees who later became part of the wider Syrian diaspora. While the Iraqi-Syrians could apply as Iraqis, Palestinians were considered stateless, because Germany does not recognise Palestine as a legitimate country (chapter 6). Their asylum applications would thus display a code that marked uncertain nationalities, and specified whether the declared nationality was believed or not by the BAMF employees – all of which further slowed down the already clogged assessment of their applications.

In the context of the Dublin regime, this 'spatial fix' becomes twofold, because the spatial ordering of asylum allocates refugees not only to their supposed 'country of origin' but also to the one responsible for the assessment of their application. Thus, within the European order of asylum, 'the national order of things' (Malkki 1995) confines refugees to an utterly different realm from the 'post-nationality' bestowed on (the majority of) EU citizens.

4.3. BECOMING DUBLIN: NORTHWARD MOBILITIES AND SPATIO-TEMPORAL BORDERS

Daud, originally from Somalia, lived in Egypt for a couple of years, registered as a UNHCR refugee and studying Computer Science at Cairo University. He attempted a first sea crossing in 2014 but was caught by the police and detained, while his girlfriend boarded the boat and safely landed on the other shore. UNHCR facilitated his release from prison within a week, but it then took him another year to collect the smuggler fee for a second attempt. In August 2015, after more than a day adrift in the high seas, his boat was rescued by the Italian authorities and the seventy-three passengers were brought to the harbour of Taranto, in south-eastern Italy, which shortly afterwards would become one of the official 'hotspots'. Under the coordination of the local office of the Ministry of Interior, the disembarked migrants were photo-identified and medically screened, and then redistributed across different reception structures in the Apulia region. Daud's group was brought to the Police Headquarters of Bari, and divided into two queues with a policeman guarding each:

> They told us we had to give our fingerprints because we were illegal and we had no documents. Because of anti-terrorism laws in Italy they needed to know who entered the territory. So they said the fingerprints would just be local, for security reasons. They said: 'Don't worry if you want to go to another European country, it's fine!' The people who tried to refuse were beaten. By the end of the day, everybody gave their fingerprints.

At the accommodation centre of Bari Palese, there were no translators, and Daud acquired some information only from his roommate, a young Nigerian man, who had been waiting there already for a year and still had no news about the status of his application. This disheartening prospect persuaded Daud to leave the facility and autonomously attempt the long journey up to Hamburg, where his girlfriend was waiting for him. With the help of his roommate, he bought a train tickets to Rome and a SIM card. On the next day, he stayed in 'Anagnina' a formerly abandoned building in the south of Rome which, from the early 2000s, has been squatted by Horn of Africa's refugees. 'Anagnina' had an entry policy restricted to residents only, but a Somali friend managed to sneak Daud in, and he never left in those ten days, because going out potentially meant not being able to make it in again. As soon as he received money from a relative, he boarded a bus to Munich, where he was again hosted by a Somali acquaintance. The trip involved the risk of being caught and fingerprinted both at the Italian/Austrian and the Austrian/German borders but, in summer 2015, the patchwork of internal controls was arbitrary and intermittent, and it thus left an interstice for Daud's good fortune.

On September 1, he finally arrived in Hamburg and re-joined his girlfriend after a year and a half of separation. He hid at home for a few days, worried about the possibility to be transferred somewhere else once registered. Upon registration, however, he was once again lucky and the redistribution algorithm allocated him to Hamburg. In that period, the city was at its busiest, processing hundreds of registrations each day, so that Daud's fingerprints were not taken until January 8, in the course of his first asylum hearing.[4] Here, he declared that his fingerprints had not been taken anywhere else, confident that the information given by the Italian police was trustworthy. In March, however, he received a letter communicating his subjection to the Dublin procedure, because his fingerprints had hit a match on Eurodac, and Italy had not objected to the transfer request. When a 'take charge' request[5] is submitted, the receiving state must reply within two months, but since the Italian Dublin Unit never replies, Dublin signatories have adopted a policy of implied assent. Daud was painfully aware of this carelessness; in his words: 'through that law I became Dublin, because the Italians never answered'. He was subsequently invited for a Dublin interview,[6] where he explained that he should not be deported back to Italy because his fiancé had been recognised in Hamburg; they planned to get married and he wanted to continue his studies, for which an English-language programme was available in the Hanseatic City. However, because the Dublin Regulation's criteria do not contemplate unmarried partners as a reason for family reunification, in April his appeal was rejected, and he received a transfer order to Italy.

His lawyer stated that his only chance to stay was to wait for six months, because if the deportation was not carried out within that time frame, Germany would become responsible for Daud's application. Waiting for that period was nonetheless complicated: going into hiding would have extended the period of 'Dublinability' to eighteen months and, in order not to fall into this 'absconding' status, Daud still had to collect his post from the camp, as well as renewing his *Ausweis* (ID card) at the Ausländerbehörde.

Moreover, because of the myriad bureaucratic quibbles of the Dublin procedure, the exact end of that period was uncertain, and his lawyer failed to obtain this information from the BAMF. It was a delicate matter, because Daud's *Ausweis* would expire on August 23. That day, for some lucky coincidence of the bureaucratic clog, the BAMF decision had not reached the Ausländerbehörde, so that Daud received a further three-month residency permit. The six-month period eventually ended up in September, and Daud was invited for his second hearing which led to a positive outcome. He received subsidiary protection[7] in spring 2017, almost two years after his first arrival in Taranto. That year he also got married, and later had a child.

As in Daud's case, many other Dublin transfers were ultimately *not* carried out, thanks to a combination of asylum seekers' determination and the system's inefficiency. Already in 2014, my research interlocutors who had either been fingerprinted or submitted previous applications elsewhere invariably reported that, at the Police Headquarters, they had been told to wait for six months, after which Italy would become responsible for their cases. At the time, Italy's Dublin unit was too busy with the disproportionate number of incoming requests so that it had almost no capacity to submit outgoing requests in the established times. Moreover, although Dublin signatories are supposed to mutually recognise other states' negative decisions, the latter are not inserted on the Eurodac database and, finally, the Dublin Regulation includes a 'sovereignty clause',[8] under which Member States can take charge of asylum claims regardless of their responsibility under the regulation's criteria.

The everyday messiness of state practices implies a flexibility that can be often positively exploited by refugees, but, as Bernd Kasparek (2015: 75) notes, 'flexibility implies volatility. A particular migratory practice that works today may not work tomorrow, and in this sense it is the opposite of a right'. This regime of flexibility re-inserts hypermobile refugees in an oppressive process of 'containment through mobility' (Tazzioli 2017) – whose main characteristic is the constant reproduction of their deportability. As refugees' hypermobility reproduces their illegalisation, they are simultaneously re-rendered disposable labour (Apostolova 2017: 210). This particular aspect is a reminder to resist any uncritical celebration of refugees' embodied enactment of freedom of movement, for doing so risks equating movement and freedom under a liberal prism (Apostolova 2018). Instead, the unruly mobilities I have described so far as 'necessarily limited, compromised, contradictory and tactical' (De Genova et al. 2018).

Returning to Daud's case, even though his trajectory was definitely more straightforward than those of the Afghans that opened this chapter, or those that will follow in the next section, his life plans had still been decelerated by both illegalised transit and the Dublin procedure. He had been spared the deceleration of detours, pushbacks and detention (Andrijasevic 2010) that many other 'Dubliners' undergo (Picozza 2017a), but he had, regardless, undergone repeated moments of self-confinement in order to avoid capture and detention, and had been suspended in a zone of 'spatio-temporal waiting' (Della Torre and de Lange 2017) for the whole duration of the Dublin procedure. This zone makes clear that the effects of the Dublin Regulation are more disciplinary rather than effectively controlling. The regulation most effective outcome is in fact not actual deportation but 'deportability' (De Genova 2002), in this case better understood as 'Dublinability' (Picozza 2017b) – a disciplinary condition that affects refugees' self-regulation and spatial mobilities. It is this condition of *potential* deportation that often diminishes refugees' involvement in overt political action, although this was precisely not the case neither for Lampedusa in Hamburg's members, nor for Daud, who was an active member of Never Mind the Papers (chapter 5).

4.4. BECOMING NUMBERS: SOUTHWARD MOBILITIES AND THE UNSAFETY OF EUROPE

The trajectory of Abdullahi, a close friend of Daud, was neither marked by lucky coincidences, nor by a clear migratory project that would sustain

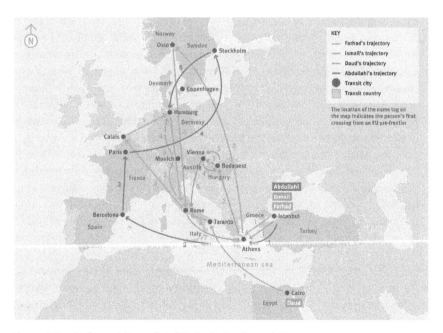

Figure 4.1   Refugees' Convoluted Trajectories through Europe.

him in taking somewhat hasty but eventually positive decisions. Rather, the estrangement and alienation that marked his convoluted trajectory shows that Europe is often not at all 'safe' for many refugees. Purportedly desired destinations in the north may end up confining them, through allocation to remote areas or detention, as well as the degrading ethics of disbelief of the asylum procedure, which ultimately can lead to deportation. This runs counter to the 'traditional' narrative of legal anti-Dublin struggles, which reproduce a simplified and dichotomous image of a 'civilised', democratic and humanitarian north-western Europe, and an 'uncivilised' south-eastern Europe, oblivious to the humanitarian culture of the former (Hristova et al. 2015: 10).

Abdullahi arrived in Europe in 2011, entering Greece via Turkey, and his fingerprint records were not inserted on Eurodac, because Dublin procedures to Greece were still suspended.[9] The account unfolding in our interview was confused, paced by different moments of detention and pushbacks, long walks in the attempt to cross borders, the continuous irruption of the police, and a general disorientation. Differently from Daud's autonomous tactics, Abdullahi's journey towards the European north was strictly structured by the smugglers' strategies, who were in touch with an uncle of his who lived in the UK:

> Everybody told me different things. I was confused. They gave me a paper: I had to leave Greece in one month. Some told me I should say I was under twenty. But I said I was twenty-two. After three days, I was out of jail and I went to Athens. I stayed for a month in Omonia, near Victoria Square. It was a place of drugs and prostitution, like Reeperbahn.[10] I was surprised. I was in a small flat with lots of people, all packed together. Every week we paid like three euros. Officially, there were only two people in the home; it was a business. Sometimes someone called the police and we had to run. My uncle called a man to pick me up and he gave me the passport of someone who looked like me; it was somewhere from Africa and it had a Schengen visa. Then I got a plane from Athens to Barcelona. I didn't know anywhere before. I just heard: 'this is here, that is there'. If only you could see the way I've come. . . . Nights in jungles, in the dark, I couldn't see anything. The police caught us . . . we ran. . . . This was in Turkey, to get to Greece. I didn't know anything of Europe before, just that life was better and that I would be safer there.

From Barcelona, Abdullahi travelled to Sweden on a bus with intermediate stops in Paris and Hamburg, and the credibility of his fake passport spared him from fingerprinting and registration along the way. Once in Gothenburg, he returned the passport to a smuggler's contact and applied for asylum. Under his uncle's advice regarding the avoidance of the Dublin procedure, he declared that he had lost his documents and tickets on a direct flight from Athens.

On the day of his asylum hearing, he was asked about geographical information regarding his city of origin, in particular on the exact routes he would take from his house to other locations. Exhausted by the journey and alienated by the procedure of the interview, Abdullahi did not understand the nature of these questions, and was thus unable to respond convincingly. At a later stage, he was contacted by a Somali translator who asked him specific questions about regional dialectal expressions, gastronomic traditions and cultural norms in order to corroborate his story. Abdullahi was astonished by those questions: 'You know all these things' – he told the translator – 'I'm Somali; you are Somali. Why are you asking me?' When his application was rejected, he was incredulous: 'We spent forty minutes on the phone, but the translator said that *two* of the words I told him were actually from another area!' With the aid of a public solicitor, he appealed against the decision and was thus granted a second interview. By then, he had become acquainted with the procedure and thus asked for a printed map on which he could draw the exact routes from his home to other places. The appeal, however, was again rejected, because the officials thought he had just better prepared to lie to them. He appealed a second time but was, again, rejected: 'These lawyers work for the Immigration Department' – he commented – 'they are paid by them, they do not work for us'.

Abdullahi's legal predicament lasted for three years and turned him into a rejected but undeportable asylum seeker, entrapped in a 'waithood' (Khosravi 2014, 2018) that was all the way more alienating because it stemmed from an incomprehensible, Kafkaesque trial, which asked him to prove things that were to him mere matters of fact. In the accommodation facilities, rumours would spread alternately over possibilities of regularisation or the threat of resumed deportations, but Abdullahi kept the hope that, one day, the Swedish state would believe his case or, at least, issue some kind of alternative papers. In the worst-case scenario, he would have been able to submit a subsequent application after four years of residency.

Eventually, in September 2015, he gave up on Sweden and, following the advice of a cousin who resided in Hannover, took advantage of the chaos sprung by the 'crisis'. The German clog, in fact, provided a number of loopholes not only for those who had been fingerprinted en route but also for those who had been previously rejected elsewhere. After his first registration in Hannover, he was relocated to Hamburg, where he slept in a temporary tent-camp set up in Jenfeld Moor Park, together with some eight hundred asylum seekers. In December, however, after his first asylum interview, he was inserted in the Dublin procedure. Sweden accepted the transfer request, but the deportation never happened because the police always looked for Abdullahi when he was away from the camp. After the six-month period expired, his asylum application fell under the legal responsibility of Germany, where he was finally accepted, five years after his first arrival in Europe.

In 2014, I had registered such alienating and convoluted mobilities in Italy, including also the 'outward' ones of those who had been deported to their home countries and subsequently travelled back to Europe and attempted a second asylum application in a different state. Invariably, their experiences spoke to the violence and estrangement of being literally 'bounced' back and forth – especially in those cases in which the trajectory of their illegal journey had been 'reversed' by a deportation. For instance, Ali had been detained and deported back to Afghanistan from the UK in 2011, after his underage status had not been believed and his asylum application rejected. In our interview in Rome, three years after that deportation, he was still incredulous of the medical procedures[11] to which he had been subjected for the assessment of his age – a puzzled account extremely resonant of Abdullahi's one about language testing. From Afghanistan, Ali had again embarked on the journey to Europe and, in 2012, submitted an asylum application in Denmark, where he had also been rejected. Eventually, in 2014, his asylum application was accepted in Italy and, in 2015, he irregularly returned to the UK to work.

Similar predicaments happened to many 2015 newcomers, especially those who transited through Hamburg's Central Station and followed the

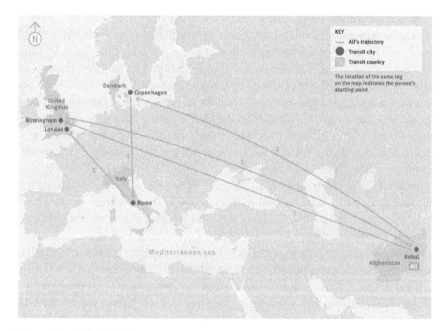

Figure 4.2   Ali's Trajectory.

volunteers' repeated calls and printed signs indicating 'Sweden'. Facing the overcrowded conditions of Hamburg's camps and registration centres, and with rumours spreading over the intention of the German government to immediately deport those who would be rejected, Sweden and Norway appeared as 'safer' and less-crowded destinations. However, a number of those who arrived in Scandinavia, faced equally 'unsafe' conditions there, and later decided to return to Germany. In March 2016, I met Ayoub in Schnackenburgallee, one of the biggest refugee camps of Hamburg, hosting about three thousand refugees. A middle-aged man, originally from Syria, Ayoub was extremely distressed from his arrival in Europe and the asylum process itself. He had entered Germany in 2015 via Rosenheim and, at the border, had been given a paper stating that he was transiting through in order to reach Norway, so that his asylum claim was not registered in Germany. He was not sure of what had happened throughout: perhaps some people had recommended Norway, or rather something had been lost in translation during the first identification at the German border. Whatever the reason, once at Hamburg's Central Station, he had been dragged by the wave of people heading to Norway, where he was registered, and reallocated to a small town, at the border with Sweden. There, he suffered the harsh weather, as well as the exorbitant life costs; the camp's residents who had been already legally recognised used to cross into Sweden to buy cheaper goods, but this was not an option for him, as his asylum application was still pending and border controls were strictly carried out between the two countries.

Ayoub joined a group of refugees protesting the camp's bad food and the lengthy procedural waits and, eventually, they joined forces with about a hundred asylum seekers across Norway and met in Oslo, where they demanded to be transferred back to Germany. Ayoub did not know whether the transfer had happened under the legal framework of the Dublin Regulation, nor whether the cost had been subtracted by the benefits they received in either of the two countries. On the SAS flight from Oslo to Hamburg, he just handed his papers to the Norwegian police – his asylum application, his Syrian passport and ID, and his Saudi Arabian driving licence, as in the past he had been working there as a truck driver. The Swedish police handed the documents to the German one, and Ayoub was told he would get them back after the outcome of his asylum application – a practice that granted a smoother deportation procedure in the case of rejection. Due to the volatility of many such protests, he had not kept in touch with anyone else of the refugees transferred from Norway.

He arrived at Schnackenburgallee in December 2016, but did not receive any official communication until February 2017, when a letter communicated the date of his first asylum interview: May 20. This lengthy wait was like a slow illness consuming his body: he suffered a heart attack and complained about the incompetency and carelessness of the camp's social workers for whom, he felt, he was 'just a number'. As in the case of Abdullahi, discussed in chapter 2, the main laceration of his legal precariousness was the separation from his beloved ones, who were stuck in Palmyra, under ISIS' control and besieged by the regime forces. Even if he submitted an application for family reunification, under those circumstances, there was no way for his wife and children to reach Turkey or Lebanon, where the German Embassies could take care of the paperwork. Moreover, under the new regulations concerning subsidiary protection – the most common status granted to Syrians from 2016 onwards – family reunification requests could not be submitted before completing two years of residency. In any case, waiting times for reunifications were at the very least around six months. He felt a heavy personal responsibility over this stuckness, because until 2015, Syrians could still request family reunifications after three months from their first registration, and they were also allowed to take up part-time jobs after five months, provided that no German worker had applied for that particular position. Had he settled his position before, he thought, perhaps his family would have been already on the way to join him. But there he was, and the multiple borders separating him from his beloved ones seemed unsurmountable. He often thought of returning to Syria, but his health conditions, as well as his economic and legal precariousness made that return all the way more unfeasible.

This stuckness and anxious obsession with return were shared by many others in similar predicaments; in particular, in the beginning of 2016, with the closure of borders and the massive clog in the application system, I recall many refugees coming to the Bieberhaus' *Beratung* office or Cafe Exil, asking for information about voluntary repatriation programmes which, however, were limited to very few nationalities and, significantly, did not including those of most refugees.

4.5. BECOMING FRAGMENTED: THE LEGAL SUBORDINATION AND REFUGIFICATION OF NONWHITE 'TWOFOLD MIGRANTS'

The fragmentation of mobility and labour rights that refugees experience in Europe is part of a wider process of legal subordination of migrants who are racialised and classed along colonial lines and consequently inhabit variously precarious statuses. While the 'post-nationality' of 'Europe' is premised on EU white and middle-class citizenry, migrant 'Others' are continuously confined to the twofold national belonging described above, even when they are legalised through statuses different from asylum. In particular, the residency restrictions which are a by-product of the Dublin Regulation are mirrored by another EU directive regarding third-country (non-EU) nationals.[12] Whether recognised refugees, migrant workers or relatives of other legalised foreigners, third-country nationals can apply for a long-term residency (LTR) permit – which grants unrestricted freedom of movement within the EU – only if they demonstrate that they have stayed put for five years and are thus 'well-integrated' in a national context. The LTR Regulation thus creates a zone of spatio-temporal suspension (Della Torre and de Lange 2017), but the promise of freedom of movement bestowed by this waiting is not always upheld, since national regulations over residency and labour can severely limit the rights of these permit-holders. In Hamburg, I discovered that many LTR permit-holders, as well as naturalised citizens, underwent experiences of intra-European south-north migration that resembled more closely those of refugees than of 'native' white middle-class citizens. Indeed, through their physical movements, they were subjected to a process of 'refugification', amounting to fragmented spatio-temporalities, racialised precariousness and a suffocating humanitarian government.

To my great surprise, while I volunteered at Cafe Exil, Italian and Spanish were some of the most needed languages, because a great proportion of the Cafe's guests had re-migrated from the European south. For the vast majority, they were born in Morocco or Tunisia and had lived in Italy or Spain for a couple of decades; some were Arab residents of Ceuta and Melilla,[13] thus EU citizens; and others were Black Portuguese from the former colonies. Their cases were enlightening of the racialised politics of both migration and citizenship, not only in terms of state regulation but especially of social networks and class position. I never met any white Italian, Spanish or Portuguese citizen who would attend Cafe Exil seeking for legal or bureaucratic support; nor any who would sleep in the same homeless shelters in which these marginalised citizens – or quasi-citizens – did.

Omar, Youssef and Hamza, all in their early twenties, were among the most cheerful and energetic recurring 'guests' and, from the beginning, we easily established a complicity over our shared languages. They attended Cafe Exil with similar quandaries – regularising their residencies, finding jobs, accessing professional trainings programmes, learning German – but they had very different legal statuses. Omar and Youssef were children of the Moroccan migration to Italy of the 1980s and 1990s, a migration that was massively irregularised with the new visa impositions of the Schengen agreement (Castles et al. 2014: 2). Omar's father had never regularised his position and, following several arrests for drug dealing, was eventually deported back to Morocco. Conversely, Omar's mother managed to access a regularisation programme and worked hard in badly paid but regular jobs, until she managed to apply for a LTR permit for herself and her son. At the time of Omar's arrival in Hamburg, she had just applied for citizenship. Differently, Youssef had only a temporary permit for family reasons, which did not allow him to legally reside in Germany, but only to sojourn there for up to three months, just as the asylum permits described above. Finally, Hamza was born in Melilla and, holding Spanish citizenship, had the most valuable legal status among the three.

Despite these profound legal differences, their lives in Hamburg were woven together by the room they shared in a homeless accommodation centre, where they had originally met and then never separated. Their mobilities were pushed into a grey socio-legal zone, distinct from both the migrations of white EU citizens and the ones of asylum seekers. Precisely because of their status as citizens, quasi-citizens or permit-holders in other EU states, they could not access specific refugee support and services, such as state benefits, free health care, free language classes and specific *Ausbildung* (professional education) programmes. Moreover, in line with other countries concerned about 'excessive' EU migration, Germany had started to put restrictions on EU citizens' access to benefits: at the time, these could be requested only after six months of legal employment, and a new law under consideration would further subject access to five years of legal residency (Wagstyl 2016).

Together with these three young men, at the Cafe, I would meet every day older ones in similar predicaments, all men of the generation of Omar and Youssef's fathers. This generational gap implied different responses to their situations: the young ones were better equipped to face cultural change and legal difficulties, animated by a thirsty curiosity for the world and the desire to leave Italy behind; the older ones missed Italy dearly, hated Germany and were gripped by a deep sense of failure. Because they mistrusted the Germans' 'obsessions with rules' and their 'cold character', at the Cafe, they would speak to me only, treating me as a 'fellow countrywoman'. 'If only I could get a poorly paid job, even just 500 euros a month' – one of them used to repeat – 'I wouldn't think twice about going back.' Their outbursts spoke about a feeling not only of 'forcedness' regarding their remigration out of Italy but also of nonachievement and time loss – 'structures of feeling' (Williams 1977: 128) that cut across the experiences of these 'twofold' migrants, rejected asylum seekers, those who had been 'Dublined', and deportees (Khosravi 2018: 8).

LTR permit-holders faced specific restrictions: within a maximum of three months from their arrival in Germany, they had to convert their Italian permits into German residency and working ones. The conversion, however, was bound to an employer offering work and could be obtained only with an official registration of residency (*Anmeldung*). In turn, the latter could be registered only in a legally rented or owned accommodation – an almost impossible requirement due to the housing and rent crisis in Hamburg, particularly impacting on people racialised as nonwhite, who would be often turned away by landlords because of their names, accents or appearances. Moreover, due to the virtual impossibility of finding employment before obtaining legal permission, most of them simply did not have the money to rent a room and thus slept in night-only homeless accommodation centres managed by Fördern und Wohnen, the same state company that ran refugee camps and secondary accommodation centres (chapter 5). The state covered the accommodation fee only for asylum seekers and unemployed refugees, so that non-refugee homeless people needed to pay it by themselves. Night-only centres, open during the winter emergency programmes were exempted by the fee, but guests were allowed to stay only on a daily basis, so that every evening, they had to queue before the opening in order to secure a sleeping place for the night, a daily meal and a hot shower. Omar, Yussef and Hamza slept in a shelter in the Münzviertel, just on the backstreet of Cafe Exil, which comprised four hundred beds inserted in two-level containers – the same structure of most refugee camps, which architecture included intense policing carried out by security guards. Due to the night-only policy, and to the legal impossibility to access the job opportunities they had often already been offered, my interlocutors spent the mornings hanging out at Cafe Exil, semi-sleeping on the chairs and sofas, and trying to cobble pieces of information useful to develop strategies for overcoming the vicious cycle of work – *Anmeldung*.

Only in those days did I realise that I had been living semi-irregularly in Hamburg for several months because, as a EU citizens staying in Germany for longer than two months, I was supposed to register my *Anmeldung* within two weeks from my arrival. The *Anmeldung* was needed for any formal activity, such as working, studying, and registering for health care, but this irregularity had never had any consequence for me, thanks to the social capital of my whiteness (Lundström 2017: 84), *incarnated* in a body that was never subjected to racial profiling, and *institutionalised* in a class position that facilitated my migration in multiple ways. In Hamburg, I smoothly moved between short-term sublets found through my activist/academic social networks; I received my salary from a British university on a British bank account and, lastly, I could rely on my EU card in case of any urgent healthcare necessity. While the authorities never checked whether I had complied with administrative regulations, my Maghrebi counterparts were often stopped and searched. As in the case of refugees recognised in other member states, such as the Afghans or Lampedusa in Hamburg's members, the police would stamp their permits in order to count from then the three-month period of allowed stay. This practice subjected them to an internal EU deportability akin to the 'Dublinability' of asylum seekers; it implied the same strategies to avoid capture, and a disciplinary precariousness and conditional legitimacy to stay on the territory, particularly because an expulsion would have jeopardised any further application for a residency permit.

Finally, their experiences of socio-geographic fragmentation closely reflected those of hypermobile refugees: Hamza, who had left Melilla at a young age to join his uncle in northern Spain, had lived in both France and Italy before moving to Germany, in the attempt to emancipate himself from agricultural labour; after staying in Hamburg for a year, working in cleaning jobs, he again left to Melilla to visit his family, and was planning to move to the UK before Brexit restricted the movement of EU citizens. Youssef managed to circumvent the prohibition to work implied by his family reasons-permit, and took a loader job in a warehouse; however, he soon lost it, after being caught in a petty theft in the same supermarket chain. Some of their friends were planning to move to the Netherlands, others had just arrived from Belgium. Every day they waited for news about a place in Europe that could offer them work opportunities and some stability. By the beginning of 2017, they had all left Hamburg.

The 'refugification' of these migrations, pertaining to fragmented hypermobility and the humanitarisation of their everyday lives, testifies to uneven legal and economic geographies that structure the exploitation of precarious and racialised migrant labour. Throughout the chapter I have shown collective and individual examples of fragmented refugee trajectories that connect Hamburg to other European sites in order to destabilise both the linearity of transit and the ontological understanding of the governmental categories of 'migrant', 'refugee', and 'deportee'. In chapter 5, I am going to re-focus on the struggles for asylum from the standpoint of the camp and the asylum interview in Hamburg – that is to say the place and moment in which many of the refugees who have appeared in this chapter found themselves upon their arrival there.

Chapter 5

The Battleground of Asylum

Navigation, Co-optation and Sabotage

I visited for the first time some of Hamburg's refugee camps in February 2016, in the course of a 'mobilisation-tour' arranged by Never Mind the Papers prior to the imminent International Conference of Refugees and Migrants. Co-organised by Lampedusa in Hamburg and Never Mind the Papers, the conference would be held at Kampnagel[1] shortly afterwards, and host hundreds of refugee activists and supporters from around Europe and beyond with the aim of discussing self-organisation and solidarity in the light of the 'long summer of migration'. Key to its organisation was to involve as many refugee newcomers as possible and that was the purpose of that particular 'mobi-tour', a well-established practice before larger political actions, meant to break the isolation of camps' residents and create bridges with activist networks. We were a mixed group of refugee and non-refugee activists, comprising speakers of the most common languages of the camps' residents – Arabic, Persian, English, French, Tigrinya and Serbo-Croatian – so that we could directly speak with them, while also distributing flyers with the conference information and contacts details of free legal aid organisations.

In the piercing cold of a sunny Sunday morning, armed with a sound system and a tea-wagon, we stood outside Schnackenburgallee – at the time, the largest camp of the city, hosting more than three thousand refugees crammed in dire living conditions. The music pumping out of the sound system attracted the residents to come outside, and they gathered around us in small groups, sipping a warm cup of tea, grabbing the conference flyers and chatting with us. The camp was located next to a highway in the industrial area of Stellingen, a north-western suburb, and it took about twenty minutes to reach it by foot from the nearest railway station. An hourly bus service was available on weekdays, but on weekends, it ran only for three hours in the evenings. Living units were built with containers placed on two levels, each hosting four people in bunk beds. Some units were reserved to families and women travelling alone; the rest were inhabited by single men, usually sorted out by nationality. Other units were used as kitchen and canteen – the only closed spaces in which food consumption was permitted – and, in the emergency of the 'crisis', huge tents had been erected by the military and the Red Cross in order to increase the camp's capacity.

That day I met two key figures of the conference organisation, Omar and Habib, respectively, a Syrian and Afghan asylum seekers, both of whom had arrived in October, at the peak of the 'crisis', and had been allocated to Schnackenburgallee. At the time, Never Mind the Papers was thriving: the excitement of the 'long summer of migration' was still in the air, and meetings registered a very good attendance by both long-term members of Lampedusa in Hamburg and refugee newcomers who had sought the activists' support to their struggles inside the camps. In particular, the conference organisation produced great excitement and a horizon of possibility over transversal alliances between refugees and supporters and across the internal differences within these groups.

Omar spent his first months in Hamburg in one of the large tents pitched on the ground at the entrance of Schnackenburgallee, which lacked heating and thus made difficult to tolerate the rigid winter temperatures, reaching several degrees below zero. This particular issue, as well as other grievances of fellow residents regarding the slow processing of their asylum applications and the scarce access to health and social work services, pushed him to seek the activists' support to put pressure on the camp's management. He soon became involved in the organisation of the conference and started building a solid network of friendships and collaborations, which soon enabled him to leave the camp and find accommodation elsewhere. Later, his diplomatically minded attitude allowed him to keep good connections inside the camp, and these proved crucial to our mobi-tours to Schnackenburgallee, as security guards and social workers would often let us enter the camp instead of standing outside its precinct. These connections also made possible for Omar to take me inside the camp's premises on a weekday, to explore the space more calmly and conduct an interview. We had some troubles passing through security, as my Italian ID did not display a Hamburg address, but Omar's intercession persuaded the guards to let me in, as just a one-off exception. That day, with the help of Omar's translation, I interviewed his friend Ayoub (chapter 4) in the only cosy space of the camp, the 'Chai Lounge'. Referring to the Persian and Arabic word for 'tea', this space consisted of a hexagonal set of connected tents decorated with carpets and cushions and equipped with a tea and coffee point and a study area where several German books were available.[2] Once the interview was over, Omar insisted to sneak me in the canteen to have lunch together. He had previously had a mini-job[3] there and since he kept good friendship with the other workers he was convinced that my presence would not cause concern. We exchanged some reflections regarding the life in the camps, ate hamburgers and fries, and joked about possible ways out in case the security guards noticed me, but we had not realised that it was already late. As the time allowed for lunch ran out, one of the security guards repeatedly shouted that the canteen had to be cleared. Omar told me to ignore him and finish my meal calmly but, as we were not moving, the guard intimated him directly: 'My friend, time is over!' Omar instinctively played the card he had so well learnt to deploy during his stay, and said that, since he was not allowed to eat in his room, he had the *right* to finish his meal in the canteen. The security guard, however, was not in the mood to be fooled and, while pointing at me, retorted: 'What is *she* doing here? You know visitors are not allowed in the canteen. Pack your things and go!' It so became apparent that my presence had indeed been noticed all the while but had not been addressed until it became a bargaining chip to render Omar more docile and compliant. We finished our meal on the unpaved road separating the containers, while Omar ranted about the way the security guards took advantage of the power endowed by their position. Most of them, he underlined, had a 'migrant background', and it was thus particularly frustrating to him that they completely aligned with the management's restrictive policies, instead of standing up for the refugee residents.

Being the place where refugee newcomers spend their daily lives, the camp entertains a topical relationship with the state and it exemplifies the twofold mandate of humanitarian care and securitised control that characterises contemporary migration government (Fassin 2005; Walters 2010). However, the above vignettes of my first two visits to Schnackenburgallee testify to the fact that these camps are far from the paradigm of a 'state of exception' reducing refugees to 'bare life' (Agamben 2005), and are rather spaces of negotiation and contestation (Agier 2008). In particular, the fragmented economy of the camps' management complicates the question of where to seek the manifestations of 'the state', because the strict regulation of refugees' daily lives is enforced by both outsourced workers – particularly security and catering staff – and social workers employed by Fördern und Wohnen which is a nonprofit state company (Zeveleva 2017). For the whole duration of the asylum procedure, encounters with state officials are contingent only to the first registration and the two asylum hearings at the BAMF offices, as well any visit to the Ausländerbehörde to obtain or renew residency permits, or to the unemployment office to claim asylum benefits.

This chapter explores these fragmented encounters with 'the state' by focusing on the two main *battlegrounds* of asylum: the camp and the asylum procedure. It thus returns to the contested and unstable relationship between societal refugee support and state-led refugee oppression but, differently from chapter 3, it extends this analysis beyond formalised volunteering, and rather explores refugee solidarity as a *diffused* commitment that concerns also institutionalised actors, such as social workers and lawyers, who move in-between navigation, co-option and sabotage, and refugees themselves who are often 'supporters' of other refugees but can, at times, imbricate themselves in state discourses and practices of subordination of refugee newcomers. The analysis of these *battlegrounds* will thus disaggregate any unitary conception of 'the state' and its 'margins' (Das and Poole 2004), that is to say, of the expected *stateship* and *collaboration* of some actors who are *internal* to the state, and the expected *allyship* and *antagonism* of others who are *external* to it. This disaggregation occurs not only because asylum materialises in a hybrid terrain composed of different entities, such as state institutions, NGOs and self-organised grassroots groups, but also because particular individuals can simultaneously occupy diverse positions across these entities.

5.1. ASYLUM AGAINST THE STATE: SELF-ORGANISATION AND MUTUAL SUPPORT

On his first night at Schnackenburgallee, in October 2015, Habib could not sleep a wink, too shocked by the camp's architecture and living conditions. Moreover, following the government's public announcement that Afghanistan would be rendered a 'safe country of origin', rumours and panic about imminent mass deportations were spreading across the camp. Because in Afghanistan Habib had engaged in human rights activism, it was to him a natural impulse to start organising politically in Hamburg: 'When you live in a camp, the tent is your home' – he explained to me once – 'You get out and walk around, and you listen to people's thoughts, you feel their mood. They're so worried, they spend their days thinking.'

Habib was very perceptive of the camp's generalised mood of disquiet, which was all the more aggravated by the fact that, due to their purportedly bad 'prospect to stay', Afghan asylum seekers were not admitted to official German courses and thus had little to do in the camps than *waiting* until the date of their asylum hearing. 'Imagine what it means' – he continued – 'to come this long and dangerous way, only to find out that the German government wants to decide about your future and send you back'. Under those circumstances, he pointed out, it took only a moment for any kind of tension to explode among camps' residents; just brushing against someone while queuing for lunch would immediately cause fights, because people were 'angry at their own lives'.

Habib attempted to soothe these tensions and render that collective waiting collectively productive by organising language learning groups in the Chai

Lounge, with the aid of books available on-site and mobile apps. These self-organised learning sessions were a genuine form of mutual support among refugees and aimed at their emancipation from the dependency from social workers and volunteers; gradually, and spontaneously, they morphed into political meetings held every other day, whereby grievances and preoccupations were discussed together with potential actions. Officially, the purpose of the gatherings was always declared as group language learning, in order not to attract the management's attention. As Habib had gained the trust of social workers, he was given the key of the container where official language classes were held and, there, he explained to others that even if they were 'refugees', they were still entitled to human and legal rights: 'Nobody can be deported randomly, without questions' – he reassured them – 'I don't know much about asylum, but I know how the law works' – and he was right: the people who then resided in Schnackenburgallee had barely gone through their first asylum interview – the one checking for their potential subjection to the Dublin procedure – and were, at best, waiting for the second one, the proper hearing regarding the causes of their flight. No deportation order could be issued until a final decision was reached and, even in that case, rejected applicants could still appeal twice. Habib and Omar themselves did not go through their second interview until the end of 2016, and were recognised only in 2017.

Habib thus suggested that the next steps be bringing in a lawyer who could explain to the group the details of their legal situation, and organising a demonstration against deportations – for which support was needed from other networks in the city. As he was not connected to any local group yet, he first contacted some of the preexistent Afghan communities, but, to his great surprise, they did not show much empathy to the plight of the new refugees; they lacked time to engage with them and were also fractured along ethnic groups. Some weeks later, however, one of the camp's cooks mentioned over lunch that some Germans were outside distributing flyers about a demonstration. Rushing out of the canteen to talk to them, Habib found Never Mind the Papers' activists who were on a mobi-tour prior to the demonstration 'Refugees Welcome! Equal Rights for All' which, on 15 November, would see a large participation of about eight thousand protesters. The people that Habib had been looking for had ultimately come to the camp to look for him, and they were setting to the streets to protest precisely those living conditions that had concerned him, Omar, and the other residents of Schnackenburgallee.

In the camp, the presence of workers who were not merely sympathetic to the refugees' plight, but indeed critical of state policies – like the catering employee alerting Habib to the presence of activists *outside* – was crucial in terms of building bridges, raising awareness and supporting refugees in their demands and struggles *inside*. Significantly, the success of Never Mind the

Papers' mobi-tours differed greatly depending on the stance of the camps' workers, which was largely polarised. In some instances, both security guards and social workers were surprisingly kind to us: they allowed us to bring the sound system and tea-wagon inside the camp, or else escorted us to the refugees' living units to directly distribute flyers. In other cases, they were extremely aggressive, even to the point of calling the police to remove us from their premises. Once, we were told by a Red Cross social worker that our loud music was 'traumatising' the distressed refugee residents, which sounded particularly ironic, for a group of Afghans had come outside in the warm May sun, connected a mobile phone to our speakers, and were dancing the traditional *Attan* in a circle. That day, the police did not intrude our festive atmosphere, but they asked us, nonetheless, to move to the opposite sidewalk, away from the camp's private property, and asked for the ID of one of us who would be responsible for the whole group in case the social workers complained again.

Differently, during another mobi-tour in autumn 2016, the police called by the camp's management accused us of putting up a political demonstration without the required twenty-four-hour notice, and asked for everyone's documents, while intimating us to leave the area. Furthermore, after reading our German flyers, they asked for a copy of the Arabic and Persian ones, to corroborate that no 'radical' information was secretly transmitted in languages not immediately intelligible to them. In this case, that the mobi-tour was ostracised both by the camp workers, and the police carried an implicit twofold message: first, it capitalised on the sense of fear and uncertainty of asylum seekers waiting for the assessment of their applications and, by suggesting that we were somewhat 'outside the law', it implied that they should not get involved with us. Second, the disciplining warning was also directed to ourselves: Never Mind the Papers was on the watch-list of the Verfassungsschutz, the German domestic security agency in charge of surveilling 'radical' and 'extremist' groups, particularly right-wing, left-wing and Muslim ones (Schiffauer 2008; Hafez 2014). Against this background, the racialisation of Arabic and Persian as 'Muslim' – and thus potentially 'dangerous' – languages, called the attention of the police unlike the flyers in Tigrinya, French or Serbo-Croatian. Other activists explained to me that, as our ID numbers had been recorded, we may have been called in for a 'chat' about our activities, since the Verfassungsschutz was always eager to add information to their files. While this 'invitation' was not compulsory, the intrusion of the police was particularly perilous for the foreign activists who were in a precarious legal position. Recall Daud (chapter 4), who had a pending Dublin transfer order and thus, if apprehended, would have been detained and deported to Italy; his alertness and prompt reflexes allowed him to vanish as soon as the police car approached the site – even before anyone else among us actually noticed it. However, this episode exemplified the asymmetries that permeate transversal political organisation and was reminiscent of Amir's provocation (chapter 3) depicting volunteering at the station as 'a joke'; those with EU passports among us ran no risk in engaging with grey (il)legal zones, but illegalised or precariously legalised refugee activists faced the risk of deportation.

5.2. SOCIAL WORK WITHIN AND AGAINST THE STATE

In winter 2016, a year after Habib's arrival, the effective deportation of Afghans had become a much closer horizon. The first deportations involved those who had been in Germany for some years on a *Duldung* and had criminal records, but, by the end of 2015, many of those who had arrived in the 'long summer of migration' had already received negative decisions over their asylum claims. For this reason, Johannes, a social worker employed in a secondary accommodation camp, contacted Cafe Exil and asked us to co-organise an info-day for Afghan refugees, who were the most precarious camp's residents and had no access to detailed information about their cases. His precise request was that we provided not only official legal information but also specifically 'subversive' hints and practical suggestions – even if not strictly 'legal' – that could be useful to those who had been rejected but were determined to stay.

Johannes had entered that camp in early 2016, in a period in which Fördern und Wohnen was undertaking a massive employment of social workers and interns, in order to confront the surge in refugee arrivals. From the very beginning of the 'crisis', camps mushroomed throughout Hamburg, counting about ninety accommodation centres already in July 2015, with about forty new container-camps under construction, conceived as temporary solutions and built in industrial areas in which residential construction was otherwise prohibited. The need for workers in these new structures was so urgent that the requirement for a degree in social work was temporarily lifted, and anyone with the relevant interests, expertise or experience could apply. Johannes' profile was good enough for the job: he spoke a little Arabic, had previously worked in harm reduction with drug users, and had been active in anti-racist education projects. As in his case, the massive employment of social workers became an avenue for many other anti-racist activists to enter the camps, and thus occupy a privileged, though ambiguous, position to support the refugee residents' struggles and connect them to the outer political networks.

At the height of the 'crisis', Mareike, a humanities student then, took up an internship in a primary accommodation camp on Dratelnstraße, in Wilhelmsburg. The process was simple: about twenty people attended the job interview, gave a short introduction of themselves and their studies, and were all hired as interns for three months. Their tasks mostly involved administrative procedures for which the social workers lacked time, such as booking medical appointments or translators. In the beginning, Mareike had taken up the position just because she needed a job and she vaguely felt that that type of work could be politically interesting and valuable; she was unsure as of what to expect, and she had not reflected much on the role of the camps within the border regime. In an interview in summer 2017, she recalled that at the time of her employment she was still unfamiliar with anti-racist and no-border critiques. However, as she later became involved in the Refugee Conference's organisation, Never Mind the Papers' actions, and other anti-racist and feminist networks, she confessed that she felt all the more confused about the role of social workers, and generally about how activists should relate to asylum institutions:

> On the one hand, I think that you can't work inside the system, you should work against, and thus outside of it. On the other, I feel that there should be some cool people inside, who are able to show the guests how to get help, and how to get out of there, in a kind and political way. If none of the political people is inside, then only the shitty people are left. Sometimes I think that I should have never done it and I should never go back to it. But then I also think that somebody *has* to do it.

The conflict that Mareike expressed here was not merely ideological; it rather pertained to which possibilities for contestation and sabotage working in the camps foreclosed, and which ones it opened up. In turn, these possibilities also varied depending on the camps' formal organisation and on the pool of social workers gathered in any specific one. Primary camps, supposed to host only asylum seekers who were still waiting for the assessment of their procedures,[4] were more heavily structured and policed, and included the on-site presence of catering, security and BAMF personnel, as well as social workers. They were usually located at the outskirts of the city and hosted large numbers of people. Differently, secondary camps, meant for those who had already been recognised as 'refugees', were inhabited only by them, equipped with kitchens and more evenly spread across the city. Precisely because of these distinct structures, Johannes had applied exclusively for positions in secondary camps, feeling that, in the primary ones, it was impossible to build lasting relationships, because asylum seekers were meant to stay only temporarily, and the job merely consisted in redistributing them to other offices. The contradictions of the system were really 'in your face', he claimed, because security guards policed the residents, and often an actual police car was outside the precinct. 'It's such a bad system' – he repeatedly remarked

– 'how refugees are treated, how accommodation works. . . . It's a long story, but I don't support it at all, and I'm not convinced about my job.' Mareike too pointed to the way this internal conflict grew heavier inside her while working in a primary camp, particularly because she felt that she had become numb to the continuous injustice and abuse that residents experienced:

> It's scary how you get used to the presence of security inside and police out-side, showing your ID, checking on guests because they are not allowed to have visitors over. . . . Once there were ten Eritreans who were shouting 'transfer!' because they had been there already for a year, and the camp's management called the police. All this stuff gets normalised. It wasn't weird for me anymore that the security was shouting at people. And now I find it scary that this was happening *to me*.

Here, Mareike gestured towards the banality of the everyday encounters in which refugee oppression is reiterated – a banality that was mostly evident in both Mareike and Johannes' 'euphemisation' of the camps' residents as 'guests'. Inherited by social work discourses, this word aimed to avoiding the detached connotation of service 'users', but, simultaneously, it naturalised the camps as spaces of 'hospitality' rather than control and subordination (see also Jansen 2015: 23–24) – very much like in the case of the volunteers 'decorating the *Lager*' discussed in chapter 3.

Like Omar, Mareike was especially struck by the behaviour of security guards: 'Some of them were so violent towards the people they were sup-posed to "secure" that they enjoyed humiliating them.' She particularly recalled how they mocked women who went to ask for sanitary pads, by keeping asking them why they were coming. 'They knew why' – she high-lighted – 'They did it just to humiliate them.' What puzzled her all the more was that the division of labour – and thus of the kind of power a worker could exert – within the camp was classed and racialised. While social worker vacancies required university degrees, security jobs were usually taken by low-skilled workers who, in turn, were minimally trained for the purposes of their job. Racially wise, this translated into most social workers being white Germans, while most security employees having a so-called migration back-ground.[5] In this way, people who were racialised as nonwhite or otherwise migrantised as non-German – even though not strictly as 'refugees' – were those materially responsible for the immediate policing of refugee residents.

While Mareike left the camp after the end of her first contract, Johannes stayed much longer, and thought every single day of quitting his job. Under those circumstances, he deemed impossible any commitment to 'proper social work' which, in his words, should have meant the 'unconditional support' to the individual needs of the camp's residents, 'even when you think that they're not nice people'. The camp where he worked hosted five hundred refugees, for which there were only six social workers, implying a proportion of one social worker each eighty residents, and with no continuity:

> I have two-hour shifts at the office and I'm responsible for anyone standing in front of my door so, basically, for everyone. Often, people come in with complex cases, like their families are stuck in Syria, but I'm not even allowed to really go in depth or solve anything, because I'm supposed to just tell them: 'go to that office, do it on your own', and then attend to the next one. I can't really care for each individual and build relationships with them, because there are just too many people.

Yet, Johannes still believed he could make a difference, especially because all the social workers in his camp were, politically, on the same page, and they attempted all possible strategies to sabotage deportations – countering Fördern und Wohnen's official direction to quietly let them happen. For instance, between the lines, they would suggest to the concerned resident that it was 'better to sleep somewhere else' on a particular night, or rather 'avoid going to the Ausländerbehörde' on the next morning. They would recommend that the resident looked for a lawyer through Cafe Exil or Fluchtpunkt[6] – the two organisations that they trusted the most or, whenever possible, they would directly find a lawyer themselves, even arrange an alternative sleeping place in the direst cases. If the guests asked why, they just said that something was 'not right' and, especially, that that talk 'had never happened'. Usually, the Ausländerbehörde officials would go to the social workers' office to pick a copy of the keys of the unit where the people to be deported lived; Johannes would thus give them the wrong key, but this strategy did not always work, because the officials would sometimes directly break into the unit. The social workers thus had to devise different and creative strategies each time, also because they knew from past experience that if the officials realised that they were trying to prevent deportations, they would stop telling them in advance and rather plainly break in at night. Furthermore, at the time of our interview, the new regulations implied that there was no obligation for the Ausländerbehörde to communicate in advance a deportation order, neither to the concerned person, nor to the camp's management. In those cases, Johannes and his coworkers would realise that someone had been deported only after weeks. Finally, the secrecy of those strategies was not only important for the success of the actions of sabotage themselves but also because, if they came to the surface, the social workers could lose their jobs: 'And if that happens' – Johannes remarked – 'it ends up making no sense that people like us are trying to change things from the inside.'

The economic relation between the social workers and the state, however, revealed all the ambiguity of their position; while it allowed for particular actions of sabotage, keeping that position also meant sacrificing something in terms of the relationship to refugee residents. Like a tightrope walker, Johannes daily worked out an impossible balance to keep the trust of both Fördern und Wohnen and the refugees, attempting not to fall too close to any of the two sides, and not to make any of them feel betrayed. Falling would have cost him either his job or his political integrity. He could thus not establish friendships with any of the camp's residents, because treating everybody equally was imperative to avoid jealousy and conflict: 'If I give a new mattress to someone but not to the next person' – he explained – 'then I'll have ten people queuing at my office's door because they all want it. I can't even accept if they invite me at home for coffee, otherwise the distance is gone.' This sacrifice of personal relationships, however, meant to him not only an allegiance to professional ethics but also to *collective solidarity*: what really mattered, in his view, was to make clear that although he was not 'their friend', he was 'in solidarity' with all of the residents, and they could talk to him about any problem – while, in other camps, the workers would have not really cared about them and just reasserted 'the rules' and their limited time available for each one.

One cannot escape the irony that although Johannes did not politically support it, through his labour he still sustained, and financially benefitted from, the system of refugee accommodation. The asylum industry provided the material conditions for his subsistence and thus, from a political economy perspective, his alliance with the refugees hosted in the camp was intrinsically problematic. However, it was precisely his location *within* the institution that provided him with particular possibilities to contest, disrupt and sabotage the state in ways that would have simply been impossible from the outside. For this reason, the new wave of politicised social workers was trying all along to bring political awareness inside the camps, not only suggesting to their friends that they applied for vacancies but also organising anti-racist training for social workers, and networking with support organisations that could bring independent information to the residents. However, even within the pool of the most critical social workers, the willingness to risk one's job for the sake of political commitment was not a given. Johannes was adamant about the fact that he would have always chosen to be fired before supporting a deportation, but he was also aware that he was a single young man with no particular financial needs, and that he could have lived out of state benefits while figuring out what to do next.

While Johannes clearly stated that working 'from the inside' meant accepting many contradictions, he also felt that there were actions that it was possible to undertake only 'from the outside', particularly the anti-deportation demonstrations, in which he constantly participated, but could do so only as an individual, because Fördern und Wohnen did not allow any official affiliation. He had appreciated that this shifted the perception of many camps' residents who, by seeing their social workers present at the demonstrations, understood that they were 'really on their side': 'We're not just here to give them a mattress' – Johannes argued – 'and it is at demonstrations that they see that we're really pro-refugee, that we care about their situation on a higher level, not only for the tasks for which we're actually employed'.

5.3. LAWYERS AND VOLUNTEERS NAVIGATING BUREAUCRACY AGAINST THE STATE

Cafe Exil was strategically located straight across the Ausländerbehörde on Spaldingstraße, a short walk away from the Central Station. Founded in 1995 by a network of anti-racist and anti-fascist groups, it was run on a voluntary basis, and provided independent legal and bureaucratic information to migrants and refugees, with the aid of lawyers present on-site on Tuesdays. It was open four days a week and it looked like something in-between an office and a cafe. Upon entering the glass door, one first encountered wooden tables, leather chairs and sofas, where people waited for their consultations. On the side opposite the entrance, there was a cupboard from where they could grab coffee, tea and juices; and along the left wall ran a counter, behind which volunteers worked through two computers, several folders and some law books. A whiteboard on the wall behind it contained a list of relevant contacts within the city, divided into areas of interest, such as housing, women support, childcare, healthcare, language classes and employment support.

When I first entered the space, in March 2016, it looked way cosier than the austere soup-kitchen atmosphere of the Bieberhaus (chapter 1), where food and drinks were strictly distributed to the queuing refugees by volunteers wearing gloves. At Cafe Exil, those waiting for consultation could autonomously pour their own drinks but, at a second glance, they too ended up appearing as 'the poor' of a soup kitchen. During winter, many did not even come in for consultations; especially those who were sleeping in the night-only homeless shelter located on the back street were rather seeking shelter from the piercing cold in a safe space where they could grab a free coffee and connect to the Wi-Fi, as well as often just fall asleep on the sofas. Moreover, the distribution of the space drew a clear demarcation line between 'the activists', who provided information behind the desk, and 'the guests' who sought it before it. Although named under the purportedly deracialised and anti-discriminatory terminology of social work, the nonwhite 'guests' did not enjoy the same unrestricted access to the space of their white-majority 'hosts': in particular, they were not allowed to cross the counter line, behind which lay all the documentation, the volunteers' personal belongings and the project's financial donations. This rule had been established to prevent thefts, but it relied on an implicit trust of volunteers and, by extension, an implicit mistrust of 'guests'. In the months I volunteered there, thefts of money were reported at least twice, despite the fact that it had been kept in a locked box behind the counter, of which only some volunteers retained the keys. Simultaneously, the guests' own belongings were sometimes stolen from the open space but no surveillance rules were in place there. That this rule replicated the widespread societal suspicion towards refugees produced in me a particular discomfort: there were countless episodes when, being the computer at the front already engaged, I had to turn the monitor of the one behind the counter and place the mouse and keyboard at the reach of the person I was attending to. I always felt embarrassed while telling them that they were not allowed to cross the counter's line; after all, I had little knowledge of the other volunteers, and there was no real reason I should trust them more than 'the guests'.

This architectural division was only one of the examples of how Cafe Exil replicated the power and trust asymmetries of other support spaces, despite their claims of a political commitment that should have been utterly different from apolitical, humanitarian 'helping'. Significantly, the cafe's activists mostly supported foreigners in the *navigation* of state bureaucracy, which did not leave much space for disruption or radical change. Even though we were already past the moment of 'crisis' – and the project had run for way longer than any particular 'crisis' – consultations still occurred within an overarching structural emergency: almost invariably, we needed to focus on the immediacy of the guests' troubles, retaining the wider structural horizon as a mere given. In the words of Jacob, one of the activists who had been there for the longest, the cafe was not about 'working against the system', but rather about 'helping the guests to work *within* the system, to *navigate* them through'. In his view, the very structure of the cafe, with its constant turnover of people and limited resources, as well as the little space left for reflection within the day-to-day business, did not allow for wider political actions.

This stance stroke me because Jacob, as well as most other Cafe Exil's members, had been very critical of the modalities of support enacted at the Central Station (chapter 3); however, the narratives of the two groups deeply resonated regarding how the primacy of material and legal urgencies justified the absence of explicitly political actions. Members of both groups argued that facilitating the navigation of bureaucracy, or the illegalised logistics of transit, were already subversive acts in their own right. Ella, who had been formerly active at the cafe, and was now one of the coordinators of the Info-Mobil – a twin project that provided information and assistance to unaccompanied minors directly outside the camps – remarked that what thrilled her the most about that work was precisely gathering the information that the state tried to hide with the aim of preventing unwanted foreigners from ameliorating their living conditions. In helping them doing so, the cafe's purpose was, in her view, to take 'a little step into what the state doesn't want you to do'. Nevertheless, during my volunteering there, I was often frustrated by the fact that, among endless photocopying, e-mailing and translating, we were often unable to materially help individuals. As I have described in the end of last chapter regarding the compulsory registration of residency, at times the state bureaucracy was plainly too strict to be navigated.

Furthermore, although the cafe purportedly offered support to all, regardless of their putative 'deservingness', one of the lawyers present on Tuesdays often reproduced a mimicry of state partitioning, deeming some guests deserving of our support, while others not. In these instances, she acted through a twofold stance that illuminated the limits of both the state politics of deservingness and the one of societal 'assistentialism' and charity. As I assisted her with translation, I witnessed how she often became annoyed at asylum seekers who, amidst a consultation, disclosed having previously paid for a private lawyer; she saw these instances as abuses of an independent antiracist project meant to assist destitute refugees who could not, otherwise, afford legal support. Her stance was twofold because, on the one hand, she recognised class differences among refugees, and thus did not posit them as *a priori* vulnerable subjects – an issue to which I will return in the chapter 6, and which potentially allowed to avoid the reductionism of patronising charity; on the other, she reinstated the hierarchies of deservingness present in both state and non-state humanitarianism. Her crude and straightforward interactions with guests embodied the opposite of the 'maternalism' (Cunningham 1995) that is so widespread in refugee support (see chapter 7), but the possible equality that this framework could have implied was jeopardised by the implicitly colonial framework about state legibility that oriented her. For instance, during a translation from Persian, I witnessed her incredulousness at the fact that, upon his first asylum registration, a young Afghan had declared a different name from the one printed on his school documentation – which had later been sent to him from Afghanistan. This was actually a widespread problem among Afghans, because the country is way less bureaucratised than Germany, and has thus less stringent practices of birth registration and school documentation. It was really puzzling for the lawyer that someone educated at high school level could so carelessly make a 'mistake' like that: 'After all, you are not illiterate', she insisted, 'I can't believe that you didn't think about writing down a name that was not official'. In her eyes, it was way more possible that the young man was presenting false documents, hence the difference in names. However, that purported 'obviousness' of the state's practices of *legibility* (Scott 1998: 53) was not at all obvious to the young Afghan, who repeatedly explained to us that he was called different names in different situations, and he had plainly given to the BAMF the name he was called by his family, rather than the one he was registered at school with.

The lawyer reproduced a typical asymmetry of the actual asylum hearing, whereby there is a 'translation' gap between the state (in the embodiment of the asylum officer) and the asylum seeker, who both operate with different systems of knowledge (Kynsilehto and Puumala 2015: 446). The capacity to translate one's own biography into the bureaucratic grammar of legibility – both through narration and material proofs – ultimately grounds the prospective recognition or rejection (Khosravi 2010: 33; Bohmer and Shuman 2007a: 135). Although asylum seekers can easily learn the required narrative codes, they are often unable to produce the papers that can fit the requirements of Western bureaucracy, precisely because their countries of origin are less heavily bureaucratised – and it is for this reason that forgery, not only of travel documents but of any other kind of official documents useful for an asylum application, has become a business within the smuggling industry (Whyte 2015).

Furthermore, legibility does not only affect legal documents but also narrative codes of coherence; interviews are carried out with a systematic disbelief that tests the consistency and credibility of the applicant (Bohmer and Shuman 2007b) and can thus be an extremely alienating experience, as in the case of Abdullahi (chapter 4). For these reasons, one of the main activities of the cafe was to support asylum seekers in the preparation of their interview, covering advice on the cultural aspects of how stories are narrated; the importance of temporal linearity; the purpose of seemingly irrelevant questions which are asked just to test coherence; and the role of body language and mimics, in particular relating to how to discipline one's body through the codes of victimhood, since an applicant should not display too much confidence. In the course of preparation, applicants were further familiarised with their procedural rights, in particular the right to bring an independent translator or another trusted person to the interview, and the fundamental importance to wait for a printed translation of the interview report, rather than signing the German one, even if that could take several hours. During these preparatory meetings, the cafe's 'guests' were not asked to explain their personal story, in order to avoid both interfering with their own narration and triggering potential trauma by re-staging it. What really mattered, the volunteers explained, was that, if someone they trusted would accompany them to the interview, that person should know the story in detail, so that they could intervene in case the applicant forgot anything important. Nevertheless, many instinctively started telling their story in the course of the preparation. In Ella's words, they felt like they had to tell the whole story so that 'the volunteers would feel sorry for them and believe that they were really refugees'. And that was ironic to her: 'If it was for me, they could just get a German passport on the spot; I don't care if they are 'really' refugees' – she remarked in an interview – 'This whole asylum interview is horrible, it's a horror show, we don't need it, it's bullshit.'

Her commitment to both the freedom of movement and the right to stay, however, was not at all transparent in the eyes of asylum seekers who, in the course of the interview's preparation, could easily perceive her as just another branch of the state, subjecting them to an incomprehensible trial. Continuously asked for details and proofs in any office they visited, they were already inclined to provide them, even when they were not actively asked to do so. Within this confused landscape of support and policing, Cafe Exil itself could easily be perceived as somewhat related to the state, particularly due to its physical proximity to the Ausländerbehörde, which lay just across the street. Significantly, at the peak of the 2015 'crisis', the Ausländerbehörde employees capitalised on this confusion and distributed maps featuring their own and the BAMF's offices, as well as Cafe Exil itself. This attempt to outsource counselling to an independent project caused outrage among the activists who, by no means, wanted to be associated with the state in the eyes of the refugee newcomers. However, that 'the state' itself attempted to credit them for their work suggested that their position may have not been as antagonistic to it as they believed.

5.4. ASYLUM WITHIN THE STATE: LAWYERS, TRANSLATORS AND THE SUBORDINATION OF REFUGEE NEWCOMERS

When Johannes contacted Cafe Exil regarding the info-day to be organised at the camp, I offered to contribute in team with Habib and Jacob. Johannes had previously asked the organisation 'Refugee Orientation Partnership' (henceforth ROP),[7] but our group was troubled by the idea of collaborating with them, because they were involved in a programme of 'assisted voluntary return' – a highly problematic practice which represents a form of 'soft' government, mostly pursued by putting pressure on migrants who are otherwise threatened with forced removals (Blitz et al. 2005; Andrijasevic and Walters 2010: 22). Habib and I thus decided to attend ROP's info-day in order to get a sense of what kind of information they would circulate, and devise our own info-day accordingly.

At the camp, ROP brought in a white German employee and an Afghan lawyer, who had himself come as a refugee in the 1980s and was there to deliver the legal training in Persian. Upon entering the room, the man barely greeted the guests and immediately asked them to provide their *Ausweise* (ID cards). In the room, the echo of that word resonated with many instances of policing in which refugees were asked to submit their papers, and it sounded particularly threatening to those with the most precarious legal statuses, who were already overflown with rumours about deportations to Afghanistan. Johannes got anxious: he had not been informed about this detail before and thus waved to ROP's German employee to request an explanation. In the back rows, she explained to the social workers that due to EU funding regulations, they could only provide advice to people who were still in the asylum procedure, and they were thus compelled to keep a detailed record of the number of beneficiaries, as well as evidence of their legal status. This detail, however, was not made explicit to the asylum seekers in the audience; among ROP's flyers there was indeed a paper stating that the programme's beneficiaries were not obliged to give their data, but it was only in German and never shown or translated to them.

After the ID check, the lawyer started speaking with a patronising tone that made Habib, Johannes and I very uncomfortable: he first reassured the guests that they had been very 'lucky', because that was a 'good' camp, close to the city centre, and with containers designed 'only' for three people, instead of four. Then he asserted that 'integration' was paramount to refugee newcomers and detailed how ROP could help them pursuing it through language classes and job orientation. The whole speech hinged on a Eurocentric colonial rhetoric regarding human rights (Maldonado-Torres 2017), resumed in their absence in Afghanistan as opposed to their protection and promotion in Europe, for which the listeners in the audience were now definitely 'safe'. He then proceeded to an explanation of the asylum process' stages, which was utterly redundant because that was a secondary camp, accessible only to people who had already undergone their second interview. A refugee woman raised her hand, but the lawyer, with a teacher-like condescending tone, said she should keep her question until the end. After a full hour, one of the men in the audience abruptly interrupted the lawyer, without raising his hand, and said he had already received a negative decision. Only then did the lawyer stop and asked who else had already had their interview; upon seeing the entire audience raising their hands, he exclaimed: 'Why didn't you tell me before?' Although out of respect no one said it, the answer was plainly that he had not let the audience speak, nor had he considered that being in a secondary camp meant attending to people at the later stages of their asylum procedures. However, he then carried on with other legal details, without asking what the people in the audience really needed: when the outcome letter would reach the refugees, they would have two weeks to appeal against it; exceeded that time, the case would be closed – he concluded. The lawyer's attitude was resonant with the one of the Bieberhaus' volunteers during consultations:

refugees were infantilised as passive recipients of aid (Andersson 2014: 185), approached with a preconception of what they would or should need. Despite having been a refugee himself, the lawyer was very much aligning his position to the one of the state: he never pointed to the injustice of the system, nor to the responsibilities of European states in subjugating refugees, and much less to their responsibilities in the Afghan war. 'This is Europe!' – he kept repeating with a rhetoric similar to the one of the Kleiderkammer's volunteers (chapter 3), meaning that Europe was *not* Afghanistan and suggesting, among the lines, that if someone was rejected, it would have been their own fault, because they were undeserving.

The attitude of this former refugee was representative of the friction that Habib had felt when interacting with the already established Afghan organisations, who treated him with a mixture of unemphatic and patronising attitudes. The lawyer's alignment to the state perspective, however, was not only a matter of different generations. Throughout my involvement in refugee support around Europe, I met many refugee newcomers who, once they had accessed a relative position of power, would deliberately implicate themselves in the subjugation of refugee newcomers. Recall the episode of Abdullahi, in chapter 4, puzzled by the Somali translator who actively sought the most minimal mistake that could prove him as a 'bogus' refugee lying about his 'real' regional origin. Many accounts I registered in Hamburg, by both refugees and volunteers, reported translators trying to direct the interviews, providing unsolicited (and untrained) advice, modifying the applicants' stories, or even straightforwardly discrediting them, in particular in the case of dialect recognition. These interferences bore direct effects on the recognition or rejection of applicants (Reath 2004; Translators without Borders 2017), and they resonated with many cases I knew in Italy, whereby former Asinitas' students would be employed as translators either by the state itself, or by other institutions to which it had outsourced its responsibilities of policing and care. Translators were employed in asylum hearings, appeal trials, accommodation centres, and, later in the registration of arrivals at the Italian and Greek hotspots. In one case, I even found out that an old acquaintance had been employed directly by DIGOS – the Italian anti-terrorism and anti-smuggling police – in order to assist their operations with translation from several relevant languages. Beyond taking care of Internet and phone surveillance, this person had to accompany the officers in the course of apprehensions and, because this implied significant safety risks, had to wear a full face cover during the whole duration of operations.

In all these cases, refugees were employed merely for their linguistic and cultural knowledge and, as they were given little or no training on the ethics of their work, the outcome completely depended on their own sensitivity. While it is obvious how these refugees partook of the subjugation, policing and management of other refugees, it may be less transparent how, in turn, this process of co-optation by the state affected them too. Most of the translators and cultural mediators I met were highly qualified in their own countries, but, because of the limited recognition of international degrees, continuing their studies in Europe or finding qualified employment were conditional upon specific training or educational procedures, at times even tracing back to achieving middle or high school diplomas in their new countries of residence. Facing dramatically limited work opportunities, many ended up employed by the very asylum industry through which they had transited as 'recipients', 'guests', 'users' or 'applicants'. Their language skills and their mere experience *qua refugees* allowed for a double-edged inclusion: on the one hand, they emancipated themselves from their 'refugeeness' – intended as a state of dependency from the assistance of others; their asylum process was over, they had been recognised, and they were now officially employed and remunerated. In Amir's words, for instance (see chapters 3 and 6), he 'stopped being a refugee' when he started working for Paritätische, because 'integration is work'. On the other hand, however, their 'refugeeness' was redoubled, because working as translators in refugee camps, NGOs or state offices, they were re-absorbed into the social and economic world of asylum, and constantly re-marked with the refugee label, made unable to become something or someone else; simultaneously, they were constantly re-exposed to the narratives of refugee newcomers, who expected from them an unconditional *allyship*, based on cultural commonalities, national belonging or legal status, and thus also reimposed the 'refugee' label on them.

This deployment of refugees as agents of the state and its bordering practices is a classical tactic of purportedly 'post-racial' politics (Lentin and Karakayali 2016), whereby 'cultural' and racial diversity is co-opted and depoliticised by the state (Vickers 2012). In turn, because of the induced need to look 'good' in the eyes of the hosting state and its society, some refugees who do not occupy any directly internal position to the state are nonetheless eager to assert their loyalty to it, especially by reporting purportedly 'bogus' or 'criminal' refugees. I often witnessed this particular stance at Cafe Exil, when someone would come in asking how to report asylum seekers who had allegedly been fighters in their countries of origin and were thus supposed to be 'terrorists' and not genuine victims of war – and thus genuine 'refugees'.[8]

The variety of examples I have provided in this chapter disaggregates the image of 'the state' as a unitary or coherent entity. Neither the 'stateship' of social workers, nor the 'allyship' of refugee translators can be given for granted; furthermore, these examples testify to the way refugees not only partake of the production of 'civil society', as discussed in chapter 3, but also of 'the state' itself, and this pushes for a reconsideration of the true heterogeneity of the political category of 'refugee'. Here, I have shown how refugees can adopt different positions, alternately colluding with, or antagonistic to, the state and also how the category is fractured temporally through older and newer communities. Chapter 6 will elaborate on these frictions and dwell on the thresholds through which people *become* or *cease to be* refugees, as well as the manifold racialised, classed and gendered divisions among the group.

Chapter 6

Thresholds of Asylum

'Refugeeness', Subjectivity and the Resistance to the 'Coloniality of Being'

In May 2016, while I was participating in the organisation of the anti-deportation demonstration 'Migration is a Right, Deportation is a Crime!', I was asked by a London friend to get in touch with Alaa, a young Syrian who had recently come to Germany to pursue a master's degree in computer science. She had previously met him in Istanbul through common friends, and they had kept in touch throughout his first months in Germany, where he felt deeply isolated and unsettled. He was unable to navigate the bureaucracy of his residency registration and was torn between the possibility of applying for asylum and returning to Syria. Already from my friend's brief account, Alaa's impulse to physically move in order not to feel existentially stuck, deeply resonated with the predicament of many friends and research interlocutors I had witnessed becoming suspended in-between stuckness and restlessness (Picozza 2017a). At the time, he was in Oldenburg, about 150 kilometres south-west of Hamburg, so we arranged a Skype call. His own account rang true with sociologist Abdelmalek Sayad's (2004) concept of the 'double absence', being caught in-between a physical absence from Syria and a psychic absence from Germany, and he felt that only the horizon of return could possibly disentangle this dissociation, projecting 'real life' into a possible future and relegating the present to a temporary, disembodied stage.

During that first conversation, I sensed that Alaa could use a chat with my two closest Hamburg friends, Ahmad and Omar, who had both arrived in October 2015, at the peak of the 'crisis', albeit under very different circumstances: the first, on a plane from Cairo; the second, walking through the Balkan corridor with a large refugee group. Despite their different legal statuses, in the following months, both had become painfully acquainted with the condition of exile in Europe. Ahmad was originally from Gaza and was a biomedical engineering master's student; legally, it was possible for him to

105

return home, but the intermittent opening of the Rafah crossing[1] implied that entering Gaza may mean not being able to leave again, so that he had started doubting he would ever return there. Omar was an asylum seeker from Syria who had been politically engaged against the state regime during the beginning of the revolution and, while waiting for his lengthy procedure, was now very active with Never Mind the Papers. Both were convinced that Alaa was depressed and that that was an obvious response to the sociocultural shock with the northern European way of life, which was, in their view, way too different from the one of us, 'Mediterraneans'; with time things would have eased down, as it had happened to 'all of us', and they were thus determined to dissuade him from returning to the extremely precarious and violent conditions of his country.

Alaa agreed to a short visit in Hamburg, meant to test whether, once in a positive social environment, he would still feel the urge to return to Syria or rather reconnect to his initial migratory project. He arrived at the Central Bus Station on a warm spring evening, carrying all his belongings, consisting in a large suitcase and a laptop bag, just in case he ended up deciding to leave directly afterwards. After dropping his luggage at my place, we took him for a stroll along the harbour, the spot of the city we found the most soothing when anxiety gripped us. Along the walk, Omar and Ahmad insisted that what Alaa was experiencing 'had happened to all of us', but Alaa was reluctant to committing to the patience implied in that statement: 'I've been in Germany already for five weeks!' – he vented out – 'And nothing seems to move in any good direction.' The mention of that timeframe made Omar burst out laughing: 'I've been here for six months!' – he retorted – 'I've done really little and I still have no papers but, honestly, I don't feel bad about it.'

In the next days, many among my activist community showed support to Alaa in various ways: Jacob from Cafe Exil asked the KoZe squat to give Alaa a room for a few days; Sofia from Never Mind the Papers brought a mattress, and Omar, a reading lamp and a sleeping bag. As the four of us were involved in the organisation of the anti-deportation demonstration, we invited Alaa to join us in our commitments, such as weekly meetings, trips to stick posters across the city and, eventually, a mobi-tour. We were all convinced that participating in a socially meaningful context would make Alaa change his mind and it truly looked like my community was trying to 'hold' him in a moment of deep fragility. I found it significant that we had not got in touch with him through support structures, and thus our interactions were far from the depersonalising dynamics of those spaces; Alaa was not treated as 'one of the refugees', but rather as just a friend of friends who needed some rest and peace of mind in order to make a difficult decision.

During our long walks across Hamburg, he gradually unpacked the core of his dilemma. He already wished to leave Syria long before the regime's repression of the revolution and, in 2010, was accepted in a master's programme in Switzerland. His family, however, denied him of any moral or financial support, because they had conservative views and other plans for him: he would finish his studies in Syria, pursue a good position within the state regime and, finally, marry. Confronted by the choice between his dreams and his family, Alaa renounced to moving abroad. Yet, as the revolution erupted, the situation reversed. His native Homs became an opposition stronghold and underwent a three-year siege that resulted in most of the population fleeing the city. Alaa's brother was arrested during an anti-regime demonstration and, to the date, his family had no news of his whereabouts; eventually, they fled to Idlib, which would soon become another crucial opposition stronghold. With the deteriorating situation, Alaa's parents themselves persuaded him to leave and, once accepted at the University of Chemnitz, he got a loan[2] from a contact he knew from a previous IT job, a German man who was sympathetic to the plight of Syrians and confident that Alaa would successfully pursue his studies and pay his loan back whenever he settled his financial position.

To reach Germany, Alaa smuggled himself through the Syrian/Turkish border and then waited about a year in Istanbul for the German embassy to issue his visa. When he finally got it, however, he had lost all his motivation to leave and, as he used to say, had become 'a different person': he missed his life in Syria and felt torn by the impossibility of supporting his mother's search for his disappeared brother. And yet all was set: he had the visa and the flight ticket to Germany – an easy way out that countless Syrians displaced in Turkey could only dream about. On the set departure day, he flipped a coin which, upon falling, suggested to stay, but he boarded the plane, regardless, knowing only too well that it may have been his only opportunity to get out and 'see Europe'. Missing it, he thought, may have later caused him unbearable regret.

It was, however, his very arrival in Germany that caused him painful regret: it was already the second semester and, not being allowed to sign up for classes until the next academic year, he could not find the concentration for studying on his own. Germany was too cold, both in terms of temperature and social environment, and he had not had yet any nourishing or meaningful encounter. Hearing his despair on the phone, the man who had sponsored him invited him to stay with him and his wife in Oldenburg, but this move to a different federal state further complicated his residency registration. Spending empty days at home in Oldenburg only reinforced the creeping thought of returning to Syria, which would have been possible only if he again smuggled himself backwards, since his brother's involvement in the uprising would have resulted in his arrest at Damascus airport. Simultaneously, it felt scary to renounce to any legal possibility to stay in

Europe, and that was why he started exploring the possibility of applying for asylum.

In this chapter, I will connect Alaa's dilemma and its subsequent developments to other threshold narratives of *becoming*, and *ceasing to be*, 'refugees'. These thresholds shed light on the interconnected, though distinct processes of 'asylum', intended as a socio-legal relationship to the state, and 'refugeeness', as a dimension of subjectivity produced along socio-existential lines. In particular, while Alaa, Ahmad and Omar's biographies were caught within the broader coloniality of borders, they unravelled on the *threshold* (Fontanari 2015) of the asylum regime, entertaining, alternately, a prospective, imaginative or rejecting relationship to it. As already suggested in chapters 1 and 4, thinking of both asylum and 'refugeeness' as processes with manifold temporal, spatial, legal and social thresholds contrasts the dominant linear and static imagination of the 'refugee' category as a fixed ontological identity; it foregrounds the complexities of the lived experience and subjectivity of people who may *become*, and may also *cease to* be, 'refugees', depending on the stages of their migratory trajectories.

In particular, I will delve into four main aspects of the formation of the subjectivity of my interlocutors: the refugification produced by the subjection to either the legal procedure of asylum, or to other precarious legalisations that entail deportability; their racialised socialisation *as refugees* through assistance, support and solidarity; their quest for 'existential mobility' through physical mobility (Hage 2009: 98; Jackson 2013: 227–230); and self-organised political action intended as a form of resistance to the 'coloniality of being' (Wynter 2003; Maldonado-Torres 2007) – that is to say the way coloniality and race affect refugees' lived experience.

The intersection of these manifold processes is meant to convey that subjectivity is an impermanent terrain – different from any fixed conception of identity – in which power relations and cultural scripts intersect with individuals' sense of agency and self, historical awareness, experience of embodiment, and modes of 'being-in-the-world' (Jackson 1989; Ortner 2005). Importantly, the relationship between colonial power and subjectivity is not univocal; it also produces individual and collective resistance (Fanon 1963), as well as manifold interstices of autonomy and subversion (Papadopoulos et al. 2008; Fontanari 2019; De Genova et al. 2018), because subjectivity is always in excess of the power relations that overdetermine it (Foucault 1982; Jackson 2013: 4).

Hence 'refugeeness', as only one dimension of subjectivity, and not necessarily its foremost one, is in no way a clear-cut condition inhabited in the same way by different people. Rather, it can be experienced, claimed or rejected in a variety of ways, alternately pertaining to the experience of exile, the traumas of war, the living conditions attached to the asylum procedure, the dependency from others' support, and legal precariousness. People have different political and existential reasons to identify (or not) with it, and different strategies to make their way out of it, depending on specificities relating to class, race, gender, sexual orientation and physical ability – markers that deeply differentiate their experiences as 'refugees'.

6.1. CHOOSING TO BE A 'REFUGEE'

Alaa's movements through Hamburg drew an almost entire map of my fieldwork's geographies; everything felt new and dreadful to him, particularly the sight of the refugees' crammed living conditions in the camps and the convoluted legal struggles of those who had been rejected. On the mobi-tour day, we visited six camps, the last of which, located in a former school in Wilhelmsburg, surprised us with an extraordinarily warm security team. The three men were, respectively, from Egypt, Afghanistan and Italy, and our very first exchanges produced an atmosphere of cultural mutual recognition with our mixed group, which comprised, among others, an Afghan, two Syrians, a Somali who had lived in Egypt, and two Italians. Feeling sympathetic to the demands of our imminent demonstration, the guards escorted us through a courtyard and brought us to the sleeping areas, where the residents were lying in bed, killing time in the weekend's absence of educational activities or bureaucratic commitments. The former school's gym had been converted into a male sleeping room, improvised with dozens of bunk beds clumped by the walls, on which the refugees had placed sheets by way of curtains, in order to make some privacy. 'Wake up! Wake up! There are some people that want to give you flyers!' – shouted the security guards in Arabic, Persian and English. Although we appreciated their good intentions, we also felt uncomfortable about our intrusion, and we thus hurried up to explaining about the demonstration and distributing Cafe Exil's flyers to those who most manifested concern about their legal situation. Next, the guards guided us to the women's sleeping area which was separated by the corridor through some scarves, but, as no one replied to their shouts, we dissuaded them from insisting, thanked them for their collaboration, and left the camp. Back in the outer parking lot, Alaa was visibly shaken. He commented on the camp's living conditions but hastened to the conclusion that 'Well, yes, it's bad. But they *choose* to live like that. *They choose to be refugees.*'

Just a few days afterwards, we held a last preparatory meeting prior to the demonstration. The refugees in our group were organising the speeches to be held during the demonstration in a variety of languages and hinging on the different political claims regarding repatriations, Dublin transfers and the struggles of deportees' organisations in West Africa (Lecadet 2017).

Everyone aware of Alaa's situation tried their best to make him feel included, and someone asked him whether he would like to speak during the demonstration. 'You'd better not let me take the microphone!' – he mocked us in response – 'The only thing I'd tell the crowd is: Don't let them deport you! Go back yourself!'

This cynical remark stayed with me for a long time; it spoke to a kind of agency that is utterly disregarded within the conceptualisation of 'forced migration' and which has been criticised by anthropologists Liisa Malkki (1995: 515) and Shahram Khosravi (2010: 13), who highlight that, in the face of many fleeing wars, others always stay behind, and not merely because of a lack of financial capital. There is an agency and a choice in remaining emplaced as much as there is in migrating, and refugee communities are obviously aware of this mixture of mobility and permanence within their own close relationships; however, the two experiences often prove mutually unintelligible between those who stay and those who leave. For one, Omar was adamant about the worth of his exile and had made it impossible to take his parents out of Damascus to Amman, hoping that Jordan would be less of a cultural and geographical shock for people at a later stage of life. However, precisely because of their old age, his parents did not project much into the future and, shortly afterwards, returned to Damascus, where they had lived all their lives and wanted to age and die, in the face of the war. Omar could not get to grips with their stance, less so agree with it, and this untranslatability, coupled with other generational and political conflicts and their geographical distance, rendered their relationship increasingly colder. Alaa's situation was rather the opposite: while he was increasingly persuaded to return to Idlib, his parents could hardly picture that his life in Europe may in any possible way prove harder than in Syria.

In the couple of weeks he spent in Hamburg, Alaa's dilemma did not easily disentangle. One day he resolved to go back home; the next one, he contemplated applying for asylum, both to fix his residency status and be eligible for unemployment benefits, as a Syrian asylum seeker with 'a good prospect to stay'. On a Tuesday, he came to Cafe Exil to speak to the lawyer about that prospect, and she explained that his asylum application and student visa would not be mutually exclusive. As she detailed all the relevant legal procedures, Alaa interrupted her continuously, asking general questions such as if it was 'a good idea' to apply for asylum as such, to which the pragmatic and impatient woman replied: 'You're not asking me for a legal opinion. *Your question is an existential one.* What do you want to do with your life? Do you want to live your life as a student in the next years? Would you rather do something else?' Then she looked at me expecting some agreement and manifested her annoyance at people who came in with 'luxury problems'. As I have highlighted in chapter 5, she was politically committed and meticulously professional, but, she believed that Cafe Exil's limited resources should be deployed only to support 'serious' cases, especially those of people who could not otherwise afford legal aid. Before moving on to the next consultation, she rolled her eyes and told me: 'It is incredible how many people are unable to listen to speech.' I took her point on the necessary difference between legal advice and psychological counselling, yet I was puzzled by these 'politics of speech', which left me wondering about *who* exactly was unable to listen in that conversation – and the truth was, both of them.

Upon leaving the cafe after my shift, Alaa conceded that he had travelled to Germany mostly out of the curiosity to 'see Europe' and that 'Europe' had disappointed him; no matter how many freedoms he could have had there, they were of little use in the absence of a higher purpose and a meaningful community. Had he had the chance, he would have gone back to Syria for a visit, then to Istanbul and, later, maybe, to Europe, if he found something meaningful to do there. His legal situation, however, did not smoothly allow any of such movements: 'It's a one-way ticket' – he cut the conversation short – 'Either I stay here or I smuggle myself back to Idlib and stay there.'

Such problems were indeed a 'luxury', if compared to the plight of countless refugees who, in Hamburg, as well as Istanbul, or Athens, were stuck among legal quibbles and social marginalisation, separated from children and spouses they could not bring over, and with no financial means. Alaa's past and prospective mobilities were facilitated not only by his class position, particularly relating to possessing a degree and an excellent command of English, but also by his physical condition, as an able young male body, with the confidence to smuggle himself in and out international borders more safely than a woman – less so if pregnant – as well as people with illnesses and disabilities, and families with small children. However, that problems that are ordinary for 'cosmopolitan' citizens – especially those enjoying the mobile 'post-nationality' of EU citizenship – were considered by the lawyer a 'luxury' for a foreigner racialised as 'migrant' or 'refugee' was a specific by-product of the coloniality of asylum. 'Coloniality of Being primarily refers to the normalization of the extraordinary events that take place in war' – writes de-colonial thinker Nelson Maldonado-Torres (2007: 255). When exceptional violence is inscribed unto the 'normality' of refugee bodies, any other behaviour that would be considered normal for white European citizens, becomes 'exceptional'. Alaa's desire for a mobile and cosmopolitan life not fixed to a particular location was very close to my own condition suspended between London, Hamburg and Rome; it was effectively the norm for any holder of a powerful passport who enjoys an often visa-free 'surplus of mobility', while the majority of the globe's population is condemned to 'a world of checkpoints, borders, queues, gates, detentions, and removal' (Khosravi 2018: 6).

Eventually Alaa decided *not to become a refugee* in legal terms, but he was nonetheless progressively haunted by 'refugeeness' in terms of contemplating an ever-closer prospect of exile, as well as undergoing the specific experiences of fragmentation of time, space and the self that I have described in chapter 4. A few days after the Cafe Exil's episode, he left me a thank-you note which ended saying he hoped to see me soon, but I felt like we may not ever meet again. He shortly visited some acquaintances in Berlin; then, in June, he took a plane to Greece, smuggled himself into Turkey, and later on into Syria. Towards the end of 2016, with the siege of Aleppo and the eventual evacuation of the rebels to Idlib, Omar, Ahmad and I were increasingly concerned for him. When we managed to get in touch despite the regime cutting electricity and communications, Alaa revealed that his geographical displacement to the other shore had not solved his existential dilemma, and he was now thinking of going back to Europe; the question had merely been displaced to the other shore. 'It's surprising and difficult to explain it' – he told me – 'but in a way, despite the war, I feel happy here'. The war, however, would be over one day, and he may regret not having built a life elsewhere. Was it worth to pay the price of leaving his mother alone in the search for his brother, while also leaving a whole life, culture, language and people back there? What about not being able to attend his family's funerals – a classic dilemma of exile? 'There is no definite solution, Alaa' – I suggested in our chats – 'You need to give something up. This is what war does. It tears up your life and leaves you little option.' Despite my apparent confidence, I felt totally unequipped to give that advice: I knew nothing about war, except for the experiences that other people had recounted to me; perhaps I was even *normalising* it, in the intent of suggesting practical solutions. In turn, and precisely because of their firsthand experiences, Omar and Ahmad were incredulous of Alaa's choice: they had both experienced the shelling of their houses; they had both left their families; they knew they probably would never go back, but they had chosen their piece of freedom – albeit a conditional one, based on liberalism and individuality.

In April 2017, a year after we met, and while I was already back in London, Alaa wrote me that he had returned to Germany. Attending his master's in Chemnitz was again a failure; he did not want to study anymore and anyways the financial pressure of the student visa had proved unsustainable. But he could not bring himself to apply for asylum either, because his passport would be withdrawn for the whole lengthy duration of the procedure. 'Is Italy any better than Germany?' – he asked me – 'I guess it's warmer and people are nicer. Or maybe somewhere else? Literally anywhere, as long as the asylum process is quick!' – he concluded.

As privileged as it was, Alaa's case was in no way unique; virtually every Syrian I met in Hamburg knew someone who had returned home, or else someone who wished to, but could not afford – neither financially nor psychologically – undergoing the inverse smuggling trajectory. Alaa, however, was not only mentally stuck in the 'double absence' between the *here* and *there* (Sayad's 2004); he kept physically moving in the search for something he could not find and he had become an extreme embodiment of what I have called elsewhere an 'unresolved self-in-transit' (Picozza 2017a), marked by temporariness, precariousness and the recurrence of flight (Dobson 2004: 88). In the course of a year, he had covered back and forth, in a circular manner all his lines of flight and stopovers, and, although he had never crossed the threshold of the asylum regime, he experienced the same stuckness and restlessness of the hypermobile refugees who appeared in chapter 4.

6.2. FEELING LIKE A 'REFUGEE'

Ahmad's biography was also characterised by multiple mobilities, in the attempt to build a life away from the open-air prison[3] of the Gaza strip. The first opportunity had been a permission to visit the West Bank for medical reasons[4] back in 2009, and he had ended up staying there illegally for about a year, enrolling at university and enjoying a relatively more comfortable and free everyday life. Eventually, however, he had been caught at a mobile

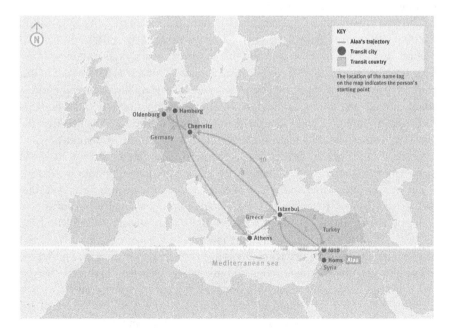

Figure 6.1   Alaa's Trajectory.

checkpoint[5] and deported back home. That forced return to Gaza hit him with a heavy depression, but, in 2010, he manged to move out again, this time to Cairo, where he lived for five years while pursuing a degree in biomedical engineering. The 2011 eruption of the Egyptian revolution was, in his words, the most significant event of his life: he took to the streets venting out his rage against the Egyptian regime's oppression of Palestinian residents, especially Gazans and, for a moment that seemed to stretch and last, he felt he could finally leave behind the horrors he had witnessed in Gaza, and breath the illusion that these would not follow him as long as he was elsewhere. In 2014, however, the political situation in Egypt had already deteriorated and, while seeking a long-term way out, Ahmad decided to visit his family back in Gaza, who he had not seen for already two years. Two days after his arrival, Israel's bloodiest war on Gaza suddenly erupted (Amnesty International and Forensic Architecture 2015), and although its horrors could barely be put into words, Ahmad was one of the few people who kept tweeting from the inside; the massacre of the civilians of Khuza'a – among which were his relatives and neighbours – left on him a profound mark in the years to come, a scar that could not heal and left no space for the tender delusions of the early period in Egypt. He applied for a master's degree in Hamburg, and waited about a year in Cairo for his Schengen visa to be issued. When he finally arrived in Germany, in October 2015, he was determined to leave behind both his political engagement and traumas, at least for some time.

The first time we met – connected by the same London friend who would later put me in touch with Alaa – he picked me up after my shift at the Central Station, and we shared a meal in one of the Turkish restaurants on Steindamm. That was the beginning of a long-lasting friendship that was paramount to our emotional survival in our first dark snowy days in Hamburg. Among endless chats, dinners and drinks, Ahmad unpacked bits of his story, together with his recurring nightmares, and I was never sure where the boundaries between the two lay. Homesickness and feelings of emptiness and loss of meaning would often haunt him in that period, but he tried to tame them, keeping his head busy with his studies, and his body with a weekend part-time job in a cafe.

He was not actively involved in the circles of refugee solidarity but, due to his friendship with me and Omar, he would occasionally participate in some of our initiatives – such as the Refugee Conference, Never Mind the Papers' demonstrations, and the many cultural initiatives organised by Omar at Kampnagel. In those occasions, due to his darker tone of skin, his Arabic name and his non-German accent, many white Germans assumed that he was a 'refugee'. At a concert at Kampnagel, we once encountered Hannah, a former Central Station volunteer, who invited us to a party that was free for 'refugees' and asked for Ahmad's number to put him on the list. Ahmad and I used to share a ruthless irony around this sort of interactions and the many prejudices that Arabs faced in Germany; our jokes ran along all the tropes of anti-immigrant discourses, from terrorism to smuggling, but we were wary not to be heard by 'the Germans', whose political correctness, coupled with a general cultural distance from that cynical humour, made our jokes untranslatable. Along those lines, Ahmad answered that he could certainly 'pass as a refugee'; yet when Hannah later texted him, he lost his patience and replied: 'I can't make it to the party. You'd better look for a *real* refugee.' On another occasion, a white German coworker prided himself of playing football with Syrians and explained how important it was that German citizens helped 'the refugees' to 'integrate': 'Look at yourself' – he told Ahmad – 'you've arrived here just in October and now you're working at this cafe with us.' My friend was outraged but lacked the energy to embark on a rant; neither was he a 'refugee', nor did he believe in that whole rhetoric of 'integration'. Had he believed it, table waiting would likely not have been his most cherished prospect, as he craved for more time to focus on his studies, and on some other meaningful activity but, instead, he needed that job to fulfil his visa's financial requirements.

In similar ways, Alaa often described experiences of 'overkindness' by German people upon realising that he was from Syria. He felt that these reactions implied a legal, political and moral projection: being Syrian equalled being a refugee, with no nuance regarding the fact that not all Syrian nationals in Europe had arrived as asylum seekers or that there were still Syrians living in Syria, not because they were waiting to leave, but because of an active decision to stay emplaced. Differently, in Ahmad's case, his nationality was an intractable problem: the German state does not recognise Palestine and, in everyday debates, the collective memory of the Holocaust makes discussions around Israel and Palestine a very heated subject, particularly within the German radical left, whereby many uphold an unconditional support to the Israeli state, to the detriment of the Palestinian cause.[6]

Ahmad's racial marking as an Arab, however, was usually enough for others to attach the refugee label to him. Moreover, despite his rejection of the 'refugee' category and its racial and moral subtexts, Ahmad had strongly internalised the condition of 'refugeeness' attached to war, revolution, trauma, exile, deportation and deportability. As in the case of Alaa, his legal status in Europe – derived from his middle-class and higher education background – spared him the technical label of 'refugee' but subjected him, regardless, to legal precariousness and deportability. In particular, every six months, he struggled to put together the approximately 4,000 euros which the Ausländerbehörde requested to be in his bank account.

In July 2016, while I was temporarily in London, he texted me asking for the contact of a deportation lawyer. I suggested Cafe Exil but did not for a second think that the question concerned himself. The next day, however, I discovered through a common friend that he had received a letter from the Ausländerbehörde rejecting the renewal of his residency permit, because his proof of financial support had been deemed insufficient. He was asked to leave Germany and warned that failing to do so would have resulted in the issuance of a deportation order. He did not want to worry me while I was away, but I immediately called him back and, considering the worst-case scenario, we discussed places where he could sleep so as not to be found by the police at his official address. It took us some time to realise that a deportation to Gaza was not really on the table, since Germany does not recognise Palestine as a state, nor does it have any agreement with Israel for the repatriation of Palestinians – let alone Gazans, whose passport is issued by the Hamas authorities, at the government since 2007 to the date.[7]

Here Ahmad's 'refugification' was apparent particularly through his 'deportability': it was as if the gaze of the German volunteers projecting the refugee label onto him was now performed, in a much more threatening way, by the German state itself. Despite resolving his residency status with friends' loans, the recurring financial pressure often made Ahmad think of applying for asylum. He was not only made *feel like a refugee* because of his racialisation and precarious legal status; he was likely to, literally, *become one*. However, as it was the case for Alaa, Ahmad was reluctant to enter the asylum regime, because it would have implied giving up his passport for the whole duration of the procedure, and the outcome would have anyways been uncertain. Throughout his first year in Germany, he often felt 'breathless' and his short trips abroad to visit friends were among the few moments in which he could really 'breathe'. Without a passport, those trips would have been impossible and, in addition, his nationality would have likely enmeshed him in an unsuccessful asylum case: because Germany does not recognise Palestine as a state, Palestinian asylum applicants are registered as stateless and, usually, they are not granted protection[8] but only the *Duldung*, given their 'undeportability'. Only after eight years of *Duldung* renewals, they may become eligible for a permanent residency permit (Wari 2015: 22–23).

Discussing the Ausländerbehörde's letter on the phone, I pointed out that the way the state treated him and countless others, was effectively to *make them feel like refugees* – precarious, docile and grateful, so that they would not engage in much contestation. The state officials who issued the letter threatening his deportation may not have known about the actual impossibility of deporting him to Gaza, but, most importantly, they likely did not care. It is not deportation per se that matters to the border regime, but rather 'deportability', for it renders migrant bodies 'a distinctly disposable commodity' (De Genova 2002: 438), and a distinctively docile one; deportability imposes a further 'coloniality of being' on particularly racialised and classed migrants, one that is premised on temporariness and precariousness as protracted experiences of everyday life. 'That's why a lot of people are scared to fight for their right to stay' – I concluded. 'Fuck that' – replied Ahmad – 'I don't want to fight for my right to stay here.' This last comment was resonant of Alaa's remark on people's 'choice' to become refugees and be at the mercy of European states. Both stances gestured to the reductionism of the widespread representation of refugees as victims who seem to have literally no choice other than to be in Europe; both were seeking strategies to resist the 'coloniality of being': first, through their very migrations out of the places where they had grown up; second, through the navigation and contestation of the border regimes to which they were subjected in Europe. While Ahmad kept a certain stability in Germany and travelled abroad only for short visits, Alaa's hypermobility was a predicament that allowed him to retain a sense of autonomy, but to the detriment of achieving a legal and social stability. As discussed in chapters 1 and 4, one of the main predicaments of asylum is the imposition of a choice between autonomy and protection; in the cases of Ahmad and Alaa, applying for asylum would have meant submitting their passports and thus being deprived, at least for a certain amount of time, of their relative freedom of international movement, as well as limiting their national mobility though the *Residenzpflicht*.

6.3. ENDURING THE 'COLONIALITY OF BEING'

Alaa's cynical remark on how people 'choose to be refugees' mirrored another unempathetic statement by Khaled, an Afghan refugee who I had first met through Habib and who argued that the fragmentation of hypermobile refugees' lives was the outcome of their 'bad choices'. I used to bump into Khaled at the University Library, where he studied German and prepared for his asylum hearing, while I transcribed my notes in the company of Ahmad, who studied for his exams. In one of those occasions, Khaled asked about my research and, as I explained my past work on the Dublin Regulation, stuckness and restlessness, he hastened to the conclusion that I should not be fooled: those hypermobile refugees were responsible for their suffering; they had foolishly lost their time and should have rather waited patiently wherever their application had been allocated, while planning their next steps. I retorted that the machinery of the law was so complex that often the people subjected to it would not even be able to understand the rules they were supposed to follow; moreover, it was unfair to expect such a superhuman patience from asylum seekers, who should have had the right to start their new life immediately.

In a way, Khaled's choices were based on future projections and were thus the opposite of Alaa's ones, who instead sought to soothe the discomfort of his immediate present; both, however, were not merely based on practical or legal matters, but rather on a quest for 'existential mobility', namely, the sense of 'going somewhere' (Hage 2009: 98; see also Jackson 2013: 227–230) and reappropriating one's own subjectivity in the face of the coloniality of being. Importantly, existential mobility is achieved not only through physical movement but also through emplacement and investment in social networking, studying or training professionally.

Alaa and Ahmad had undergone a temporal, spatial and existential suspension in the lengthy wait for their visas, the issuance of which was marked by uncertainty, and they had felt stuck throughout the whole process; understandably, they were then trying to avoid a further suspension through the asylum process, which spatio-temporality weighs heavily on applicants, particularly if they reside in the camps, whereby humanitarian management normalises a particular kind of everyday life. As Shahram Khosravi (2010: 70) notes, the camp enforces 'refugeeness' as a 'mode of being' and thus actively produces refugees through its 'pathologising bureaucracy', medicalisation and infantilisation (see also Andersson 2014: 185). Many refugee interlocutors in Hamburg described their first period in the camps as one of estrangement and irreality. Habib could not sleep a wink in his first night at Schnackenburgallee and just repeated to himself, all night: 'Oh my God. What is this place?' Amir, upon entering his camp in Billstedt, felt like he was back in Syria: 'They treated us *as if we were nothing, as if we had nothing*. We have everything in our country, even more than the German people! I have my car, my apartment, my job, my studies. I have everything. Well, I *had*' – he added laughing. 'If I sent a picture of the container to my family they would have said: "Come back here!" Of course, the problem is that I can't go back because I had problems with the government in Damascus' – he concluded. Daud described how, for four months, he slept in a tent with about three hundred people, and woke up every morning scared that his belongings may have been stolen, or that the BAMF may have decided to send him to another federal state, far away from his girlfriend.

The three of them were, in their countries, middle-class young men with university degrees, but their physical displacement to Germany had entailed a misplacement in terms of class position, and they had found themselves at the mercy of the state and NGO's support. However, feelings of estrangement and anonymisation in the camps were shared also by asylum seekers with working-class backgrounds, who had formerly been truck drivers, construction workers or farmers. Recall Ayoub (chapter 4) who somatised his distress into a chronic medical condition and lamented feeling 'just a number' to social workers. This was an important trope also for the Messehallen's protesting refugees (chapter 3) who repeatedly shouted 'We're not numbers'. 'Invisibility and dehumanization are the primary expressions of the coloniality of Being' (Maldonado-Torres 2007: 257) and are enforced through the camp's politics of 'sleep and eat', as many refugees described it. They are experienced as a form of psychological torture, imposed during uncertain and long times characterised by waiting (Khosravi 2014; Fontanari 2019), in which asylum seekers are not allowed to work, and those with a 'bad prospect to stay' are not even allowed to study, so that most of them feel as if they have 'not yet arrived' (Khosravi 2018: 8) and that the beginning of 'real life' is, once more, postponed. Here asylum weighs heavily in terms of temporality, because it exercises a coloniality that involves all tenses: refugee's past is the stone of judgement of the asylum procedure and needs to be relearnt and narrated in particular ways in order to be believed; their present is colonised by the life in the camp and the experience of waiting; and finally, their future is also colonised, in terms not only of being continually postponed but also of never appearing as definitely achievable, but rather invariably conditional.

This temporal postponement affects different refugees in different ways. Ayoub, who was in his fifties and a father, was worried about his family stuck in Palmyra and, as he had lost over a year in his movements between Germany and Norway, he felt responsible for his predicament. This stuckness weighed heavily on his parental and marital role, as he could not provide for his family neither economically nor in terms of bringing them to safety. Habib and Amir, who were in their early thirties and single men, felt this temporal postponement in a different way. Both were hoping to pursue a master's degree in Germany, but the possibility to do it was conditional to finding programmes in English, as well as having their former degrees recognised. When they met me and heard that I was doing a PhD, they felt disheartened; we were about the same age, but they had 'lost' several years because of war and displacement, and felt that they were now too late in life, also because the legal process of asylum had further 'robbed' them of their life time (Khosravi 2018: 7). The same had happened to Daud, who had been suspended in the Dublin procedure and was continually postponing both his studies and his marriage. Importantly, this delay did not only mean that they could not feel any sense of 'going forward' but rather that they utterly felt as 'going backwards', being stuck in a time of youth that 'seems to be no longer a transitional stage but an indefinite position of *not becoming* . . . of not making achievements in life' (Khosravi 2018: 8).

6.4. MOVING OUT OF 'REFUGEENESS'

It was at this early stage of waiting for their procedure that Amir, Habib, and Omar found a 'way out' of refugeeness through self-organisation – the former one at the Central Station and the latter two in Never Mind the Papers, starting with the Refugee Conference. Both at the social and legal level, Amir and Habib's experiences were very different: Amir arrived in spring 2015, shortly before the 'crisis' peak and, as a Syrian national with a 'good prospect to stay', obtained his papers in just a few months; conversely, as an Afghan arriving in summer, Habib was suspended in a lengthy asylum procedure that lasted over a year. Amir slept in a camp only for a few weeks, and soon found accommodation at a friend's place; Habib lived in Schnackenburgallee for the whole duration of his asylum procedure and, after his legal recognition, moved to a secondary camp in a suburb, as finding a room in Hamburg had proven almost impossible, due the unaffordable price of rents and the racial and class prejudices of landlords who did not want to rent to refugees and other benefit claimants.

Both Habib and Amir got involved in self-organisation shortly after arriving in Hamburg, and that involvement changed dramatically their experience of the city. Habib argued that political organising had produced a psychologically positive effect also on the other Afghan residents of Schnackenburgallee, whose mood of disquiet had been his main concern throughout his first period in the camp (chapter 5). After participating in his first Never Mind the Paper's demonstration in November 2015, he appreciated how people's sense of their own self and political collectivity had transformed: 'We gathered in the street and discovered that we can take our voices out there and say "Stop deportations!" It's not like we can really change the politics – he clarified to me – *but the mind changes.* After that, I saw a lot of people calming down.' Away from the passivity and anonymisation of humanitarianism, political organising within and without the camps allowed for these refugee newcomers to reappropriate their subjectivity and the agency 'over their destiny' (Agier 2008: 64). Habib's insight grasped that their resistance to the coloniality of asylum was not only unfolding along legal lines (against their prospective deportations) but was a true resistance to the coloniality of being; protesting refugees could, at least partially, emancipate themselves from their refugeeness through political contestation, in a way that resonated with the words of anti-colonial thinker Franz Fanon (1963: 37), for whom 'the "thing" which has been colonized becomes man during the same process by which it frees itself'.

Nonetheless, this analysis risks romanticising border struggles through a common trope of the 'autonomy of migration' literature that depicts migrants/refugees as embodiments of heroic resistance (Bojadžijev 2006; Scheel 2013: 280). Self-organisation is only one aspect of the re-appropriation of subjectivity, because the 'coloniality of being' shapes the condition of refugees' everyday lives not only at the psychological or legal level, but precisely at the *material* one. Possibilities to improve these living conditions, particularly relating to paid employment, are unevenly distributed along classed, racialised and gendered lines, and intersect with legal status, educational background and social networks.

Amir's case is enlightening to understand how participation in self-organised networks can fulfil a particular role at times of unemployment: volunteering at the Central Station offered him a way out of 'refugeeness' not only in sociopolitical, but also economic terms. Being one of the most active volunteers at the Central Station, at the time of the project's move to the Bieberhaus (chapter 1), he was employed as coordinator by Der Paritätische, for which he has kept working to the date. In an interview that is worth quoting at length, he argued that, in Hamburg, he had truly 'found himself', and that volunteering at the station had been the crucial threshold towards his 'integration':

> When I arrived, I wasn't doing anything, I didn't speak English and I didn't know any German people. The station was like a job but without money: I was there for eighteen hours every day, all summer, until we entered the Bieberhaus. Because of the Station, now I have work, an apartment, a social network, and also a girlfriend, 'cause I met her there. Now I'm not a refugee anymore, I'm an immigrant. I'm still an immigrant because I've got black hair. The difference is integration: after finding a job and a flat, everyone becomes an immigrant, because when you work and you pay your taxes, you are like everyone else here. So now I'm an immigrant, I think. *Integration is work*, this is my slogan. Here is like Dubai for me because I'm working. *Syrians are not 'refugees' in Dubai.*

This interview's excerpt masterfully illustrates the unstable and contingent meaning of the 'refugee' and 'migrant' categories, unveiling their temporal, spatial, legal and racial subtexts. While the connection between 'finding oneself' and 'not being a refugee anymore' speaks to a subjective-existential dimension, Amir frames 'refugeeness' as an objective, collective and temporary passage of *stillness* – marked by 'doing nothing' and coupled with the dependency from others' assistance. This narrative unfolds along well-defined steps: the experience of displacement implies a process of *becoming* a 'refugee'; later, by virtue of integration into citizenship through labour and tax paying, people *cease* to be 'refugees'. This chronological succession is not individual; for Amir, through 'integration', *all refugees become 'immigrants'*. In turn, the condition of 'migration' is more static, because no process of integration can overtake the spatial and racial displacement of a racialised 'black hair' into the purported whiteness of Germany.

While it is worth noting how political refugees internalise state discourses of 'integration' in terms of participation in capitalist labour markets, Amir's remarks also point to the geopolitical instability of the 'refugee' and 'migrant' categories: in Dubai, Syrians are not *legally* recognised as 'refugees' because the Gulf Arab States are not signatories of the 1951 Geneva Convention, and thus do not legally constitute 'refugees' as such (De Bel-Air 2015). In fact, many exiles originating from conflict areas migrate to these countries, but they do so through a variety of different visas and residency permits, relating to work, study or family reasons. While this legal aspect is often posed as a lack of rights for refugees in the Gulf, from a different perspective, Amir argues that it rather has a positive effect on migrants' own self-perception, because being able to work 'as anybody else' partly bridges the gap between the 'refugee' and the 'citizen' – a poignant reminder against any humanitarian reductionism of 'refugees' as passive subjects of assistance.

Significantly, Amir's words reflect a temporal perception of one's own 'refugeeness' that I have observed elsewhere, particularly in the conversations between my Afghan friends presented in chapter 4; being 'semi-legal' refugees who had been in Germany already for several years working and living in private accommodation, implied a distance between them and the refugee newcomers. As they picked me up after my weekend shifts at the Central Station, they would take me on nightlife tours of Reeperbahn and talk about 'the refugees' I was attending to as a group to which they plainly did not belong. For them too, 'refugeeness' was a temporary passage stemming from the need for assistance rather than from the experience of war or exile.

Similarly to Amir, Omar also found an avenue for social networking, personal development and financial autonomy through his initial participation in self-organisation. The Refugee Conference – of which he was among the most active promoters – was held in February 2016 at Kampnagel, a well-established performance theatre which attempted to keep connections with grassroots groups. Shortly after the conference, Omar decided to dedicate his energies to cultural politics and started organising an 'Oriental Karaoke' at Kampnagel, a bimonthly event attended by Syrians and other Arab Hamburg residents, as well as many white Germans involved either at the theatre or in networks of solidarity. Soon, Kampnagel contracted him as an event curator, and he organised several live concerts featuring Arab musicians from around the world.

While I witnessed this process through our friendship, Jana later recounted it to me from a different critical angle. During the organisation of the Refugee Conference, Omar had easily made his way into the core team, and established a direct relationship to some of Kampnagel representatives. Differently, the Lampedusa in Hamburg and Lampedusa in Hannover groups seemed to suffer from the mediation of Never Mind the Papers' activists between them and Kampnagel. Jana sensed that they may have been thinking that, as a middle-class Syrian, Omar 'knew how to deal with the Germans', but he did not know what it meant to land in Germany 'as a refugee' because he was 'just out of university'. During our interview, Jana found it particularly difficult to untangle this node and paused many times, but her overall hypothesis was that refugees and supporters entertained very different relationships depending on the social and educational background of the former:

> To put it in an extreme way: many people in LiH are illiterate in their own languages, they have been tortured and they've been on the run for something like eight years. For people like Omar it took just a few weeks to arrive in Hamburg from Istanbul. If I do this strange comparison, the Syrians I met in 2015 were better educated, more reflected, more outspoken and willing to connect with their old life. They smiled, they knew how to talk. But of course this narrative is slippery, it is exactly what Merkel said, that we needed all these well-educated people to fill our decreasing demographics.

While in the course of just a year and a half, Omar had obtained refugee status, found a job and a place to stay, most LiH's members had been suspended, for years, in the legal precariousness of a *Duldung*; others had no German paper at all and, although they had not renewed their Italian residency permits, lived in an ever-present deportability to Italy. They had no access to formal and stable employment, and the structures of solidarity formed around them were now more concentrated on the refugee newcomers. Jana recalled that the disconnection was so profound that, even though their protest tent was just a couple of minutes away from the tents erected by Paritätische and the volunteers outside the Central Station, it had taken ages for Lampedusa in Hamburg's members to find out that there was such an extensive support structure there. Again, with growing unease, she attempted to explain to me the (implicitly racialised) politics of deservingness that underpinned grass-roots refugee support in Hamburg:

> In 2014, many Germans hosted the Lampedusa people, but with the next winter the question arose: 'Why should we host these poor guys who have not yet managed to decide if the accept a *Duldung*? They still have no job, no clue about what's going on, and they reject our offers for German classes. They're still sad guys who cannot support their families back home. Why shall we get them in, now that we can choose? Shouldn't we take these dynamic Syrian women and children instead?'

This crude depiction of the supporters' changing mood illuminates particular hierarchies of deservingness that, to a certain extent, run counter to the ones previously presented, for it is not passive victimhood that is sought here, but rather active entrepreneurship. However, it is also a painful reminder against any romanticisation of refugee self-organisation: that after five years in Europe, Lampedusa in Hamburg's members still had to recur to support networks for their own subsistence lay in stark contrast to the fact that someone like Omar, coming from a different national context and class background, had already developed a certain autonomy after just a year of presence in Germany. This contrast was mostly apparent to me in the last meeting following the Refugee Conference, whereby many organisers – comprising both refugees and supporters – were upset by the lack of conclusions from the conference, and wanted to draft a document listing some points on 'how to carry on with the struggle'; others found it pointless to draft such a document in a small group that could not be representative of the larger conference participation. Significantly, Omar stated that he already knew 'how to go on': his future plans had been sown in the networks that he had established through the conference, most notably in its involvement at Kampnagel.

If self-organisation had allowed for a re-appropriation of many of my interlocutors' political and existential agency, both in the case of Lampedusa in Hamburg and many Afghans, it had not acted upon the material and legal conditions of their lives, and this caused a decrease in political participation in both groups. Even Habib, who had initially been so enthusiastic about political organisation, saw his feelings swing through time: Never Mind the Papers' meetings became increasingly tiring and time-consuming and, although he had sorted out his own legal status, countless people around him were still in precarious, deportable situations. Furthermore, he was tired and burnt-out from all the trust and expectations that other Afghans were placing on him, as well as from the ethnic politics that ran through their groups. He wanted to focus on studying German instead and was hoping to pursue a university degree in Law and Human Rights. One of the last time I saw him, he was contemplating ways to move to Canada or the United States, as Europe had somehow deceived him and made him lose any sense of 'going forward'.

Through these last examples, I have highlighted how the strategies of resistance to the coloniality of being are articulated differentially along classed and racialised fractures. In chapter 7, I am going to build on this intersectional approach, exploring the topic of coloniality in its direct relationship to solidarity and looking at the ways it produces a contested arena in the relationship between 'refugees' and 'supporters'.

Chapter 7

Refugees Welcome?

The Production of Whiteness within Visual, Moral and Social Economies of Solidarity

During a live concert at the Rote Flora – the oldest squat of Hamburg, located in the gentrified neighbourhood of Sternschanze (Naegler 2012) – I once lamented to the group I was with the pervasive whiteness of that space and the resulting disconnection between the omnipresent pro-refugee posters and stickers and the absence of refugee bodies. Marija, A white Croatian activist who had just moved to Hamburg, retorted that it was *obvious* that there were no refugees around us, because 'we' had the privilege to party, while 'they' had 'more urgent things to do', such as worrying for their asylum cases, finding jobs or resisting prospective deportations. Although in Hamburg she was working as a waitress, she saw a clear-cut boundary of 'privilege' defined not by class, but rather legal status. This flattening of 'refugees' in a seemingly bound dimension of mere suffering is a common trope of the coloniality of asylum and one that ceases to recognise that the obstacles posed by legal status do not determine an inability to enjoyment, leisure and socialisation per se. In fact, at the time, I used to attend many other parties that were highly participated by people who were still in the asylum procedure, such as those organised by Omar at Kampnagel. Marija's comment struck me precisely because it deprived 'refugees' of the normalcy of leisure, and it deeply resonated with Cafe Exil's lawyer's idea of 'luxury problems', which stripped 'refugees' of their desires for a cosmopolitan mobility (chapter 6).

That night, I also noticed a poster hanging on the walls of the squat that furthered my thinking of these naturalised divisions: in a comic like drawing, there was a female superheroine wearing a black mask, a red cape and a 'Refugees Welcome' T-shirt. Her skin was white, her hair, red; her facial expression firm but reassuring. With her hands she held the feet of a figure whose face was not visible but whose body had arguably masculine features.

Figure 7.1   The Fluchthilfe Poster at the Rote Flora.

The poster's caption translated as 'Organise the Escape Aid! Trafficker, Smuggler, Superheroines',[1] and it referred to the history of humanitarian smuggling – in German *Fluchthilfe* – which traces back to the networks that facilitated the flight of politically persecuted people from the Eastern GDR to Germany between 1961 and 1989 and, previously, from Nazi Germany to other countries between 1933 and 1945 (borderline-Europe et al. 2017: 266; Frei 1992). The poster displayed three interconnected imageries of contemporary refugee support which, unwittingly, produce dichotomous racialised and gendered subjectivities, whose experiences are ultimately conceptualised as *incompatible*, though interconnected through relations of support and solidarity.

First, it reasserted a *politics of Othering*, displaying refugees as subjects defined by their *flight* and objects defined by their *need for help*, to which European supporters can respond precisely because they do not have that experience of flight. As a compound of 'flight' (*Flucht*) and 'help' (*Hilfe*), the German concept of *Fluchthilfe* emphasises the moral legitimacy of the movements of 'refugees' against the background of those of other 'migrants'. A similar discursive operation underpins the choice of politically correct words to depict 'refugees', whereby *Geflüchtete* ('someone who has fled') is currently preferred to *Flüchtling* ('someone who is fleeing') in order to avoid the negative connotation attached to the latter (Holmes and Castañeda 2016: 11). Despite this effort to use a positively politicised language among left activists, the emphasis on the act of 'fleeing' unwittingly reasserts the putative deservingness of 'refugees', and so it justifies the political commitment to supporting them.

Second, the visual elements of the poster conferred to the European *Fluchthelfer* the status of an aestheticised heroine, in a peculiar German version of white saviourism. 'Refugees' are alternately criminalised, victimised and heroised in both activist and research discourses (Bojadžijev 2006; Scheel 2013: 280; Steiger 2016: 230) and, by extension, so are the very 'supporters' who help their border crossings, material survival and legal struggles against state regimes of illegalisation. From the Second World War to the Cold War and, later, the Yugoslav wars, changing border regimes in Europe have produced multifarious socio-legal imaginaries of humanitarian smuggling, alternately pertaining to their illegalisation and straightforward criminalisation, or their moral heroisation (borderline-Europe et al. 2017: 266).

Third, the differential visibility of the activist made superheroine's face, juxtaposed to the occultation of the refugee's one, was resonant of practices of face-blurring that I had often seen circulating in both academic and volunteering contexts: here, white researchers or volunteers would show photographs that displayed their own faces, while those of the nonwhite refugees standing next to them were blurred or blanked out, purportedly for protecting their anonymity and countering journalists' insensitive and intruding practices. I remember, each time, wondering *why* exactly they were displaying those pictures in the first place, since they did not add anything illustrative or critical to their presentations. Rather, those images produced an objectification of refugee bodies which, once deprived of the singularity of their faces, became *interchangeable*, with a remarkable similarity to the widespread diffusion of X-ray security images, which represent refugees as faceless and disembodied commodities (Khosravi 2010: 27). Ultimately, these photographs that showed white faces while blanking out nonwhite ones seemed to merely fulfil a 'display' value (Land 2015: 245), guaranteeing a moral legitimacy to the white speaker as *witness* and *advocate* with a direct relationship to 'refugees'.

These three interconnected elements of the contemporary visual culture of refugee support play a pivotal role in the production of racialised subjectivities, specifically the nonwhite victimised 'refugee' and the white heroised 'supporter'. Both at the representational and material level, white supporters often end up occupying the central platform of border contestations, and produce a morally positive imagery of whiteness, alternately through paradigms of hospitality (Danewid 2017), innocence (Wekker 2016) and anti-racism (Ahmed 2004). This chapter will thus revisit the coloniality of asylum away from any direct relation to the state and the law, and rather examine the (re) production of whiteness and Europeanness in the direct encounters between 'refugees' and 'supporters', through racialised, gendered and classed imaginaries, tied to political ideologies, moral superiority, and the disposability of time. In particular, I will highlight how 'refugees' continually risk becoming *objects* rather than *subjects,* of white European humanitarian support and/or political struggles. Such objectification responds to a wider logic of *Othering* which reproduces refugees as victims, and white Europeans as their saviours.

7.1. ABOLITIONIST GENEALOGIES OF WHITENESS

The 2015 *Fluchtilfe* poster described above was a prophetic one. Between 2018 and 2019, the mediatised border spectacle of the criminalisation of solidarity featured many white heroines and heroes who were legally sued – but eventually never found guilty – for supporting the transit of illegalised migrants in the Mediterranean and the Alps. These events partly represented a re-politicisation of humanitarianism (Borri and Fontanari 2017; Tazzioli 2018b; Tazzioli and Walters 2019), for European states were criminalising mere acts of support to the very physical existence of irregularised migrants, such as rescuing, sheltering or feeding them. Yet, by recentring white subjects at the core of border contestations, they also unwittingly invisibilised refugee struggles, and reproduced a particular politics of race, which displayed a heroised imagery of whiteness, while it objectified nonwhite bodies as victims to be rescued.

One of the cases that became more well-known was the one of the boat captain Carola Rackete who, on 29 June 2019, docked the *Sea Watch 3* in Lampedusa in order to guarantee the rescued passenger's safety, and did so against a naval blockade imposed by the Italian minister of interior Matteo Salvini. This action produced a particular polarisation between a part of the public criminalising her and another section heroising her. Italian artist Tvboy drew a graffiti in the Sicilian city of Taormina titled 'Saint Carola, Protector of Refugees', which was later destroyed by supporters of Salvini's xenophobic party Northern League. The graffiti portrayed the German white woman as a saint who held a black refugee kid in a life vest, and the imbalance between the strength of the former and the helplessness of the latter was very resonant of the one of the superheroine I had seen at the Rote Flora.

The dramatic media visibility of white supporters, and their frequent positive connotation as 'heroes' by a part of society invisibilised nonwhite and non-European subjects who had long engaged in that kind of illegalised support, but had invariably been portrayed in the media as criminal 'smugglers' (Garelli and Tazzioli 2018). As it has emerged in the previous chapters, refugees themselves are often 'supporters' of refugee newcomers, through informal practices of assistance and hospitality during the journey, self-organised mutual aid within the camps, participation in wider networks of solidarity together with European citizens, and collective political struggles. This nonwhite solidarity, however, has been continuously criminalised through anti-smuggling politics that particularly target nonwhite people who are part of the same communities of incoming refugees – one of the prime examples of which have been the repeated trials of Tunisian fishermen depicted as 'smugglers' because of rescuing migrants in distress at sea already from the mid-2000 and significantly, again in 2018 (Fekete 2009; Albahari 2015).

Crucially, many networks active in contemporary *Fluchthilfe*[2] in Europe and the United States hold as fundamental political reference the so-called Underground Railroad (Golden and McConnell 1986; Mezzadra 2020), namely, a scattered network of escaped slaves, white and black abolitionists, and Quakers which, between 1780 and 1862, helped the escape of slaves from the Southern United States to the North and Canada. However, critical historical accounts of the Underground Railroad point out that the relevance attributed to this network is in fact a foundational myth, which responds to the need for white heroes in mainstream Western history (Gara 1961). This northward escape trajectory was in fact the least used at the time, as most fleeing slaves rather sought refuge in 'Spanish Florida, Mexico, the Caribbean, Native American communities in the South-east, free-black neighborhoods in the upper South, or Maroon communities – clandestine societies of former slaves' (Schulz 2016). Similarly, Mediterranean routes towards Europe represent a minimal part of contemporary refugee flows which, instead, for the wide majority are directed to countries neighbouring conflict areas, in Asia, the Middle East and Africa. As I have repeatedly argued throughout the book, the right to asylum is hypocritically upheld as one of the core 'values' of Europe and the public emphasis on state generosity and society's practices of assistance and welcoming invisibilises the wider violent structure of European borders. Furthermore, NGOs' search-and-rescue operations bring to safety a very minority of those embarking in the perilous journey and, while this is used to counter the argument that NGOs would constitute a 'pull factor', it actually reveals that search-and-rescue operations are far from having a dramatic impact against the coloniality of borders (Garelli and Tazzioli Forthcoming). Importantly, the implications in the displacement of these marginal activities to the centre of past and contemporary histories lie in the imbalance in the portrayal of white saviour and nonwhite rescued subjects, particularly relating to the way politicised humanitarianism re-signifies whiteness in liberal discourses, while silencing the protracted legacies of racism and colonialism (Hesse 2002).

First, mainstream histories of the abolition of slavery not only marginalise black voices, while privileging white ones (Hesse 2014), but particularly invisibilise slave revolts which were rather fundamental events that oriented the political discourses of abolitionists (Trouillot 1995; Gopal 2019). A particular legacy of this invisibilisation is that the *critical analyses* that circulated at the time were entrusted to white abolitionists, while slave narratives were reduced to mere *experiential accounts*, crafted in accordance to particular moral and voyeuristic literary codes in order to attract the sympathy of whites (Hesse 2002: 146). This division of discursive labour between experiential and critical accounts bears particular similarities with the contemporary diffusion of refugee narratives as opposed to critical and political discourses disseminated by white academics and activists, who become the privileged witnesses and commentators of refugees' oppression. In turn, very much as it happened with slave rebellions, refugees' own struggles are rarely taken into account in public discourses.

Second, the emancipation of black slaves was achieved within a historical, political and material structure that did not shake the foundations of whiteness; instead of highlighting the constitutive role of colonialism and slavery in the development of liberal democracies and global capitalism, the history of slavery has rather become the history of its abolition (Hesse 2002: 149), thus reinstating it as an aberration to the norm of progressive liberal democracies. Similarly, whether in its more explicitly humanitarian or politicised forms, contemporary refugee support in Europe occurs within a social, material and representational regime of whiteness that determines its political and moral claims; it upholds the democratic, liberal value of asylum, reducing it to a question of welcoming, hospitality and humanitarian assistance, and rarely engaging with the colonial past and present. The result is not only that, as in the case of white abolitionists, the most visibilised voices and bodies in circles of refugee support are those of white Europeans, but also that their very specific whiteness – a 'democratic' one, alternately rooted in human rights, anti-racism or no-border discourses – is (re)produced, rather than questioned, through their very involvement in refugee support.

7.2. COLOUR BLINDNESS, PRESENTISM AND THE NEED FOR HELP

Anti-racist and no-border activists in Hamburg and beyond share the principle that solidarity should not be about asymmetric charity, that is to say, merely 'welcoming' and 'helping' refugees as vulnerable subjects; it should rather be about recognising them as actors of, and supporting them in, their own struggles. To highlight this principle, Jacob, a Cafe Exil activist, reported a speech given by a Lampedusa in Hamburg's spokesman during the demonstration 'Equal Rights for All':

> Keep in mind that you, as German people, are the reason for which we had to flee. In my home country [Niger], you're extracting minerals to produce your mobile phones. So I had no chance there and now I'm here. But then, the only thing you're offering me are second-hand clothes or that we can sit together once a week drinking coffee and eating cake. What we need are sleeping places, jobs and learning German. We want to buy our clothes by ourselves; we don't want to ask for a new pair of shoes.

Jacob considered this perspective key to understanding the problematic stance of supposedly 'apolitical' help and consequently posited a hierarchy between 'activists' and 'helpers' within the Refugees Welcome movement. In turn, this reasoning produced an internal Othering within refugee supporters themselves, as many activists revendicated a moral superiority at the detriment of cooperation with helpers networks. However, as I have extensively shown in chapters 3 and 5, both humanitarian and politically radical tendencies ran across the two poles and drew hierarchies and differences in the relationships between 'supporters' and 'refugees'. In fact, the activists' aspiration to an egalitarian, transversal solidarity was difficult to achieve in a context shaped by political, legal, economic, racial and social inequalities.

Paying attention to the different subject positions of 'refugee activist', 'European activist', 'refugee volunteer', and 'European volunteer' calls into question any simple understanding of 'self-organisation', for there is no unique 'self' at play in these struggles (Gauditz 2017: 51; Ünsal 2015). In particular, while contesting borders is paramount to the survival of some, for others it is rather a matter of political values; it does not immediately impact on their everyday lives. Upholding a clear-cut division between the two groups risks reproducing colonial distinctions between colonisers and 'natives', and yet any naive brushing off of this question overlooks the material and political conditions of existence and mobility that are often diametrically opposite in transversal alliances between oppressed and oppressing groups (Land 2015: 84–85).

As mentioned in the beginning of the chapter, the most common reductionism at play in the distinction between 'refugees' and 'supporters' – and, by extension, 'civil society' – defines refugees around their legal status and their experience of flight; it displaces the question of racialisation, imagining both 'supporters' and 'refugees' through the 'colour blindness' (El-Tayeb 2011: xvii) that is proper of Europe's 'post-racial' imagination (Hesse 2011). In turn, that European supporters are imagined as (implicitly white) privileged citizens is often the very motor of their sociopolitical engagement.

Lukas, a German law undergraduate student, told me in an interview that he felt that 'we, as people living in Europe, don't know anymore how tough it is to cross borders and apply for visas; we got used to crossing borders without any troubles, but it's quite tough for people from other regions'. Through his engagement with incoming refugees at the Central Station he progressively focused on the question of *why* it was so difficult for them, and he came to the conclusion that 'everyone should be able to choose where to live' and, thus, a quest for freedom of movement should be at the core of asylum and migrant support. His reflections grasped the wider coloniality of borders and migration and thus did not naturalise 'refugees' as victims to be 'helped'; however, his use of the pronoun 'we' was enlightening of the 'colour blindness' that underpins the widespread imagination of 'Europeanness' which, in turn, is premised on an unnamed middle-class whiteness. In the course of that interview, both of us smoothly, instinctively navigated that 'we' and understood what it meant: those who seamlessly cross EU borders are usually white citizens, who also benefit from visa-waivers in other regions of the world. Yet the smoothness through which 'we' cross borders is dictated not only by our citizenship status but also by 'our' bodies that are read as white (Schwarz 2016: 254), 'our' names that do not call attention as Arabic or Muslim (Ahmed 2007: 162), and 'our' economic possibilities to materialise those movements.

There are indeed many Europeans who exceed the premises of that 'we', and are Othered, racialised and policed in very different ways, such as blacks, Muslims and Romas. As discussed in chapter 4, many of the people I attended to at Cafe Exil were indeed EU citizens but, originating from former European colonies, their histories of border crossings and attempts to settle were radically different from those of white middle-class 'Europeans', and much closer to those of refugees. Both national and EU citizenship are racialised and classed as white, and they erase the presence of 'native' citizens racialised as nonwhite, as well as 'natives' who never acquire citizenship

– such as many Roma and those who are widely categories as 'second-generation migrants' – and foreigners who acquire citizenship after long-term residence – all of whom usually have severely different experiences of border crossing than the one described by Lukas.

The racialised reductionism and incompatibility implied by the refugee/citizen dichotomy assumes 'Europeanness' as a site of privilege, normalcy, mobility, leisure and freedom, and 'refugeeness' as a site of oppression, disruption, immobility and unfreedom; it reduces refugees to the experience of flight and subjugation to the law – whether by calling them *Flüchtlinge* or *Geflüchtete*. This asymmetry is best exemplified by another logo that became widespread with the Refugees Welcome movement, stencilled on the walls of many European cities, and that I have often seen displayed on the *Facebook* walls of my European activist interlocutors: *Fuck Tourists! Welcome Refugees*. While the anti-capitalist and anti-racist narrative that distinguishes 'tourists' from 'refugees' seems self-evident at first, upon a second glance, denying refugees of the possibility to be tourists, and vice versa, implicitly reduces refugees to the spatio-temporality of flight, while their 'European' counterparts are entrusted to the one of free mobility.

Mahdi, A Syrian musician who played in the course of the 'Migration is a Right, Deportation is a Crime!' demonstration described to me his rage for the way the 'refugee' label was invariably attached to him by German supporters: he was often invited to conferences and events as a 'refugee artist' or, at best, a 'refugee activist' while, in fact, to him, his political subjectivity was first premised on his participation in the Syrian revolution, not on his being a 'refugee' in Germany. In 2017, he visited Italy, where he had previously lived while pursuing a master's in economics, and subsequently, recounted to me his perplexity upon seeing the abovementioned stencil on a building facade in Naples: 'Who am I supposed to be now?' – he asked me – 'Am I the *welcomed* refugee or rather the *unwelcome* tourist?'

Another example of this racialised reductionism was expressed by Hannah, the white German volunteer who invited Ahmad to a party that was free for 'refugees' (chapter 6); she argued that in Greifswald – a small provincial town close to the Polish border where she had previously lived – most immigrants had always been 'Polish or Russian, *white normal people* wearing T-shirts and jeans'; however, with the 2015 'crisis', she had 'suddenly' noticed other people whose clothes 'were not really fitting', because they were donations from support groups. 'Their skin was darker and they smelled differently' – she commented, positing that the novelty of 2015 was the irruption of foreigners racialised and classed in novel ways:

I don't want to sound racist but they have a different perfume. You really feel the difference in Greifswald, it's visible. I don't know if I've ever talked to or had a refugee friend before; *I didn't really care.* Many of my friends have a 'background', but *it just didn't matter,* I never thought that 'refugees needed help'. I just always thought that shit happens and people need help and you help them.

Here, the racialisation of refugees is imagined both by bodily characteristics – skin colour, smell and clothing – and by their description as subjects that need to be rescued and helped, a political configuration that is paramount to contemporary asylum narratives. In this regard, Charles, a Central Station volunteer who was some fifteen years older than Hannah, recounted that he had grown up with many refugee children from Iran, Afghanistan and the Horn of Africa, both because they were classmates and because his priest father was involved in sanctuary practices in the 1980s. He specified, however, that the social landscape was dramatically different, because those earlier generations of refugees were politically persecuted individually, while 'right now, it's so anonymous; it's about incoming masses'. He also mentioned the particular neighbourhoods in which he had lived and attended school, gesturing to the way class stratification and urban segregation structure the possible encounters between white Europeans and migrants. It is precisely when these are 'missed encounters' (Bouteldja 2016: 49) that, in the public imaginary, migrants seem 'always just arrived' (El-Tayeb 2008: 653). Jana, who was born a decade earlier, lamented not having been exposed to that contact; she had become aware about the high presence of Afghans in Hamburg only in 2017, when they started protesting deportations together with refugee newcomers. Significantly, Hamburg had been a preferred destinations for Afghans already for several decades and, at the time of my research, they were the third largest migrant group of the city. Syrians, instead, had started settling much later and occupied the nineteenth position in the list of foreigner residents; yet, the spectacularisation of the 2015 'crisis' and the volunteers' response to it made their presence much more visible to the wider white German population.

Because Charles was very conscious about the historical comparison in people's attitudes towards refugees, he also noticed that, for many nonwhite Germans whose parents had been refugees, it was extremely complicated to deal with the new people arriving, mostly due to cultural and political changes in their countries of origin: 'My friend's family is from Iran but he was born here. He speaks Farsi and he'd be a great helper but he doesn't like the feeling of it. He can't stand the gender thing and the religious issue' – he recounted, highlighting how refugee children often grow up under European sociocultural influence and can thus experience particular conflicts when relating to newcomers belonging to their same communities of origin. An old friend of mine, whose family was also from Iran, shared similar concerns: she lived in Cologne and, as she struggled to find a job after finishing her studies, was torn by the prospect of applying to the many open vacancies in the field of refugee support. She had the relevant languages and skills to fit the profile, but she was also reluctant because, as a nonwhite German, she was struggling to come to grips with an institutional and everyday racism that she had previously thought of inexistent in Cologne. The 'presentism' widespread in pro-refugee volunteering unwittingly displaced her again, as one that did not fully fit neither the category of 'refugee' nor the one of 'supporter'.

7.3. GOOD WHITES AND BAD REFUGEES

As it has emerged so far, the question of 'whiteness' – as a political regime simultaneously based on race, class, citizenship and sociopolitical values – is crucial to the (re)production of the distinction between 'refugees' and 'supporters' but is, nonetheless, 'invisible and unmarked' to 'those who inhabit it' because support spaces are mostly 'oriented "around" whiteness, insofar as whiteness is not seen' (Ahmed 2007: 157). Left-wing activist spaces in Hamburg and elsewhere in Europe are supposed to be open and welcoming for bodies who are read as nonwhite; yet the question emerges of *whose bodies are actually at home* in those spaces. As I will describe in greater detail in the end of this chapter, there is a specific economy of time – and thus, by extension, of class, race and gender – underpinning activist engagement. In particular, as activists spaces are also often spaces of leisure and entertainment, the absence of refugees therein is often justified through assumptions of *who has the privilege to leisure* – as I signalled in the opening vignette.

However, what actually makes spaces such as the Rote Flora unlikely to be inhabited by refugees is rather their 'orientation to whiteness' (Ahmed 2007: 157), that is to say how their politics and the consequent structures of socialisation are premised on 'the dominance of the value system of "whites"' (Fadaee 2015: 783), namely, Eurocentric conceptions of anticapitalism, anti-racism, queer feminism, environmentalism and ethical consumption. Political activist Houria Bouteldja (2016: 43) terms this 'political-ideological apparatus' of the left the 'white immune system', namely, a platform through which white people shake off their complicity in global coloniality and perform a positive version of whiteness, as opposed to the negative one of white supremacy, authoritarian nationalism and xenophobia (see also Ahmed 2004; Green et al. 2007: 407). Yet, European solidarity and radical politics occur *within* a sociopolitical environment structured by coloniality, they don't emerge *outside* of it; historically, the conditions of possibility of radical struggles in Europe and the United States, in particular feminism, have been indirectly premised on, and enabled by, the racist foundations of colonialism, imperialism and capitalism (hooks 2000: 376; Bouteldja 2016:

89). While the 'white immune system' displaces such conditions of possibility, it also engenders a second effect, which is an implicit imagination of the political and moral superiority of white European radical ideologies. Again, in Bouteldja's words (2016: 43) white subjects are re-centred as 'the greatest antiracists . . . the most appalled by anti-Semitism . . . and the greatest anti-colonialists' – to which, I would add, also the most courageous abolitionists and the most criminalised no-border activists.

Differently, refugees are easily relegated to conservative 'bad politics' externalised to their communities of origin, and this displacement is paramount to the *coloniality of asylum*, for it reduces them to subjects whose speech is sought and valued only as mere testimony of their direct experience with flight and asylum, and not as a provider of critical analysis on these and other topics. In this regard, Mahdi recalled an episode in which he had been invited to speak at a conference on the rise of right-wing movements in Europe, held in Berlin. During the event he felt that the speakers envisioned a form of 'good', democratic, egalitarian and anti-racist 'Europeanness' which should have protected refugees from the threatening rise of neofascism and xenophobia. When he was given the platform, he was hoping to speak at length about Syrian activism in exile but, instead, the audience solely sought his input on the condition of refugees in Germany. The subsequent panel turned to the larger political context of Europe, and he was warned that the discussion would be held in German. This linguistic exclusion, he concluded, meant that the Germans implicitly saw refugees as incapable of providing insights on European politics and identity.

Likewise, Mahdi complained about not being taken seriously when talking about Syria, and less so about Palestine, because 'Arabs are supposed to be sectarian. The Germans think that our political stances are not neutral. They see them as inborn, influenced by psychological or social issues.' His words made me think about many remarks I had heard by anti-racist activists regarding the racism of refugee newcomers. There was in these instances a displacement of racism, as well as anti-Semitism, sexism and homophobia as *problems of the migrants* and not precisely *problems of the Europeans*, rooted in a long historical tradition (Lucassen 2005; El-Tayeb 2011: xxvii–xxviii; Wekker 2016). In this instances, it seemed that anti-racist activists felt that they had expunged racism from their circles, while the refugees were less 'enlightened'. In such confrontations, Mahdi criticised the Eurocentric assumptions in-built in the universalisation of anti-Semitism – a specifically European phenomenon (Bouteldja 2016: 59) – and its displacement to Arab communities.

Along similar lines of displacement, Jana commented the racist discrimination that Arab refugees perpetrated on black refugees at the Messehallen, and how there had been attempts to solve these conflicts by dividing people by ethnicity or nationality. In our interview, however, she presented white work-ers in the camps as characterised by either 'a general racism' or 'a general open-mindness' and this implied two misplacements: first, it was predicated upon a reification of race that lacked any acknowledgement of how whiteness is unstable and 'graduated' (Anderson 2013: 37) depending on specific times and locations; different groups come to be included into it at certain times, both at the local and global levels. Such has been the case of Jews after the Second World War and the foundation of Israel (Brodkin 1998; Bouteldja 2016: 57), as well as the Irish in the UK (Anderson 2013: 37), and Italians in the United States (Guglielmo and Salerno 2003).[3] Second, the umbrella 'people of colour' – which she used to characterise all refugees – is an intrin-sically Eurocentric one; it can have uses in European or other white Western majority contexts, but elsewhere erases the specific histories of anti-blackness and colourism imported by colonialism (Hashim 2006; Pierre 2013), as well as other historical imperialist or colonialist expansions, such as those of the Muslim Arabs in North and East Africa.[4] Moreover, in ascribing a 'general open-mindness' to supposedly antiracist white Europeans, this narrative dis-places racism *outside* of Europe – 'it's bad here, but in Syria or Libya . . . ' – she concluded in our interview.

In similar ways, Mathias, a Central Station volunteer, inscribed sexism as a specific problematic of refugee men volunteering at the Central Station and not also of white Germans:

> We had a problem with the treatment of women, not necessarily aggressive behaviours, more like comments that could get annoying. At least three or four women complained about personal questions, like if they had a boyfriend, or if they were virgins. Such comments are unacceptable but we didn't have any mechanism to handle such misconduct. Even if it was reported to me, who was I to tell to that person that he was not allowed to come and help anymore?

Mathias himself had met his girlfriend, who was an Iranian student, at the station but, here, the gendered relationship was reversed: it was not a Muslim man who approached – and thus implicitly 'threatened' – a white German woman, but rather a white German man who got together with a Muslim woman. That some gendered behaviours are considered more predatory than others is racialised in particular ways (Gianettoni and Roux 2010).[5] Like any other man, refugee men can obviously perpetrate sexist behaviours, such as insisting with unwanted approaches, however, an exclusive focus on their sexism erases any recognition of the sexism that is indigenous to 'Europe', that is to say 'white patriarchy' (Bouteldja 2016: 79). Importantly, Mathias' narrative was premised on an externalisation of patriarchal oppression as something that occurs *outside* support spaces; the solution would thus have

been the mere expulsion of 'sexist men' from the helpers network, instead
of the production of spaces of reflexivity and dialogue in which structures
of oppression could be analysed by a collectivity within its specific ways of
operating.

A last point of coloniality in the relationship between 'refugees' and
'supporters' is the displacement of unethical habits of consume. During the
organisation of the Refugee Conference, there was an important controversy
over the catering menu. The collective who would run the kitchen offered to
cook vegan food, due to costs, health regulations and ethical reasons, but the
refugee organisers wanted to cook their own regional food, including meat.
Jana pointed out that this was not a trivial matter; some of the refugees conceptualised it as '*we* are inviting *our* people and want to offer *our* food', and it
was thus a matter of belonging and ownership of the space of the conference.
Significantly, a similar conflict had already emerged during the Freedom
March to Brussels, whereby the refugees had lamented 'the dominance of the
value system of "whites"' (Fadaee 2015: 783). Upon recalling this episode,
Jana highlighted her awareness about the coloniality that bestows more decisional power to supporters than to the refugees they are supposedly organising *with* (and not merely *supporting*) and concluded with the question: 'Who
were "we" to impose vegan food?'

7.4. WOMEN* SPACE IS EVERYWHERE: AGAINST MATERNALISM AND THE 'PATHOS OF SMILE'

Academic and activist Nadiye Ünsal (2015) describes the gendered structure
of refugee solidarity, in which refugee men and German men build alliances
that further silence the voices of both refugee and non-refugee women.
Refugee men and male supporters dominate public speeches, networking and
decision making, while women undertake 'the invisible jobs, such as cooking,
infrastructure, cleaning, translation, taking minutes of meetings, emotional
and legal support, [and] conflict resolution' (Ünsal 2015: 9). Furthermore,
white European women frame their commitment as one of empowerment and
emancipation of refugee women who are conceptualised as culturally stuck in
oppressing gender relations (Braun 2017: 41). Some of my women interlocutors, including Jana, shared these concerns, highlighting how in the course of
several years of involvement in refugee support, they had mostly got in touch
with male refugees and, as a result, felt stuck in particular relations of maternal caring. This was also very much my own experience both in Rome and
Hamburg and, while sharing these reflections with fellow academic/activist
Leslie Gauditz, she suggested that refugee support is characterised by a paradigm of 'maternalism' (Cunningham 1995), as opposed to state paternalism.

Baudrillard's (1998: 159) conceptualisation of the 'mystique of solici-tude' as a major characteristic of the third sector in consumer societies is enlightening in this regard. Etymologically, 'solicitude' means both 'care' and 'request'; socially, it conveys an ethics of simultaneous maternal care and 'bureaucratic charity' and sheds light on the mixture of care and social control that volunteers unwittingly reassert on the objects of their support, producing artificial intimacy through their 'pathos of the smile' (Baudrillard 1998: 160). This 'pathos' interrupts the urban habitus of disconnection and alienation, but, simultaneously, produces a 'lubrication of social relations with the institutional smile' (Baudrillard 1998: 161). This conceptualisa-tion resonates with the episode, narrated in chapter 3, in which a protesting refugee reproached Jana about the fact that the volunteers were *decorating the Lager*, while the protesting refugees *wanted no Lager* – thus implying that the volunteers were attempting to 'lubricate' the conflict between the refugees and the state. The same perspective can be applied to support in the navigation of state bureaucracy (chapter 5), which misses on the potential of radical disobedience.

However, what is crucial to my argument here is that intimacy is produced through a gendered, maternal ethics, one in which I myself felt particularly entrapped while volunteering at Cafe Exil. As I have described through the interactions with the lawyer in the previous two chapters, usually, the Cafe was not experienced as a particularly emotional or maternalist setting; for instance, Ella, felt burdened by people suddenly venting out their stories at her, and would instead offer to organise therapy for them: 'If they put this on me' – she argued – I would lose my sleep. I can't deal with it, I'm not as strong as they might think.' This unpreparedness to listen was shared also by Jacob, who had told me from the onset that the purpose of the Cafe was to redirect people to other services and initiatives that could help them. In his view, we were not trained in listening and there was no expectation that we did that – a stance that recalled Johannes' critical description of the ethics of social work in the camps (chapter 5).

Differently, in my case, a combination of factors produced a particular dis-position to listening – namely, the languages that I shared with the 'guests', my training as an educator at Asinitas, and my temperamental inclination to warm friendliness. This disposition offered the fertile ground for extended conversations in which the 'guests' would perceive me as an empathic lis-tener, rather than a problem-solver who could find a solution to their bureau-cratic vicissitudes. In turn, these encounters burdened me and produced conflicting feelings over the way I failed to establish boundaries. Especially the older men who were struggling with their sense of failure over the years spent in Italy often asked me questions that were 'existential' – as the lawyer would have put it – and this usually happened precisely while I was taking care of those everyday tasks that are mostly undertaken by women, such as making coffee and unloading the washing machine. At times, I would burst, feeling entrapped in an attitude to care that was expected by the male guests but for which I myself had created the preconditions. Even in those moments, however, I was unable to create a real distance; comments such as 'I'm not your sister!' would come out of my mouth, which allowed for one of the men to retort: 'and not my wife either!' – and then laugh while helping me to pour the coffee in the thermos.

A crucial conflict over the maternalist stance of white European women, as well as the paternalist one of refugee men, exploded during the Refugee Conference, organised at Kampnagel in February 2016 by (mostly men) refugees and (mostly women) supporters. A group of white German women decided to create a 'Women* Space', while another one, comprising refugee men and German white women, was responsible for the conference programme and the allocation of rooms. The group coordinating the 'Women* Space'[6] thought of it as a cosy, relaxed environment in which women participants could rest, have a tea and bring their children. With these purposes in mind, the Programme Group assigned to them the space of the Migrantpolitan, a wooden cabin located in the green space on the back of the main theatre building. The location was quite difficult to find and remote from the rest of the conference. Eventually, as more workshops were organised last-minute, some of which explicitly hinged on women issues, the Programme Group assigned the 'Women* Space' as also a venue for workshops. The refugee activist women who attended the conference, mostly from Women in Exile[7] and the International Women Space,[8] were outraged by their confinement to a remote, unorganised area, and their rage erupted into a protest: they marched through the different rooms in which workshops were ongoing, chanting 'Women* Space is Everywhere' and eventually occupied the stage of the main theatre hall, interrupting the men who were speaking there. Their speeches addressed the marginalisation of women within the conference and beyond, the oppression they underwent by refugee men, and the ambiguous invisibility of white activists, who were behind the scenes of an event advertised as a 'self-organised Refugee Conference'.

Mariam, one of the women who engaged in that protest, told me later that 'refugee women are not seen by anyone: they are not seen by refugee men, in so far as they are women; and they are not seen by women supporters, in so far as they are focusing only on the voices of refugee men'. The matter is not necessarily an utter invisibility of refugee women, but rather a *differential visibility*, for which there are particular images of refugee women that are constructed by supporters when they take them into consideration. One of the white organisers, Mareike, told me in an apologetic tone that they were expecting 'a certain kind of women'. Her judgement was based on images of refugee women that she had formed based on her experience as an intern in a refugee camp and it reflected a hegemonic understanding of them as vulnerable subjects instead of significant political voices (see also Lorde 1984b). From the perspective she elaborated after the protest, they had prepared a space 'for women who still lived in the camps and did not want to feel as being in a camp during the conference'. The aim was thus that they could avoid queuing for food and hang out on the carpet and cushions with a warm tea:

> That's what we prepared. But in the end the women who used the Women* Space were not living in the camps anymore. They were *badass activists* and they didn't like it. They wanted to be on the big stage, speaking to an audience of five hundred, not just to fifty women in a little crowded room. I think that we prepared for *other people*. When the protest happened I really loved it. I was in the big hall and we started hearing shouting, and suddenly all these women occupied the stage. I was excited. Only later, I realised that this criticism was on the stuff that I myself had been working on.

When I later mentioned to Mariam this analysis of the event, she ironically and angrily replied: 'Well, if that's their opinion, then we all need to go home and think. And I know she's not alone.' She was pointing out that refugee women, as much as men, who do not frame their politics in terms that are recognisable to European leftist activists, were dismissed as actors that were not directly 'political'. In other words, Mareike's analysis spoke of an inability to listen of white German women activists, who were caught precisely in the maternalism and 'pathos of smile' that made them imagine the women attending as passive recipients of care rather than 'badass activists'. While she did not take the criticism personally, Jana was very upset at the protest:

> The protesting women doubled up our invisibility. It was a structural systematic mistake. The women organising the Women* Space had not been involved in all the dynamics and problems of the organisation. If the protesting women were in touch only with these other women, it was the wrong address. They could have addressed me at the infodesk. Maybe it's egoistic but they could have come and asked: 'Why did you construct the conference in this way?' Then I'd had the possibility to say: 'Fuck, it's a mistake. Can we do it together?' I was looking forward to getting in touch with refugee women at the Conference, but in a productive way.

In our interview, I tried to dwell on what made her so upset about that event. I was sympathetic to her predicament, for she had undertaken an insane amount of work both relating to practical organisation and the mediation between refugee and supporter organisers. In a way, her reluctance to agree with the shape that the protest had taken was emblematic of the way white activists often do not want to give away the power that their activism confers to them: 'They treated me like these invisible activists not realising colonial relations' – she concluded – revendicating her different sensibility. From a different perspective, however, her discrepancy with the protest sprung also from an active effort to avoid a maternalist attitude. Precisely Mariam had told me once that many white Europeans were paralysed by guilt and thus never showed any disagreement with black people: 'They keep silent and they let you be the radio who's speaking all the time. They don't participate in the conversation, they don't take you seriously.' Differently, Jana had stepped away from her active participation in the support of Lampedusa in Hamburg, precisely because she felt that the group demanded an unconditional support:

> It sounded like: 'You [the Germans] *have* to help us and you don't have a voice in our decisions.' After several conflicts, I decided not to support them anymore. I did indeed *support* them with my design work for posters etc., but *I'm an activist, I have my own agenda.* Some say: 'You see? This is the proof that you're using us. You're from the upper class and bla bla bla.' I'm not from the upper class, even though I've got privileges. I don't have any savings, nor a family background that can support me financially. There are differences between us, but we can work together if you also let me tell you something about me, where I come from, and what my political praxis is. I think this is a very important point. To say: *I have a political agenda.*

However, Jana's interpretation of the protest unwittingly aligned with the one of refugee man organisers. Most of them were not at all enthusiastic, rather seeing the protest as a fracture that undermined the unity of the movement, particularly pernicious at the level of the public gaze. This only testified to the way patriarchal oppression was reasserted in that environment, following a framework – already denounced by many US black feminists – for which women should keep quiet and not wash the dirty linen in public, in order to avoid undermining the unity of the struggle against white supremacy (Guy-Sheftall 1995: 20) on the one hand, or against patriarchal oppression (Lorde 1984b), on the other. Conversely, the protesting women had decided to expose the invisible power asymmetries and oppressing structures that are proper of refugee activism, in a move that I personally found very refreshing and enlightening. I, for one, had definitely engaged invariably with refugee men throughout both my activism and research. While I had always been aware of it, I had naively deemed it a symptom of the composition of my field. From the protest onwards, I instead started realising how this gender asymmetry was an expression of a particular politics of visibility, which European activists and researchers merely reproduced.

7.5. POLITICS AS LEISURE: THE POLITICAL ECONOMY OF TIME DISPOSABILITY

The maternalist imagery of powerlessness ascribed to refugee women is often attached to refugee men too. Mahdi provocatively told me once that he felt taken more seriously by working-class, anti-immigrant, right-wing Germans, rather than by leftist 'supporters', because they see refugees as 'competitors, people who can steal their jobs, or cause other troubles. They see a threat and a strength in refugees; they don't see me as someone they can help from a superior position. But the left discourse is all about empowerment, about bestowing power.' Mariam held a similar argument, stating that, in inter-sectional terms, she would have been interested in forming alliances with anti-immigrant working-class Germans, because 'they are concerned about food, clothes, work, material things, and refugee life is also very much about this material struggle. But those Germans are mocked by the leftists. Because they see their life as *something more* than the material.' Here, both Mahdi and Mariam were pointing to the politics of class privilege that ran in spaces of organising (hooks 2000: 383) and which, most strikingly, reflected into a quantification of time disposability.

In these spaces, time and information are crucial currencies. Paul, a Cafe Exil member who was active at the Central Station described that, in spite of the supposed unstructured horizontality of the network, hierarchies of power were built depending on the amount of available time that people could spend there. The more time spent at the station, the more reliable information they could achieve. In turn, this information was not shared transparently. Charles lamented that the people behind the infodesk did not share enough informa-tion with the people doing the transfers from and to the platforms, who thus knew little about the border situation, ferry capacity or sleeping places and, consequently, often passed on inaccurate or utterly wrong information to the transiting refugees. The infodesk group justified this management of informa-tion as a protection from potential charges for aiding illegal migration, but Charles was not convinced by this argument: 'It may have been illegal but the facts were that the state was letting us do that. And we were three hundred people; what could have they done to us?'

Importantly, these hierarchies were reinforced also between 'helpers' and 'translators', along the unspoken racialised lines of the 'migration background', as 'the Germans' were the only ones who could take care of logistics, relying on a wide variety of resources and networks, and relegating refugee activists to a situation of dependency (see also Ünsal 2015: 7). This very asymmetry was also at the core of the Refugee Conference organisation, whereby mostly white Germans would be directly in touch with Kampnagel's team, and thus be responsible for logistics.

Jana was painfully aware of this imbalance; she knew that the Kampnagel's team trusted her because they came from the same circles of the creative industry and thus from the same power system: 'My role was to take a key' – she recalled – 'and then give it to refugee organisers and say: *Take it, it's your key.*' Class position, the relative disposability of time, and the consequent professional or activist networks unevenly distributed the power to participate in decisional processes, make informed decisions, and know which numbers to call – and even just to know who, when and where was deciding about a particular issue.

Most crucially, class position meant that particular people were more likely to be involved in activism, both at the level of interest and time disposability. Mereike identified this class composition within Never Mind the Papers, whereby, in her view, most white Germans had an academic background: 'Everybody there already knows about borders and how they harm migrants; they go to lectures, they know the language' – she argued – 'but if you speak to other people, like my family, their friends, or the hairdresser, the topics at hand are very different. Without this theoretical background people just think that Germany is great for taking care of all these refugees.' For Mareike, crucial to these differences was the availability and organisation of people's free time, because 'in the end all these political meetings are your *leisure time*'.

This insight into the structure of political work as something that is rooted in the availability of 'free' or 'leisure' time is crucial to the imbalances in the presence of refugees and supporters; at the earliest stages of the asylum procedure, refugees usually have plenty of time 'to kill', as it has emerged through the previous chapters; however, their participation in activism usually decreases when they obtain their papers and start working. In turn, white European activists are those who are more consistent in participation, and therefore have more decisional power.

My white activist interlocutors usually placed their political commitments and activities of solidarity out of capitalist relationships of production. For instance, Ella had never wanted to make a paid job out of her expertise on migration bureaucracy; that was 'the activist job', for which she desired no economic compensation. However, in the case of social workers who were also activists, the condition of possibility of their free time, which eventually could be dedicated to 'the activist job', lay in their participation into the asylum industry (chapter 5). For instance, at the time of her involvement in the organisation of the Refugee Conference, Mareike was a full-time BA student, and a part-time intern in the Refugee Camp on Dratelnstraße. She earned a monthly stipend of €900 for 20 hours of work per week: 'Not bad, for a part-time job' – she commented, which usually are paid around €450.

Beyond those who were actively involved in the asylum industry, other German supporters indirectly benefitted from global capitalist relationships that placed them in relatively privileged class positions. Regarding this point, while comparing international activism in Germany and Greece, Jana commented that, in Germany, there is so much wealth that, on average, everybody is able to donate something, or at least some free time and, especially, 'many have the possibility to quit a job and take a holiday volunteering somewhere else'. Many of the volunteers/activists I introduced throughout the previous chapters had put their studies or jobs on hold during the peak of the 'crisis': Jacob had quitted his job and was at Cafe Exil up to four days a week; Lukas had given up on a whole semester of exams, and Jana had spent her holidays in Lesbos and Idomeni.

This availability of time and finances places European supporters in a particularly contested position to their refugee counterparts. While both 'citizens' and 'refugees' have their own internal class divisions (e.g. some refugees may have more class privilege that some German citizens), they become more homogenous, and thus more opposed to each other, in the realm of volunteering and solidarity networks. Usually, the refugees who *seek support* are very much immersed in the 'material struggle' that Mariam mentioned, while the Europeans that *offer support* are those who enjoy a greater amount of 'free time' (e.g. students and freelancers). In turn, time disposability is distributed unevenly also along gendered lines. Mareike recognised that only relatively privileged women could attend political meetings, because they had disposable time, were not afraid to move in the dark and, those who had children, also had someone babysitting for them. She thus highlighted how a patriarchal structure was at the root of the organisation of time of both refugee and non-refugee women, and thus the gendered imbalance in participation within Never Mind the Papers' meetings was just the top of the iceberg.

Precisely the structure of those meetings became a heated issue towards the end of my stay in Hamburg, in late autumn 2016. Ella and Jana lamented that the meetings had become increasingly 'white chitchat' and the whole concept for which the alliance had been formed was fading away. They highlighted how many of the refugees who had previously participated where now too busy with work or bureaucratic paperwork; others found the meetings plainly boring, based on too much discussion rather than meaningful actions. Ella also highlighted the ethics of responsibility for which 'the Germans' would be more consistent in attending political meetings: 'It's like work: you *have to* go to the meetings'.

However, as I have signalled in the beginning of this chapter, reducing the absence of refugees from certain spaces to the mere matter of 'they have more urgent things to do' risks flattening the whole category on their supposed lack of material resources, and thus of time for both leisure and politics – or rather *politics as leisure*. Instead, it is crucial to point out that some refugees indeed have (at least some) amount of free time but they prefer not to dedicate it to this kind of meetings, for the reasons that I have highlighted in the cases of Mahdi and Mariam, who indeed felt not recognised as peer actors by their supposed 'supporters'.

Conclusions

Consuming the Pain of Refugees

In June 2017, two years after the long summer of migration, I returned to Hamburg to collect the last follow-up interviews. Jana hosted me in her flat, and we shared countless conversations about the legacy of 2015 and our concerns about the reproduction of colonial relationships between 'refugees' and 'supporters' both at the intimate/individual and the political/collective levels. Jana traced back the most significant encounters she had experienced throughout that period and recalled that, when the relationships she had established with refugee newcomers could have leant more towards friendships, they had suddenly vanished. She was puzzled as to why exactly that had happened, and the words of Hasan, a Syrian man with whom she had collaborated in cultural projects, kept buzzing in her mind: 'Fuck you and your refugee thing. I'm not a refugee, if you meet me because of that, just don't meet me.' In our last four-hour-long interview, Jana paused, and noticed that, since she had become involved in this 'refugee thing', she had become more and more interested in listening to the stories of other people and to their wide range of experiences. This interest, she speculated, sprung from the fact that she had long suppressed and downplayed her own grief for the premature death of her younger brother, thinking that others were going through much worse experiences. A German friend once argued that she was engaging in refugee support precisely to *compensate* something and Jana agreed:

> It's like a trick, I got in touch with people who suffered a lot and, in a shorter time, lost many more people than I did. I cried a lot with them and my own pain has been able to come out. Maybe it's not the best, but it's a way to cope with problems. I'm attracted to people who suffered and I want to build things together; to be constructive with pain and loss. Listening to heavy stories has

147

made me happier and stronger, because being confronted with all this suffering is like *getting more into the heart of what life is.*

Like humanitarian workers, refugee supporters are often driven by the desire to be 'out there in the world' (Malkki 2015: 1) or, in Jana's words, to get in touch with 'the heart of life'. They seem to search for the same sense of 'existential mobility' that those they are in solidarity with seek through physical mobility. But, unlike humanitarians working abroad, or refugees, they do not need to physically travel: it is the world 'out there' that comes to them, and their exposure to refugee stories nourishes their cosmopolitan, 'internationalist subjectivity' (Malkki 2015: 3). Again, in Jana's words: 'If I have a question concerning Afghanistan, now I know who to ask. I know people from every country, it's like being aware of the globe.' Being a 'refugee supporter' thus becomes a crucial part of one's subjectivity (chapter 2), and even more in the case of those who identify as 'activists' because, 'as a supporter, you can stop supporting people' – says Jana – 'but, as an activist, you cannot stop'. It determines our social relations, transnational networks and field of everyday political and moral commitment, but it does so through the asymmetry of *struggling for someone else*, instead than for our own conditions of life. While different struggles can be interlinked materially and politically, and there are several experiences in Europe of migrants *and* citizens struggling together for labour or housing rights, refugee solidarity presents specific asymmetries and, importantly, is often not sufficiently connected to the question of international solidarity, and thus erases political differences among refugee communities (chapters 6 and 7). Moreover, it has come to play a particular role at a historical juncture in which the predominance of representational politics in Europe has long alienated direct collective political action. 'Refugees' have come to fill a political void, as if they were, at least potentially, new revolutionary subjects. Marco Carsetti, who was my coworker between 2010 and 2012, and one of the founders of Asinitas, traces back this process with merciless honesty (2014: 5; my translation):

A group of 'homeless' – the refugees – found affective abode in another group of 'homeless' [the educators and volunteers], who were, in turn, looking for an abode in the refugees, namely, an individual and collective identity, materialising into projects, networks, salaries and cultural production. *The refugees were our refuge.* . . . They brought us a healthy nectar that could heal us from alienation, fragmentation and atomisation, and help us in rebuilding home, festivity, villages, community, rites of passage and political conflicts, struggles for change and justice. Beyond human warmth, they offered us a moral and ethical imperative, they gave a meaning to our existence. After meaningless and frustrating years of university studies, it is as if volunteers are suddenly thrown, thanks to the refugees, in a tangible, material world: *in life itself.*

Here, Carsetti refers to the distortion of relationships that often occurs in spaces of refugee support, one that, I have repeatedly argued throughout the book, *socialises refugees as recipients* of support, while it simultaneously *socialises supporters as providers* thereof, but also *as consumers* of the affects and moralities that these relationships imply. This distortion creates the conditions for a particular kind of intimacy to emerge, one that is predicated upon the empathic participation in the suffering of others, but that easily turns into the consumption of that suffering.

Hannah Arendt (1990: 89) wrote that 'pity can be enjoyed for its own sake', and thus 'lead to a glorification of its cause, which is the suffering of others', but 'solidarity, though it may be aroused by suffering, is not guided by it, and it comprehends the strong and the rich no less than the weak and the poor' and is thus 'committed to "ideas" [. . .] rather than to any "love" of men'. This view of solidarity is significant for envisioning a commitment to horizontal relationships, but it can also relegate affects as pre-political or nonpolitical. Differently, black feminist thought has long remarked how individual and collective affects are a necessary part of political struggles, and they have – unfairly – long been dismissed as something peculiarly 'female', in favour of more 'abstract or 'pure' ideological views (Lorde 1984a). It is thus important to ask which specific affects are at play in any given particular struggle and whether the recognition of *difference* (Lorde 1984b) within those affects inspires action in a horizontal or vertical way. Jana's account of her relationship to her own and others' suffering envisions a 'cross-traumatic affiliation' (Craps 2013: 72) as a departure point for transversal solidarity, recognising that 'separation, loss and renewal' are common human experiences, of which migration is perhaps just an exemplification (Jackson 2013: 2). This conceptualisation, however, risks reducing solidarity to a merely psychological level and thus concealing differences in how we experience, or exert, political oppression. 'Trauma' does not exist in the abstract; it is the product of global asymmetries of power which, along the lines of poverty, racism, gendered oppression or disability and mental health stigma, subject certain populations to a stringent *coloniality of being*. Therefore, as discussed in chapter 2, what matters is the terrain that produces *the conditions of possibility of collective hardship*, and not the quality of *individual* emotional responses.

The *politics of suffering* (Fassin 2005, 2012) through which 'the refugee' is read and narrated in public discourses translates into *a politics of otherness*: one that considers refugee traumas as *qualitatively* different from the experiences of Europeans, and thus reinforces the *incompatibility* of the two categories, with the risk of naturalising refugee oppression as something ontological and not politically produced. Establishing commonalities through an idea of 'trauma' in the abstract may be more common for middle or upper-class Europeans; differently, the experience of class subordination, racism and sexual or gendered oppression may establish commonalities for many others. Moreover, the kind of *witnessing* that has developed within the section of European society that is concerned with what Jana calls 'the refugee thing' moves through both the poles of innocence (Sontag 2003) and guilt, and thus can simultaneously *inspire* and *paralyse* action.

This witnessing does not merely pertain to a 'distant spectatorship' (Chouliaraki 2006), but rather to direct, material everyday relationships. What is most troubling of this politics of otherness is that refugee miseries have become an increasing *object of consumption* for Europeans who, driven by the imperative 'to be out there in the world', produce and consume a plethora of cultural artefacts regarding the 'refugee experience', of which I could name countless documentaries, films, exhibitions, books, theatre pieces and research projects. Herein, *the spectacle of suffering* of refugees is offered to some European citizens as a field of action and thought, producing the always already racialised *spectacle of solidarity* described in the previous chapters. In this process, the status of *witness* (Levi 1988; Craps 2013) does not only invest the construction of the 'supporter' – as embodiment of the 'sympathetic witness' – and advocate – responsible for the *recognition* of victims (Dalley 2016: 28) – but also of the 'refugee' herself as a *victim*. Anybody involved in asylum politics will be familiar with instances of cultural or political events in which refugees take the stage and re-narrate their traumatic life histories and trajectories, and these performances are invariably accompanied by specific affects in the audience: in a panel where no one else is being applauded, the 'refugee' will be, because of the *authenticity* of her witness stance. Liisa Malkki's (1996) formulation of the status of refugees as 'speechless emissaries' is, in this context, best understood as *inaudibility* or *selective audibility* rather than utter *inability to speak*. While Malkki's argument was about the dismissal of refugees' own accounts in favour of grand narratives by 'experts', it seems that, twenty years later, refugees' own narratives are incredibly widespread through Western societies, yet always reduced to experiential, uncritical accounts (chapter 7).

Holocaust survivor and writer Primo Levi (1988) offered an extensive conceptualisation of *witnessing* as a duty – of both the oppressed and those who listen to them – to bear testimony in a context in which material proofs of abuses and atrocities – such as archives – had been destroyed, and thus hidden from the public view. At a different historical juncture, 'the wretched of the earth' (Fanon 1963) are 'either invisible or excessively visible' (Maldonado-Torres 2007: 257), as the sheer atrocities of border enforcement – including death, torture, prolonged detention and deportation, and mental or physical illness – have extensively been narrated, visibilised and analysed in academia, art, journalism and forensic practices (Tazzioli 2018c). What scope for action is left within this regime of knowledge production?

The question here does not merely regard the lack of action, or inspiration thereof, for those who hold relatively more power; it rather pertains to what such re-narrations do to refugees themselves, in terms of forever reproducing their *refugeeness* and restaging their suffering. This topic was one of the crucial dilemmas for Mariam, a Sudanese feminist and queer activist who participated in the women's protest at the Refugee Conference, who later told me: 'Until when do white people need to consume the pain of refugees as a tool for reflection? I'm tired of consuming myself, my story, and my pain every time I need to educate them about the racism they perform without being aware of it.'

Ending the book on this bitter note is both a reminder of why many people who are, or have been, 'refugees' feel alienated from (white) leftist activism and research, and a warning not to reproduce the spectacle of their suffering and exclusion within critical *knowledge production* and *consumption*. The critique offered throughout the previous chapters has lacked any normative hint into the ways refugee solidarity could effectively be decolonised but, if 'decolonisation is not a metaphor' (Tuck and Young 2012), in the absence of political mobilisations that can destabilise the material conditions of global coloniality, claiming a decolonisation of refugee solidarity too easily becomes yet another claim to innocence. Instead, the main critical task of this book has been precisely to bring that coloniality into full view and shed light on its implications on both daily practices and critical knowledge production, *from within* those practices and production themselves.

Europe's geographies of asylum continue to be a contested field, composed of border struggles which both partake of, and seek to overturn, that very coloniality. Wars and other crises continue to produce displacement, and refugee newcomers have been temporarily immobilised through the externalisation of border controls and the institution of hotspots at the south-eastern borders. The long summer of migration seems to have been just one moment of an intermittent history, whose motor is the interplay of migrants' own border struggles and the states' attempt to categorise, capture, and punish their disobedient mobilities (Karakayali and Rigo 2010). It is difficult to predict what shapes will the new disruptions take, but the history of the European border regime shows that, once a particular route or strategy becomes more policed, new escape routes are found and different interstices are carved out (Papadopoulos et al. 2008).

As a system of subordination of nonwhite, non-European and impoverished people, asylum may be *unreformable* (Behrman 2019), but we are nonetheless confronted with the multifarious questions that contemporary (post-)colonial migrations pose. Importantly, the COVID-19 pandemic has accelerated a global process of erosion of asylum which, from the EU to the United States and Australia, becomes an ever more difficult right to access, physically, territorially and legally. Since the inception of the pandemic, Greece, Cyprus and Hungary banned entry for all asylum applicants; Belgium closed its reception centres, and Spain suspended the processing of applications; ultimately, Italy and Malta closed their ports – and almost two thousand people died or went missing in the Mediterranean throughout the period (Rubio Bertran 2020). NGOs were prevented from engaging in search-and-rescue operations, and the sinking of migrant boats did not make it through the news. Even after European border controls started relaxing between spring and summer 2020 with the weakening of the pandemic, there were still cases of boats left ramming at sea for up to nine days, because no country wanted to take responsibility for them. Furthermore, in the beginning of the pandemic, it was grotesque to see how, globally, tourists and other nationals from the Global North were rescued with state flights, while irregular migrants were abandoned or utterly deported in virtually all transit zones, from the Mexican/Guatemalan border and the Mexican/US one, to Calais and the Mediterranean. While the global lockdown made virtually impossible both the transit of illegalised people and the material support to their movements, white Western populations became increasingly concerned about their own fragilities and loss of freedom of movement. The discourses of Alt-right protesters in the United States, and those of liberal intellectuals in Spain and Italy merged in their preoccupations for constitutional rights and freedoms (Picozza 2020), but they were oblivious to the way, since the inception of liberalism, in the Euro-Atlantic area those rights and freedoms have always been reserved to white relatively privileged citizens only. Even the more sympathetic stances that try to relate the long-term privation of freedom of refugees to the new one of white citizens risk a displacement that reflects the way in which white subjects are always already *conscious* of their inviolable rights and freedoms (Hesse 2014). This stance is well expressed in queer philosopher Paul Preciado's (2020) argument that, in the management of the pandemic:

> The new frontier is your epidermis. The new Lampedusa is your skin. For years, we considered migrants and refugees infectious to the community and placed them in detention centers – political limbos where they remained without rights and without citizenship; perpetual waiting rooms. Now we are living in detention centers in our own homes.

Preciado seems to take for granted that the reader will not have inhabited the many Lampedusas scattered in this world, which have little to do with state or self-imposed isolation at home. Lampedusa is reproduced as an abstract, almost metaphorical territory, inhabited by masses of bodies which can never access the singularity of the reader, incapsulated in that 'your skin'. And yet, during the pandemic, these many Lampedusas were neither metaphorical nor overcome by the new biopolitics involving white European citizens.

In the first week of March 2020, as I edited the final draft of this book, I witnessed from afar the violent border spectacle unfolding at the Greek-Turkish border, whereby thousands of illegalised people, who had long been immobilised on the other shore thanks to the EU-Turkish deal, were now attempting to cross into Europe, taking advantage of a relaxation of border controls momentarily deployed by Erdogan as a bargaining chip with the EU (Pantazakos 2020; De Genova 2020). At the borders of the River Evros and the islands of Lesbos and Samos, the Greek police teargassed, beat up and shot dead incoming refugees (Forensic Architecture 2020), while also ramming their rubber boats at sea. Local and international neo-Nazi groups set NGOs' premises on fire, prevented their operators from entering refugee camps, and directly confronted incoming refugees, preventing them from reaching NGOs sites. The Greek state temporarily suspended the right to claim asylum, and most international humanitarian operators were ordered to evacuate by their institutions. The conflict between the necropolitics of the state and the redemptive biopolitics of humanitarianism was stronger than ever – though, through the evacuation of volunteers, the lack of political power of the latter at times of violent 'crises' was dramatically revealed. As EU officials justified the use of force by the Greek state, depicting Greece as 'the shield of Europe' (Rubio Bertran 2020) and stating that the legitimacy to fire rubber bullets at migrants depended on the circumstances (Fleming 2020), many newspaper articles proclaimed the 'death' of Europe, its moral values, culture of rights, and juridical system (see, for instance, Abdul Karim 2020).

On 5 March, TRT Arabi published the pictures taken by photographer Belal Khaled, which showed a group of male refugees in Uzunkopru, Turkey, who had been tortured, stripped to their underwear, and robbed of their few belongings by the Greek border police, before being forced to swim back the Evros River towards the Turkish side (Tanriverdi 2020). These images strongly resonated with those taken on 5 May 2009 by photographer Enrico Dagnigno, who accompanied the Italian Coastguard patrol boat Bovienzo while they carried out the first ever pushback at sea between Italy and Libya. That time, some of the shipwreck victims disembarked at the port of Tripoli took off their clothes, with the aim of showing to the Italian border guards, and the press, the scars of the tortures they had undergone in the Libyan prisons – which were directly financed by Italy's treaty with Gaddafi. One man kneeled down, grabbed a coastguard's hand and implored not to be taken back to the Libyan hell.

I was twenty-one then, and, for the first time in my life, I felt what philosopher Walter Benjamin (2003: 392) famously described as the 'amazement that the things we are experiencing are "still" possible'. Benjamin poignantly warned us that the historical perception that guides such amazement is 'untenable'. In fact, the view of Europe as the cradle, and the maximum expression, of democracy, whose history is inextricably tied to the right to asylum, precisely suffers from a colonial and fascist amnesia that conceals the fact that European liberal 'values' have never been universal, but rather always unevenly distributed through hierarchies of humanity (Mehta 1999). Furthermore, the 'amazement' that reacts to the violence of the European border spectacle suffers not only from a long-term memory loss – the one of five centuries of colonial subjugation, mass murdering, spoliation and exploitation – but also from a more short-term one, that is to say, twenty years of 'the war against migrants' (Cetti 2015), occurring in concomitance to the continued involvement of EU member states in military occupation and violent extractivism overseas.

Although the visual and narrative economy of asylum has not been a central topic of this book, it has formed its necessary background. The 2009 pictures by Enrico Dagnino prompted me to get involved with Asinitas, reflecting a common trope for which, due to social and spatial segregation, 'supporters' can hardly have any encounters with 'refugees' prior to their own engagement in support. It is now over a decade that I forensically witness the physical, legal, psychological and social violence that illegalised people undergo in Europe and, as it has emerged throughout this book, this violence does not solely manifest in the immediate necropolitics, biopolitics or abandonment of the state; it is rather woven into a fabric of everyday occurrences that reproduce that violence through protection and solidarity.

The stories recounted throughout the book took place at a time in which those 'European values' that are seemingly 'dying' today rather seemed to prosper, a time in which borders were relatively open and an important segment of the European population was engaging in solidarity and civil disobedience. Thinking back on that period at the time of submitting this manuscript provokes despair rather than hope. One cannot but wonder how and where that movement has evaporated, how and why migration politics have deteriorated so much afterwards. Recall Ella's comment in the introduction: 'Maybe, in 2015, they heard it was open, or maybe the smugglers had just bought more boats; but in a way it had always been open.' Borders keep their porosity and refugees continue arriving daily through trajectories that are scarcely visible and mapped; in addition, radical practices of solidarity are often clandestine, invisible and cannot be investigated, much less publicised.

In any case both those mobilities and solidarities have dramatically reduced in numbers.

Ten years after the publication of Dagnino's photographs, nothing of that 'amazement' is left, but only a deep bitterness and, perhaps, the capacity to still be struck by others' suffering as if it was one's own – if not for anything else, because seeing Syria turning into the bloodiest and longest war I've witnessed in my short lifespan produces the awareness that what is happening 'there' could truly be happening 'here', just at a different historical crossroad. Europeans seem to suffer from a very short memory which makes possible forgetting selectively not only the crimes they have perpetrated – as colonisers, missionaries or ordinarily citizens benefitting from the economic system sustained by colonisation – but also the ones they have endured – as a people who, not so long ago, have been precisely victims of war, antifascist fighters, refugees and migrants. Research into European refugees fleeing to the Middle East after the Second World War is scarce and is generally not a part of collective memory. As a remedy for the presentism of the 'border spectacle', that history should be more thoroughly connected to the one of present displacements, while also tracing a historical genealogy of past and present border struggles, relating to the untold ways refugees have produced 'Europe' as we know it today.

Notes

INTRODUCTION

1. The category of 'people with a migration background' has first been used in a 2005 micro-census in order to avoid any explicitly racialised or ethnicised categorisation of the population resident in Germany. It has subsequently deeply percolated in everyday usage, reproducing an exclusion of some people from the 'core national group' along negatively racialised and classed lines (Elrick and Schwartzman 2015: 1546). Volunteers and activists may often perceive it as a politically correct form that does not point to people's legal status; yet, they mostly deploy it to refer to people who are racialised as nonwhite, or ethnicised as non-Western or non-European. As Ebua (2012: 267) suggests, migration discourse entails a racialised subtext, for white Western people are never thought of as having 'a migration background'.

2. Fingerprinting and registration of asylum seekers is a requirement of the Dublin Regulation, adopted by all EU and Schengen member states (see chapter 4).

3. Upon their first registration, asylum seekers are allocated to specific Länder (federal states) under the federal system of redistribution (see chapter 3).

4. While I formally studied Persian both in Rome in 2011 and in London in 2013, I am indebted to Farhad for patiently accompanying me in the learning process during my 2014 fieldwork; among long walks and conversations, he would make this new language more accessible to me, all the while moderating his choice of words and pace of speaking, and encouraging me to speak without fearing my mistakes.

5. The Balkan region stands in a peculiar relationship to Europe's geographies of asylum and to the wider border regime (Papadopoulos 2007). While Croatia and Slovenia are part of both the EU and Schengen, other transit countries are part of neither, but still significantly contribute to the EU border regime through bilateral agreements of readmission, most strikingly materialising in pushbacks at the border.

6. For a comprehensive timeline, see Šeruga (2018).

7. Including detention centres on the islands of Chios, Kos, Lesbos and Samos in Greece, and on the island of Lampedusa and the coastal cities of Pozzallo, Taranto and Trapani in Italy.

8. All research participants' names have been changed for the sake of anonymisation; however, in agreement with them, no other information about them has been altered. Only in one case, in chapter 5, the name of an organisation has been changed in order to protect the identity of a research interlocutor.

CHAPTER 1

1. In order to speed up deportation procedures, in that period, Germany had extended its 'safe country of origin' list, including all Western Balkan countries, and had begun placing Roma asylum seekers on 'fast-track' procedures targeting 'obviously unfounded applications' (Leko 2017).

2. The 'EASY' system distributes asylum seekers' quotas to different Federal States. Its algorithm, the Königsteiner Schlüssel, is calculated yearly on the basis of tax revenues and population size of each federal state.

3. Integrationsgesetz, 31 July 2016.

4. At the time of writing, the European commission has submitted a proposal to adjust the 2020 budget in order to assist Greece in the management of irregular migration during the COVID-19 pandemic. Instead of allocating funds to the improvement of refugees' access to healthcare on the islands, the proposal allocates funds mostly to the construction of five new Multi-Purpose Reception and Identification Centres (MPRICs); to 'Voluntary Return' programmes; to security operations; and to quick return programmes for those preemptively excluded from the right to asylum (European Commission 2020).

5. Directive 2008/115/EC of 16 December 2008.

CHAPTER 2

1. The 'Interventionist Left' is a coalition of different groups and initiatives active in Germany and Austria since 2005 in the fields of anti-racism, anti-fascism, queer feminism, climate justice and international solidarity.

2. The logo was originally created in the 1990s by graphic artist John Hood, and placed on the highway at the US/Mexico border in order to warn drivers of possible pedestrian crossings. Later, it was re-elaborated by British artist Banksy, who added a kite in order to inspire the dimension of freedom relating to flight (Volpp 2018). Finally, an anti-fascist collective in Berlin added the 'Refugees Welcome' caption.

3. Under the Treaty on Friendship, Partnership and Cooperation between Italy and Libya, signed by Berlusconi and Gaddafi in August 2008.

4. Asylum seekers in Germany cannot autonomously decide where to settle and submit their application. Upon their first registration, they are redistributed through

the Königsteiner Schlüssel system, based on resident population size and tax income per region.

5. While neither Afghanistan nor Iran have ever been *formally* colonised, they extensively suffered both the effects and discourses (Monsutti 2013) of European imperialism, as well as later US, Soviet and EU imperialism and/or military occupation, most evident in the 'colonial present' of the Afghan war (Gregory 2004). That both countries have produced extremely high numbers of refugees since the end of the 1970s is exemplary of how, in the postcolonial present, colonial difference is rearticulated in manifold ways and nonlinear geopolitical relationships.

6. Founded in 1953, the Federal Office for Migration and Refugees is the agency of the Ministry of the Interior responsible for asylum and migration While its headquarters are located in Nuremberg, it has several branches scattered all over Germany.

7. This division between the BAMF and the Ausländerbehörde (the local Foreigners Office) is due to the fact that German Länder have their own residence acts, which are distinct from national asylum/migration laws.

8. By 'autonomous left movement' I mean a diverse network of anti-capitalist, anti-fascist, anti-racist and feminist grassroots militant groups, traditionally mostly active in squats in Berlin, Hamburg, Frankfurt and Göttingen; this is also linked to the wider European network of local squatting movements (Mudu and Chattopadhyay 2017).

9. The same neighbourhood is also home to the St. Pauli FC football team, traditionally left-wing and characterised by anti-fascist, anti-racist and pro-refugee politics.

10. The 'No-Border' movement is a loose global network of grassroots activist groups concerned with freedom of movement and social justice and engaging in pro-migrant/refugee action, anti-deportation struggles and the organisation of no-border camps and demonstrations (Anderson et al. 2010; Gauditz 2017).

11. 'Church Asylum', as it is referred to in Germany, has been inspired by Sanctuary movements in the United States (Coutin 1993), and is a practice that provides safe haven to individuals and families threatened with deportations (Neufert 2014: 36).

12. I think here especially of large-scale, interview-based research projects funded by the EU or by national governments, whereby high number of interviews are conducted in very short-time frameworks.

CHAPTER 3

1. Each federal state is responsible for the setup of at least one primary registration centre (ZEA – Zentrale Erstaufnahmeeinrichtung).

2. Fördern und Wohnen ('Supporting and Living') is a nonprofit housing company, owned by the city-state of Hamburg. It was founded in 2007 with the aim of supporting homeless people, including refugees, young people, people suffering from substance addictions, and people with disabilities. Occasionally, F&W shares the

management of refugee accommodation with charities and NGOs, such as Caritas, Die Johannitern and the German Red Cross.

3. The Messehallen is comprised of eight halls and usually hosts trade fairs, attracting 700,000 visitors annually. It has also been the venue of the 2017 G20.

4. In June 2016, the many scattered RW initiatives came together under the alliance BHFI (Bündnis Hamburger Flüchtlingsinitiativen: http://bhfi.de), comprising more than a hundred initiatives of refugee support.

5. Asylum seekers can register their application directly at the border, at a police station, through an immigration authority such as the BAMF, or rather at their accommodation centre.

6. The 'EASY' system is a national online platform that distributes asylum seekers' quotas to the different Federal States. It is based on an algorithm – the Königsteiner Schlüssel – calculated yearly on the basis of tax revenues and population size of each federal state. Furthermore, some BAMF branches specialise on specific countries of origin, thus allocation can also depend on the applicant's nationality. Because Hamburg is a wealthy and densely populated city-state, a greater number of asylum seekers were allocated there, compared to other cities. This system of distribution cannot be challenged legally, unless in the exceptional case in which a woman applicant is due to give birth imminently.

7. From its opening in 2014 to its eviction in autumn 2016, the KoZe also offered sleeping places to rejected asylum seekers and undocumented immigrants.

8. The Bahnhof Mission is a Christian charity that takes care of people in need who are travelling through German railway stations – mostly the homeless, the elderly, disabled people and unaccompanied children.

9. In German, the word *Lager* means 'camp'. Despite its strong association with the Holocaust in other languages, refugee activists purposefully deploy the term in order to highlight the dire living conditions in the camps (Bhimji 2016: 449). See Jansen (2015: 23) for a discussion of how, in policy language, the uncomfortable historical memory and present meaning of the 'camp' has been 'sanatised' through the word 'centre'.

10. In order to speed up the processing of applications, the BAMF circulated an informal decision to suspend the application of Dublin for Syrian asylum seekers. As the document leaked in the press, many Syrians made their way to Germany as this offered some certainty of not being deported to other transit countries in which they had been fingerprinted.

CHAPTER 4

1. Recognised refugees are allowed to travel through the Schengen area under Art. 21 of the Convention implementing the Schengen Agreement of 14 June 1985 between the Governments of the States of the Benelux Economic Union, the Federal Republic of Germany and the French Republic on the gradual abolition of checks at their common borders, 19 June 1990.

2. Until 2018 – when it was removed through the Security Decree, converted into Law 132/2018 – Humanitarian protection was a precarious form of international protection given in Italy to those who did not qualify neither for refugee status nor for subsidiary protection, but who were nevertheless considered vulnerable for reasons of age, gender, environmental disasters or political instability in their countries of origin.

3. The 'right to stay' (*Bleiberecht*) refers both to a group of precarious residency statuses, such as the *Duldung*, in legal language, and to a crucial demand of migrant/refugee campaigns, under the slogan '*Bleiberecht* for all', which often concerns rejected asylum seekers.

4. After registration, asylum seekers are invited for a first hearing that assesses their potential subjection to the Dublin procedure. This can be determined in several ways, primarily not only through the existence of fingerprints matches on Eurodac but also through the applicant's own account of their journey, and the presence of proofs, such as transport tickets found on them at the moment of apprehension. If the applicant is not inserted in the Dublin procedure, they will subsequently be invited to a second hearing, which focuses on the reasons for flight and protection seeking, and determines the prospective recognition or rejection.

5. Dublin transfer requests are divided into 'Take Charge' – concerning asylum seekers who are submitting an asylum application for the first time – and 'Take Back' – concerning those who have already submitted an asylum application in their 'competent' country.

6. This is an ad hoc interview, which provides a chance for applicants in the Dublin procedure to explain to the BAMF the reasons for which they should not be transferred to their 'competent state' – in particular in the cases in which they fit other criteria set by the Regulation, in particular the principle of family unity.

7. The concept of Subsidiary Protection has been introduced by the Qualification Directive (Council Directive 2004/83/EC) with the aim of offering international protection to those asylum seekers who face 'serious risks' in their home countries but fall outside the narrower definition of the Geneva Convention. Beneficiaries of this kind of protection have fewer rights than those recognised with full refugee status.

8. Council Regulation (EC) No 343/2003 article 3.2 and Council Regulation (EU) No 604/2013 Article 17.1

9. After being condemned by the ECHR for its systemic humanitarian deficiencies (*ECHR Grand Chamber Judgment. M.S.S. v. Belgium and Greece. 21.01.2011*), in 2011, Greece suspended its participation in the Dublin Regulation, which was resumed only in 2016.

10. Reeperbahn is Hamburg's red light district, bordering the St. Pauli neighbourhood, whereby this interview took place.

11. Medical procedures for the assessment of unaccompanied minors' age are in place in most European countries. They are widely criticised for their pseudo-scientific nature, as well as complicity in border control (Sauer et al. 2015).

12. Directive 2003/109/EC of 25 November 2003 Concerning the Status of Third-Country Nationals who are Long-Term Residents.

13. On the racialised politics of citizenship within the two enclaves, see Gold (2000: 91–118).

CHAPTER 5

1. Kampnagel is a theatre and production venue for contemporary performing arts, located in a former crane factory in the neighbourhood of Barmbek.

2. The Chai Lounge was built by the company More than Shelters with recreational and educational purposes, under the initiative of a group of volunteers and social workers.

3. 'Mini-jobs' are a part-time, tax-exempted, and low-waged form of marginal employment, with a maximum monthly salary of €450.

4. In reality, the residents of primary camps were often mixed. Access to secondary accommodation was slow and limited in numbers; families, the ill and single women were usually prioritised, so that many single men, who had already undergone their asylum interview, or had even been recognised, still resided in primary camps.

5. See Wischmann (2018), on the relationship between education and race in Germany.

6. Founded in 1994, Fluchtpunkt provides both legal advice and legal representation to refugees for free.

7. This is a fictional name, chosen for protecting Johannes' identity.

8. The topic of universal jurisdiction falls beyond the scope of this book and is too complex to be comprehensively unpacked here. However, it must be mentioned that Germany is currently holding war trials of Syrian lower-level regime officials, who entered the country as 'refugees', and are accused of crimes against humanity (Rankin 2019). On the one hand, preconceptions of incoming refugees as ontologically 'vulnerable subjects' prevent from thinking through questions of justice posed by the very refugee communities; in positing a principle of solidarity with all incoming asylum seekers, refugee supporters may well be oblivious to the question of *international solidarity* and thus fail to acknowledge the pursuit of justice of some refugees against others. On the other, the question arises of *who* can claim the authority to investigate and restore justice internationally (Hovell 2018) and this question is rendered all the way more complex through the increasing overlapping of migration, criminal and terrorism laws in Europe.

CHAPTER 6

1. The Rafah crossing, controlled by both Palestinians and Egyptian authorities, and video-supervised by EU and Israeli officials, is the main point of entry and exit for Gazan residents. It is often closed for long periods, due to Israel's security

concerns. In the few days of opening per year, transit is often allowed only for urgent medical cases (see UNHCR 2018).

2. Application for, as well as renewal of, student visas require particular financial conditions and the opening of a 'blocked account' from which money cannot be withdrawn until the applicant's arrival in Germany. In the absence of a scholarship or one's parents' financial guarantees, a person with permanent residency in Germany can guarantee for the applicant – as in Alaa's case. Subsequently, students are expected to have in their account € 8,640 euro per year.

3. Due to its geopolitical configuration, the Gaza Strip is often metaphorically mentioned as the 'world's largest open-air prison' (see, among others, Chomsky 2012). Surrounded by fences, walls and high security technologies, the Strip is extremely densely populated. The Erez crossing into Israel cannot be accessed by Gazans, except for the exceptional cases of those who are allowed into Israel for medical conditions. The Rafah crossing is seldom open and extremely over-queued, thus Gaza's population suffers from extremely limited mobility outside of its borders (Aljamal 2014).

4. After the closure of the 'Safe Passage' between the West Bank and Gaza in 2000, movement between the two territories is virtually impossible for Palestinians, with the exceptions of (some) urgent medical cases (Roy 2007: 257).

5. See Weizman (2007: 139–159) and Kotef (2015: 27–38), on the technology of 'flying' or mobile checkpoints – namely temporary and ad hoc – which render any given space a potential checkpoint.

6. In particular, within the German radical left, there is a conspicuous presence of the 'Anti-German' current, which holds as its core ideologies pro-Western and pro-Israeli discourses, as well as a critique of both German and Islamic anti-Semitism. Anti-Germans thus condemn anti-Zionist and anti-American discourses in the left as resurgent anti-Semitic ideologies (Schlembach 2010).

7. From 2003 to the present, Hamas has been designated by the EU as a terrorist organisation (Council Decision [CFSP] 2017/154 of 27 January 2017).

8. Palestinians who are nationals of neighbouring countries whereby UNRWA (United Nations Relief and Works Agency for Palestine) is present are not eligible to apply for asylum in Germany.

CHAPTER 7

1. In German 'Schlepper, Schleuser, Supeheldinnen'. While the first two nouns are gender-neutral, the third one is feminine.

2. See, for instance, the campaign Fluchthelfer.in, created by the Peng! Collective (Baban and Rygiel 2017); the network Watch the Med/Alarm Phone (Stierl 2015) and Welcome 2 Europe (Welcome to Europe Network 2010).

3. The admission into whiteness of the latter two groups has been later accompanied by their 'de-migrantisation' in the context of northern Europe, concomitant to their admission into EU citizenship.

4. At the time, Arab anti-blackness particularly appeared in the international debate through the news of slave auctions in 2017 (Haile 2017).

5. On the related topic of the sexual oppression of migrant men through the deprivation of intimacy and desire, see Ahmad (2009).

6. The * symbol was meant to encompass all gender orientations that are not aligned with 'cis man', such as 'trans' and 'non-binary'.

7. Women in Exile is a group of self-organised refugee women, first founded in Brandenburg in 2002, with the purpose of voicing the double discrimination of refugee women, along legal-racial and gendered lines. They campaign for the abolition of *Lagers* (refugee camps), which they periodically visit in order to support and mobilise the women hosted there.

8. International Women Space is a feminist collective based in Berlin, composed of both refugee and non-refugee women, and struggling against the intersections of racism and sexism. The group emerged from the occupation of the former Gehart-Hauptmann School in December 2012, following the eviction of the Oranien-Platz protest camp.

References

Abdul Karim, Jaafar. 2020. 'Europe Has Lost Its Soul at the Border.' *Deutsche Welle*. Online.

Aced, Miriam, and Veit Schwab. 2016. 'Addressing Whiteness with/in (Critical) Migration Studies.' *Movements. Journal für kritische Migrations-und Grenzregimeforschung* 1: 151–161.

Agamben, Giorgio. 2005. *State of Exception*. Chicago: University of Chicago Press.

Agier, Michel. 2008. *On the Margins of the World: The Refugee Experience Today*. Cambridge: Polity.

Ahmad, Ali Nobil. 2009. 'Bodies that (Don't) Matter: Desire, Eroticism and Melancholia in Pakistani Labour Migration.' *Mobilities* 4(3): 309–327.

Ahmed, Sara. 2000. *Strange Encounters: Embodied Others in Post-Coloniality*. London and New York: Routledge.

Ahmed, Sarah. 2004. 'The Non-Performativity of Anti-Racism.' Paper presented at Text and Terrain: Legal Studies in Gender and Sexuality, a Centre LGS Colloquium, University of Kent.

———. 2007. 'A Phenomenology of Whiteness.' *Feminist Theory* 8(2): 149–168.

Albahari, Maurizio. 2015. *Crimes of Peace: Mediterranean Migrations at the World's Deadliest Border*. Philadelphia: University of Pennsylvania Press.

Aljamal, Yousef M. 2014. 'Travelling as a Palestinian.' *Biography* 37(2): 664–679.

Amnesty International and Forensic Architecture. 2015. *'Black Friday': Carnage in Rafah During 2014 Israel/Gaza conflict. Amnesty.org*. Online.

Anderson, Bridget. 2013. *Us and Them? The Dangerous Politics of Immigration Control*. Oxford: Oxford University Press.

Anderson, Bridget, Nandita Sharma, and Cynthia Wright. 2010. 'Editorial: Why No Borders?' *Refuge* 26(2): 5–18.

Andersson, Ruben. 2014. *Illegality, Inc. Clandestine Migration and the Business of Bordering Europe*. Berkeley: University of California Press.

Andrijasevic, Rutvica. 2010. 'From Exception to Excess: Detention and Deportations across the Mediterranean Space.' In De Genova, N., and Peutz, N. (eds.) *The*

Deportation Regime: Sovereignty, Space, and the Freedom of Movement. Durham, NC: Duke University Press: 147–165.

Andrijasevic, Rutvica, and William Walters. 2010. 'The International Organization for Migration and the International Government of Borders.' *Environment and Planning D: Society and Space* 28(3): 977–999.

Antonakaki, Melina, Bernd Kasparek, and Georgios Maniatis. 2016. 'Counting, Channelling, and Detaining: The Hotspot Center Vial in Chios, Greece.' *Society and Space Open Site. A Companion to the Environment and Planning D: Society and Space Printed Journal.*

Apostolova, Raia. 2017. *Moving Labor Power and Historical Forms of Migration: The Internationalist Socialist Worker, the Social Benefit Tourist and the Economic Migrant.* PhD Thesis. Department of Sociology and Social Anthropology, Central European University.

———. 2018. 'Obstacles Before Struggles: Freedom of Movement and the Conditioning of Collective Response.' In Fedyuk, O., and Stewart, P. (eds.) *Inclusion and Exclusion in Europe. Migration, Work and Employment Perspectives.* London: Rowman & Littlefield International.

Appadurai, Arjun. 1988. 'Putting Hierarchy in Its Place.' *Cultural Anthropology* 3(1): 36–49.

Arendt, Hannah. 1943. 'We Refugees.' *Menorah Journal* 31(1): 69–77.

———. 1958. *The Human Condition.* Chicago: University of Chicago Press.

———. [1951] 1973. *The Origins of Totalitarianism.* New York: Harcourt Brace.

———. 1990. *On Revolution.* Harmondsworth: Penguin Books.

Asad, Talal. 1973. 'Introduction.' In *Anthropology and the Colonial Encounter.* London: Ithaca Press: 9–20.

Baban, Feyzi, and Kim Rygiel. 2017. 'Living with Others: Fostering Radical Cosmopolitanism Through Citizenship Politics in Berlin.' *Ethics & Global Politics* 10(1): 98–116.

Bačić Selanec, Nika. 2015. 'A Critique of EU Refugee Crisis Management: On Law, Policy and Decentralisation.' *Croatian Yearbook of European Law & Policy* 11(11): 73–114.

Baldwin, James. 1998. 'On Being "White" … and Other Lies.' In Roediger, D. R. (ed.) *Black on White: Black Writers on What It Means to Be White.* New York: Schocken Books: 177–180.

Baudrillard, Jean. 1998. *The Consumer Society: Myths and Structures.* London: Sage.

Behrman, Simon. 2014. 'Legal Subjectivity and the Refugee.' *International Journal of Refugee Law* 26(1): 1–21.

———. 2019. 'Refugee Law as a Means of Control.' *Journal of Refugee Studies* 32(1): 42–62.

Benjamin, Walter. 2003. *Selected Writings. Vol. 4. 1938–1940.* Cambridge, MA: Harvard University Press.

Bernhard, Patrick. 2012. 'Behind the Battle Lines: Italian Atrocities and the Persecution of Arabs, Berbers, and Jews in North Africa During World War II.' *Holocaust and Genocide Studies* 26(3): 425–446.

Betts, Alexander, and Paul Collier. 2017. *Refuge: Transforming a Broken Refugee System.* London: Penguin Books.

Bhambra, Gurminder K. 2009. 'Postcolonial Europe: Or, Understanding Europe in Times of the Postcolonial.' In Rumford, C. (ed.) *Sage Handbook of European Studies.* London: Sage: 69–85.

Bhimji, Fazila. 2016. 'Visibilities and the Politics of Space: Refugee Activism in Berlin.' *Journal of Immigrant & Refugee Studies* 14(4): 432–450.

Bialasiewicz, Luiza. 2012. 'Off-Shoring and Out-Sourcing the Borders of Europe: Libya and EU Border Work in the Mediterranean.' *Geopolitics* 17(4): 843–866.

Birke Peter. 2016. 'Right to the City—and Beyond: The Topographies of Urban Social Movements in Hamburg.' In Mayer, M., Thörn, C., and Thörn, H. (eds.) *Urban Uprisings. Palgrave Studies in European Political Sociology.* London: Palgrave Macmillan.

Blitz, Brad K., Rosemary Sales, and Lisa Marzano. 2005. 'Non-Voluntary Return? The Politics of Return to Afghanistan.' *Political Studies* 53(1): 182–200.

Bohmer, Carol, and Amy Shuman. 2007a. *Rejecting Refugees: Political Asylum in the 21st Century.* London, New York: Routledge.

———. 2007b. 'Producing Epistemologies of Ignorance in the Political Asylum Claim Application Process.' *Identities: Global Studies in Culture and Power* 14(5): 603–629.

Bojadžijev, Manuela. 2006. 'Does Contemporary Capitalism Need Racism?' *Eipcp .net.* Online.

Bojadžijev, Manuela, and Sandro Mezzadra. 2015. '"Refugee Crisis" or Crisis of European Migration Policies?' *Focaalblog.* Online.

borderline-europe, Bellezza, Sara, and Tiziana Calandrino. 2017. *Criminalization of Flight and Escape Aid.* Hamburg: Tradition.

Borgstede, Simone Beate. 2016. '"We Are Here to Stay": Reflections on the Struggle of the Refugee Group "Lampedusa in Hamburg" and the Solidarity Campaign, 2013–2015.' In Mudu, P., and Chattopadhyay, S. (eds.) *Migration, Squatting and Radical Autonomy.* London, New York: Routledge: 162–179.

Bouteldja, Houria. 2016. *Whites, Jews, and Us. Towards a Politics of Revolutionary Love.* Cambridge, MA and London: Semiotext(e).

Braakman, Marije. 2005. *Roots and Routes: Questions of Home, Belonging and Return in an Afghan Diaspora.* Leiden University, Department of Cultural Anthropology & Sociology of Non Western Societies.

Braun, Katherine. 2017. 'Decolonial Perspectives on Charitable Spaces of "Welcome Culture" in Germany.' *Social Inclusion* 5(3): 38–48.

Brodkin, Karen. 1998. *How Jews Became White Folks and What that Says About Race in America.* New Brunswick, NJ and London: Rutgers University Press.

Cantat, Celine. 2015. *Contesting Europeanism: Discourses and Practices of Pro-Migrant Organisations in the European Union.* PhD Thesis. School of Law & Social Sciences, University of East London.

Carsetti, Marco. 2014. 'Vittime e Vittimisti.' *Gli Asini* 21: 4–15.

Carson, Lorna. 2016. 'The Sights and Sounds of the Multilingual City.' In Carson, L., and King, L. (eds.) *The Multilingual City: Vitality, Conflict and Change.* Bristol: Multilingual Matters.

Castles, Stephen, Hein de Haas, and Mark J. Miller. 2014. *The Age of Migration*. New York and London: Guilford.

Césaire, Aimé. [1955] 2000. *Discourse on Colonialism*. New York: Monthly Review Press.

Cetti Fran. 2015. 'Fortress Europe and the War Against Migrants International Socialism.' 148. Online.

Chakrabarty, Dipesh. 2000. *Provincializing Europe: Postcolonial Thought and Historical Difference*. Princeton, NJ and Oxford: Princeton University Press.

Chatterjee, Partha. 1993. *The Nation and Its Fragments: Colonial and Postcolonial Histories*. Princeton: Princeton University Press.

———. 2004. *The Politics of the Governed: Reflections on Popular Politics in Most of the World*. New York: Columbia University Press.

Chomsky, Noam. 2012. 'My Visit to Gaza, the World's Largest Open-Air Prison.' *Truthout*. Online.

Chouliaraki, Lilie. 2006. *The Spectatorship of Suffering*. London: Sage.

Cocco, Emilio. 2017. 'Where Is the European Frontier? The Balkan Migration Crisis and Its Impact on Relations between the EU and the Western Balkans.' *European View* 16(2): 293–302.

Coutin, Susan B. 1993. *The Culture of Protest: Religious Activism and the U.S. Sanctuary Movement*. Boulder: Westview Press.

Craps, Stef. 2013. *Postcolonial Witnessing: Trauma Out of Bounds*. Basingstoke and New York: Palgrave Macmillan.

Crepaz, Katharina. 2017. 'A "Common Commitment": Civil Society and European Solidarity in the Refugee Crisis.' In Nancheva, N., and Agarin, T. A. (eds.) *European Crisis: Perspectives on Refugees in Europe*. Hannover: Ibidem: 29–49.

Cunningham, Hilary. 1995. *God and Caesar at the Rio Grande: Sanctuary and the Politics of Religion*. Minneapolis: University of Minnesota Press.

Dalley, Hamish. 2016. 'The Question of "Solidarity" in Postcolonial Trauma Fiction: Beyond the Recognition Principle.' In Andermahr, S. (eds.) *Decolonizing Trauma Studies: Trauma and Postcolonialism*. Basel: MDPI.

Danewid, Ida. 2017. 'White Innocence in the Black Mediterranean: Hospitality and the Erasure of History.' *Third World Quarterly* 38(7): 1674–1689.

Das, Veena, and Deborah Poole. 2004. *Anthropology in the Margins of the State*. Oxford, New York: Oxford University Press.

Davies, Thom, Arshad Isakjee, and Surindar Dhesi. 2017. 'Violent Inaction: The Necropolitical Experience of Refugees in Europe.' *Antipode* 49(5): 1263–1284.

De Bel-Air, Françoise. 2015. 'A Note on Syrian Refugees in the Gulf: Attempting to Assess Data and Policies.' *Gulf Labour Markets and Migration. GLMM.* Online.

De Genova, Nicholas. 2002. 'Migrant "Illegality" and Deportability in Everyday Life.' *Annual Review of Anthropology* 31: 419–447.

———. 2005. *Working the Boundaries. Race, Space and 'Illegality' in Mexican Chicago*. Durham and London: Duke University Press.

———. 2010. 'The Queer Politics of Migration: Reflections on "Illegality" and "Incorrigibility".' *Studies in Social Justice* 4(2): 101–126.

———. 2013. 'Spectacles of Migrant "Illegality": The Scene of Exclusion, the Obscene of Inclusion.' *Ethnic and Racial Studies* 36: 1180–1198.

———. 2014. 'Deportation.' In Anderson, B., and Keith, M. (eds.) *Migration: A COMPAS Anthology.* Oxford: COMPAS.

———. 2015. 'Border Struggles in the Migrant Metropolis.' *Nordic Journal of Migration Research* 5(1): 3–10.

———. 2016a. 'The European Question: Migration, Race, and Postcoloniality in "Europe".' *Social Text* 34(3): 75–102.

———. 2016b. 'The "Native's Point of View" in the Anthropology of Migration.' *Anthropological Theory* 16(2–3): 227–240.

———. 2016c. 'The "Crisis" of the European Border Regime: Towards a Marxist Theory of Borders.' *International Socialism* 150: 31–54.

———. 2018. 'The "Migrant Crisis" as Racial Crisis: Do Black Lives Matter in Europe?' *Ethnic and Racial Studies* 41(10): 1765–1782.

———. 2020. 'On Standby . . . at the Borders of "Europe".' *Ephemera: Theory & Politics in Organization.* Online.

De Genova, Nicholas, Glenda Garelli, and Martina Tazzioli. 2018. 'Autonomy of Asylum? The Autonomy of Migration Undoing the Refugee Crisis Script.' Introduction to Special Thematic Issue on 'The Autonomy of Migration within the Crises.' *SAQ: South Atlantic Quarterly* 117(2): 239–265.

De Genova, Nicholas, and Nathalie Peutz (eds.). 2010. *The Deportation Regime: Sovereignty, Space and the Freedom of Movement.* Durham, NC: Duke University Press.

Della Torre, Lucia, and Tesseltje de Lange. 2017. 'The "Importance of Staying Put": Third Country Nationals' Limited Intra-EU Mobility Rights.' *Journal of Ethnic and Migration Studies* 44(9): 1409–1424.

Dobson, Stephen. 2004. *Cultures of Exile and the Experience of Refugeeness.* Bern and New York: Peter Lang.

DuBois, W. E. B. 1947. *The World and Africa.* New York: International Publishers.

DW. 2015. 'Germany Passes Controversial Asylum Seekers Bill.' *Deutsche Welle.* Online.

Ebua, Gaston. 2012. 'Myth and Reality of German Contradiction on Migration: Lower and Upper Classes or Status? Lower and Superior "Races"? The German Intolerance with Racism.' *Part of Series: Kritische Migrationsforschung? - Da kann ja jeder kommen., netzwerkmira.* Online.

Elrick, Jennifer, and Luisa Farah Schwartzman. 2015. 'From Statistical Category to Social Category: Organized Politics and Official Categorizations of "Persons with a Migration Background" in Germany.' *Ethnic and Racial Studies* 38(9): 1539–1556.

El-Tayeb, Fatima. 2008. '"The Birth of a European Public": Migration, Postnationality, and Race in the Uniting of Europe.' *American Quarterly* 60(3): 649–670.

———. 2011. *European Others: Queering Ethnicity in Postnational Europe.* Minneapolis: University of Minnesota Press.

European Commission. 2020. 'Draft Amending Budget No. 1 to the General Budget 2020: Assistance to Greece in Response to Increased Migration Pressure.

Immediate Measures in the Context of the Covid-19 Outbreak.' *Ec.europa.eu.* Online.

Fabian, Johannes. [1983] 2002. *Time and the Other: How Anthropology Makes Its Object.* New York: Columbia University Press.

Fadaee, Simin. 2015. 'The Immigrant Rights Struggle, and the Paradoxes of Radical Activism in Europe.' *Social Movement Studies* 14(6): 733–739.

Fanon, Frantz. 1963. *The Wretched of the Earth.* New York: Grove Press.

Fassin, Didier. 2005. 'Compassion and Repression: The Moral Economy of Immigration Policies in France.' *Cultural Anthropology* 20(3): 362–387.

———. 2012. *Humanitarian Reason. A Moral History of the Present.* Berkeley: University of California Press.

Fekete, Liz. 2009. 'Europe: Crimes of Solidarity.' *Race & Class* 50(4): 83–97.

Fleischmann, Larissa, and Elias Steinhilper. 2017. 'The Myth of Apolitical Volunteering for Refugees: German Welcome Culture and a New Dispositif of Helping.' *Social Inclusion* 5(3): 17–27.

Fleming, Sam. 2020. 'Europe Shows a Harder Face on Migration as Political Mood Shifts.' *Financial Times.* Online.

Fontanari, Elena. 2015. 'Confined to the Threshold: The Experiences of Asylum Seekers in Germany.' *City* 19(5): 709–721.

———. 2017. 'It's My Life: The Temporalities of Refugees and Asylum-Seekers Within the European Border Regime.' *Etnografia e Ricerca Qualitativa* 1: 25–54.

———. 2019. *Lives in Transit: An Ethnographic Study of Refugees' Subjectivity Across European Borders.* Abingdon and New York: Routledge.

Fontanari, Elena, and Giulia Borri. 2017. 'Introduction. Civil Society on the Edge: Actions in Support and Against Refugees in Italy and Germany.' *Mondi Migranti* 3: 23–51.

Forensic Architecture. 2020. 'The Killing of Muhammad Gulzar.' *Forensic Architecture.* Online.

Foucault, Michel. 1982. 'The Subject and Power.' *Critical Inquiry* 8(4): 777–795.

Frei, Alfred G. 1992. '"In the End I Just Said OK": Political and Moral Dimensions of Escape Aid at the Swiss Border.' *The Journal of Modern History* 64: 68–81.

Funk, Nanette. 2016. 'A Spectre in Germany: Refugees, a "Welcome Culture" and an 'Integration Politics.' *Journal of Global Ethics* 12(3): 289–299.

Gambino, Evelina. 2017. 'The "Gran Ghettò": Migrant Labor and Militant Research in Southern Italy.' In De Genova, N. (ed.) *The Borders of 'Europe': Autonomy of Migration, Tactics of Bordering.* Durham, NC: Duke University Press: 255–282.

Gara, Larry. 1961. *The Liberty Line: The Legend of the Underground Railroad.* Lexington: University of Kentucky Press.

Gardaphé, Fred L. 2002. 'We Weren't Always White: Race and Ethnicity in Italian/ American Literature.' *CUNY Academic Works.* Online.

Garelli, Glenda. 2013: 'Schengen Intermittences: The On/Off Switch of Free Circulation.' In Garelli, G., Sossi, F., and Tazzioli, M. (eds.) *Spaces in Migration: Postcards of a Revolution.* London: Pavement Books: 75–95.

Garelli, Glenda, and Martina Tazzioli. 2013a. 'Arab Springs Making Space: Territoriality and Moral Geographies for Asylum Seekers in Italy.' *Environment and Planning D* 31(6): 1004–1021.

———. 2013b. 'Challenging the Discipline of Migration: Militant Research in Migration Studies, an Introduction.' *Postcolonial Studies* 16(3): 245–249.

———. 2016. 'Beyond Detention: Spatial Strategies of Dispersal and Channels of Forced Transfer.' Online. *Environment and Planning D: Society and Space.*

———. 2018. 'The Humanitarian War Against Migrant Smugglers at Sea.' *Antipode* 50: 685–703.

———. Forthcoming. 'Migration and "Pull-Factor" Traps.' *Migration Studies.*

Gatta, Francesco Luigi. 2019. 'Migration and the Rule of (Human Rights) Law: Two 'Crises' Looking in the Same Mirror.' *Croatian Yearbook of European Law & Policy* 15(1): 99–133.

Gauditz, Leslie. 2017. 'The Noborder Movement: Interpersonal Struggle with Political Ideals.' *Social Inclusion* 5(3): 49–57.

Geertz, Clifford. 1974. '"From the Native's Point of View": On the Nature of Anthropological Understanding.' *Bulletin of the American Academy of Arts and Sciences* 28(1): 26–45.

Geronimo. 2012. *Fire and Flames: A History of the German Autonomist Movement.* Oakland, CA: PM Press.

Gianettoni, Lavinia, and Patricia Roux. 2010. 'Interconnecting Race and Gender Relations: Racism, Sexism and the Attribution of Sexism to the Racialized Other.' *Sex Roles* 62(5–6): 374–386.

Gill, Nick. 2010. 'New State-Theoretic Approaches to Asylum and Refugee Geographies.' *Progress in Human Geography* 34(5): 626–645.

Gilmore, Ruth Wilson. 2007. *Golden Gulag: Prisons, Surplus, Crisis, and Opposition in Globalizing California.* Berkeley: University of California Press.

Giuliani, Gaia. 2018. *Race, Nation and Gender in Modern Italy: Intersectional Representations in Visual Culture.* London: Palgrave Macmillan.

Gold, Peter. 2000. *Europe or Africa?: A Contemporary Study of the Spanish North African Enclaves of Ceuta and Melilla.* Liverpool: Liverpool University Press.

Goldberg, David Theo. 2006. 'Racial Europeanization.' *Ethnic and Racial Studies* 29(2): 331–364.

Golden, Renny, and Michael McConnell. 1986. *Sanctuary: The New Underground Railroad.* New York: Orbis Books.

Gopal, Priyamvada. 2019. *Insurgent Empire: Anticolonialism and the Making of British Dissent.* London and New York: Verso.

Green, Meredith J., Cristopher C. Sonn, and Jabulane Matsebula. 2007. 'Reviewing Whiteness: Theory, Research and Possibilities.' *South African Journal of Psychology* 37(3): 389–419.

Gregory, Derek. 2004. *The Colonial present: Afghanistan, Palestine and Iraq.* Malden, MA: Blackwell.

Guglielmo, Jennifer, and Salvatore Salerno. 2003. *Are Italians White? How Race Is Made in America.* New York: Routledge.

References

Guild, Elspeth. 2006. 'The Europeanisation of Europe's Asylum Policy.' *International Journal of Refugee Law* 18(3–4): 630–651.

Gupta, Akhil, and James Ferguson. 1992. 'Beyond "Culture": Space, Identity, and the Politics of Difference.' *Cultural Anthropology* 7(1): 6–23.

———. 1997. 'Discipline and Practice: "The Field" as Site, Method and Location in Anthropology.' In *Anthropological Locations: Boundaries and Grounds of a Field Science*. Berkeley: University of California Press.

Gutiérrez Rodríguez, Encarnación. 2018. 'The Coloniality of Migration and the "Refugee Crisis": On the Asylum-Migration Nexus, the Transatlantic White European Settler Colonialism-Migration and Racial Capitalism.' *Refuge* 34(1): 3–10.

Guy-Sheftall, Beverly. 1995. *Words of Fire: An Anthology of African-American Feminist Thought*. New York: The New Press.

Hafez, Farid. 2014. 'Disciplining the "Muslim Subject": The Role of Security Agencies in Establishing Islamic Theology within the State's Academia.' *Islamophobia Studies Journal* 2(2): 43–57.

Hage, Ghassan. 2009. 'Waiting Out the Crisis: On Stuckedness and Governmentality.' In Hage, G. (ed.) *Waiting*. Carlton, VI: Melbourne University Publishing.

Haile, Rahawa. 2017. 'Libya's Slave Trade Didn't Appear Out of Thin Air.' *Pacific Standard*. Online.

Hamann, Ulrike, and Serhat Karakayali. 2016. 'Practicing Willkommenskultur: Migration and Solidarity in Germany.' *Intersections: East European Journal of Society and Politics* 2(4): 69–86.

Hansen, Peo, and Stefan Jonsson. 2013. 'A Statue to Nasser? Eurafrica, the Colonial Roots of European Integration and the 2012 Nobel Peace Prize.' *Mediterranean Quarterly* 24(4): 5–18.

Haraway, Donna. 1988. 'Situated Knowledges: The Science Question in Feminism and the Privilege of Partial Perspective.' *Feminist Studies* 14(4): 575–599.

Harding, Luke. 2015. 'Refugee Crisis: Germany Reinstates Controls at Austrian Border.' *The Guardian*. Online.

Harper, Ian, and Parvathi Raman. 2008. 'Less Than Human? Diaspora, Disease and the Question of Citizenship.' *International Migration* 46(5): 3–26.

Hashim, M. Jalal. 2006. 'Islamization and Arabization of Africans as a Means to Political Power in the Sudan: Contradictions of Discrimination based on the Blackness of Skin and Stigma of Slavery and Their Contribution to the Civil Wars.' *Respect. The Sudanese Journal for Human Rights' Culture and Issues of Cultural Diversity* 3.

Heck, Gerda, and Sabine Hess. 2017. 'Tracing the Effects of the EU-Turkey Deal: The Momentum of the Multi-Layered Turkish Border Regime.' *Movements. Journal for Critical Migration and Border Regime Studies* 3(2): 35–58.

Heller, Charles, Lorenzo Pezzani, and Maurice Stierl. 2017. 'Disobedient Sensing and Border Struggles at the Maritime Frontier of Europe.' *Spheres. Journal for Digital Cultures*. Online.

Hess, Sabine. 2012. 'De-Naturalising Transit Migration: Theory and Methods of an Ethnographic Regime Analysis.' *Population, Space and Place* 18: 428–440.

Hess, Sabine, and Bernd Kasparek. 2017. 'Under Control? Or Border (as) Conflict: Reflections on the European Border Regime.' *Social Inclusion* 5(3): 58–68.

Hesse, Barnor. 2002. 'Forgotten Like a Bad Dream: Atlantic Slavery and the Ethics of Postcolonial Memory.' In Goldberg, D. T., and Quayson, A. (eds.) *Relocating Postcolonialism*. Oxford, UK and Malden, MA: Wiley-Blackwell: 143–173.

———. 2007. 'Racialized Modernity: An Analytics of White Mythologies.' *Ethnic and Racial Studies* 30(4): 643–663.

———. 2011. 'Self-Fulfilling Prophecy: The Postracial Horizon.' *South Atlantic Quarterly* 110(1): 155–178.

———. 2014. 'Escaping Liberty: Western Hegemony, Black Fugitivity.' *Political Theory* 42(3): 288–313.

Holmes, Seth M., and Heide Castañeda. 2016. 'Representing the "European Refugee Crisis" in Germany and Beyond: Deservingness and Difference, Life and Death.' *American Ethnologist* 43(1): 12–24.

hooks, bell. 2000. 'Racism and Feminism.' In Back, L., and Solomos, J. (eds.) *Theories of Race and Racism: A Reader*. London and New York: Routledge.

Hovell, Devika. 2018. 'The Authority of Universal Jurisdiction.' *The European Journal of International Law* 29(2): 427–456.

Hristova, Tsvetelina, Raia Apostolova, and Mathias Fiedler. 2015. 'On Some Metholodigcal Issues Concerning Anti-Dublin Politic.' *Movements. Journal for Critical Migration and Border Regime Studies* 1(1).

Jackson, Michael. 1989. *Paths Toward a Clearing: Radical Empiricism and Ethnographic Inquiry*. Bloomington: Indiana University Press.

———. 1996. *Things as They Are: New Directions in Phenomenological Anthropology*. Bloomington: Indiana University Press.

———. 2002. *The Politics of Storytelling: Violence, Transgression and Intersubjectivity*. Copenhagen: Museum Tusculanum Press, University of Copenhagen.

———. 2013. *The Wherewithal of Life: Ethics, Migration, and the Question of Well-Being*. Berkeley: University of California Press.

Jacobson, Matthew Frye. 1999. *Whiteness of a Different Color*. Cambridge: Harvard University Press.

Jansen, Yolande. 2015. 'Deportability and Racial Europeanization: The Impact of Holocaust Memory and Postcoloniality on the Unfreedom of Movement in and to Europe.' In Jansen, Y., Celikates, R., and de Bloois, J. (eds.) *The Irregularization of Migration in Contemporary Europe: Detention, Deportation, Drowning*. London and New York: Rowman & Littlefield.

Juss, Satvinder S. 2013. 'The Post-Colonial Refugee, Dublin II, and the End of Non-Refoulement.' *International Journal on Minority and Group Rights* 20(2): 307–335.

Karakayali, Serhat, and Enrica Rigo. 2010. 'Mapping the European Space of Circulation.' In De Genova, N., and Peutz, N. (eds.) *The Deportation Regime: Sovereignty, Space, and the Freedom of Movement*. Durham, NC: Duke University Press: 123–144.

Kasparek, Bernd. 2015. 'Complementing Schengen: The Dublin System and the European Border and Migration Regime.' In Bauder, H., and Matheis, C. (eds.)

Migration Policy and Practice: Interventions and Solutions. New York: Palgrave Macmillan: 59–78.

———. 2016. 'Routes, Corridors, and Spaces of Exception: Governing Migration and Europe.' *Near Futures Online 1, Europe at Crossroads*. Online.

Kasparek, Bernd, and Marc Speer. 2015. 'Of Hope. Hungary and the Long Summer of Migration.' *Bordermonitoring. eu*. Online.

Kasparek, Bernd, and Matthias Schmidt-Sembdner. 2019. 'Renationalization and Spaces of Migration: The European Border Regime After 2015.' In *Handbook on Critical Geographies of Migration*. Cheltenham: Edward Elgar Publishing.

Katz, Bruce, Luise Noring, and Nantke Garrelts. 2016. 'Cities and Refugees: The German Experience.' Discussion paper presented at the Brookings Institution Forum, "Cities and Refugees: The European Response" - United Nations General Assembly.

Kaviraj, Sudipta, and Sunil Khilnani (eds.). 2001. *Civil Society: History and Possibilities*. Cambridge: Cambridge University Press.

Kelliher, Diarmaid. 2018. 'Historicising Geographies of Solidarity.' *Geography Compass* 12(9).

Khosravi, Shahram. 2010. *"Illegal" Traveller: An Auto-Ethnography of Borders*. Basingstoke and New York: Palgrave Macmillan.

———. 2014. 'Waiting.' In Anderson, B., and Keith, M. (eds.) *Migration: A COMPAS Anthology*. Oxford: COMPAS.

———. 2016. 'Deportation as a Way of Life for Young Afghan Men.' In Furman, R., Epps, D., and Lamphear, G. (eds.) *Detaining the Immigrant Other: Global and Transnational Issues*. Oxford: Oxford University Press: 169–181.

———. 2018. *After Deportation: Ethnographic Perspectives*. Cham: Palgrave Macmillan.

Kirchhoff, Maren, and David Lorenz. 2018. 'Between Illegalization, Toleration, and Recognition: Contested Asylum and Deportation Policies in Germany.' In Rosenberger, S., Stern, V., and Merhaut, N. (eds.) *Protest Movements in Asylum and Deportation*. Cham, Switzerland: Springer Open.

Kotef, Hagar. 2015. *Movement and the Ordering of Freedom: On Liberal Governances of Mobility*. Durham and London: Duke University Press.

Kynsilehto, Anitta, and Eeva Puumala. 2015. 'Persecution as Experience and Knowledge: The Ontological Dynamics of Asylum Interviews.' *International Studies Perspectives* 16: 446–462.

Lachenicht, Susanne. 2018. 'Learning from Past Displacements? The History of Migrations Between Historical Specificity, Presentism and Fractured Continuities.' *Humanities* 7(36).

Land, Clare. 2015. *Decolonizing Solidarity: Dilemmas and Directions for Supporters of Indigenous Struggles*. London: Zed Books.

Lecadet, Clara. 2017. 'Europe Confronted by Its Expelled Migrants: The Politics of Expelled Migrants' Associations in Africa.' In De Genova, N. (eds.) *The Borders of 'Europe': Autonomy of Migration, Tactics of Bordering*. Durham, NC: Duke University Press.

Leko, Jure. 2017. 'Migration Regimes and the Translation of Human Rights: On the Struggles for Recognition of Romani Migrants in Germany.' *Social Inclusion* 5(3): 77–88.

Lentin, Alana. 2014. 'Postracial Silences. The Othering of Race in Europe.' In Hund, W. D., and Lentin, A. (eds.) *Racism and Sociology*. Berlin: Lit Verlag.

Lentin, Alana, and Juliane Karakayali. 2016. 'Bringing Race Back In: Racism in Post-Racial Societies.' *Movements. Journal for Critical Migration and Border Regime Studies* 2(1): 141–147.

Levi, Primo. 1998. *The Drowned and the Saved*. New York: Vintage International.

Lorde, Audre. 1984a. 'The Uses of the Erotic: The Erotic as Power.' In *Sister Outsider: Essays and Speeches*. Berkeley, CA: Crossing Press.

———. 1984b. 'The Master's Tools Will Never Dismantle the Master's House.' In *Sister Outsider: Essays and Speeches*. Berkeley, CA: Crossing Press.

Lowe, Lisa. 2015. *The Intimacies of Four Continents*. Durham and London: Duke University Press.

Lucassen, Leo. 2005. *The Immigrant Threat: The Integration of Old and New Migrants in Western Europe Since 1850*. Urbana, IL: University of Illinois Press.

Lundström, Catrin. 2017. 'The White Side of Migration. Reflections on Race, Citizenship and Belonging in Sweden.' *Nordic Journal of Migration Research* 7(2): 79–87.

Maldonado-Torres, Nelson. 2007. 'On the Coloniality of Being.' *Cultural Studies* 21(2): 240–270.

———. 2017. 'On the Coloniality of Human Rights.' *Revista Crítica de Ciências Sociais* 114: 117–136.

Malkki, Liisa. 1992. 'National Geographic: The Rooting of Peoples and the Territorialization of National Identity Among Scholars and Refugees.' *Cultural Anthropology* 7(1): 24–44.

———. 1995. 'Refugees and Exile: From "Refugee Studies" to the National Order of Things.' *Annual Review of Anthropology* 24(1): 495–523.

———. 1996. 'Speechless Emissaries: Refugees, Humanitarianism, and Dehistoricization.' *Cultural Anthropology* 11(3): 377–404.

———. 2015. *The Need to Help: The Domestic Arts of International Humanitarianism*. Durham: Duke University Press.

Mbembe, Achille. 2003. 'Necropolitics.' *Public Culture* 15(1): 11–40.

———. 2016. 'Decolonizing the University: New Directions.' *Arts and Humanities in Higher Education* 15(1): 29–45.

McKeown, Adam. 2008. *Melancholy Order: Asian Migration and the Globalization of Borders*. New York: Columbia University Press.

Mehta, Uday Singh. 1999. *Liberalism and Empire: India in British Liberal Thought*. Oxford: Oxford University Press.

Meret, Susi, and Waldemar Diener. 2019. 'We Are Still Here and Staying! Refugee-Led Mobilizations and Their Struggles for Rights in Germany.' In Siim, B., Krasteva, A., and Saarinen, A. (eds.) *Citizens' Activism and Solidarity Movements*. Cham, Switzerland: Palgrave Macmillan.

Mezzadra, Sandro. 2006. 'Citizen and Subject: A Postcolonial Constitution for the European Union.' *Situations* 1(2): 31–42.

———. 2020. 'Abolitionist Vistas of the Human: Border Struggles, Migration and Freedom of Movement.' *Citizenship Studies* 24(4): 424–440.

Mezzadra, Sandro, and Brett Neilson. 2013. *Borders as Method, or, the Multiplication of Labor.* Durham: Duke University Press.

Mignolo, Walter. 2011. *The Darker Side of Western Modernity: Global Futures, Decolonial Options.* Durham: Duke University Press.

Mitchell, Timothy. [1999] 2006. 'Society, Economy, and the State Effect.' In Sharma, A., and Gupta, A. (eds.) *The Anthropology of the State: A Reader.* Malden, MA and Oxford: Blackwell: 169–186.

Mohanty, Chandra Talpade. 2003. *Feminism Without Borders: Decolonizing Theory, Practicing Solidarity.* Durham and London: Duke University Press.

Monsutti, Alessandro. 2013. 'Anthropologizing Afghanistan: Colonial and Postcolonial Encounters.' *Annual Review of Anthropology* 42: 269–285.

Mosse, George L. 1985. *Nationalism and Sexuality Respectability and Abnormal Sexuality in Modern Europe.* New York: Howard Fertig.

Mudu, Pierpaolo, and Sutapa Chattopadhyay (eds.). 2017. *Migration, Squatting and Radical Autonomy.* London and New York: Routledge.

Naegler, Laura. 2012. *Gentrification and Resistance: Cultural Criminology, Control and the Commodification of Urban Protest in Hamburg.* Berlin: Lit-Verlag.

Nakache, Delphine, and Jessica Losier. 2017. 'The European Union Immigration Agreement with Libya: Out of Sight, Out of Mind?' *E-International Relations.* Online.

Neufert, Birgit. 2014. 'Church Asylum.' *Forced Migration Review* 48: 36–38.

New Keywords Collective. 2016. 'Europe/Crisis: New Keywords of "the Crisis" in and of "Europe".' *Near Futures Online.*

Nigg, Heinz. 2014. 'Sans-Papiers on Their March for Freedom 2014: How Refugees and Undocumented Migrants Challenge Fortress Europe.' *Interface: A Journal on Social Movements* 7(1): 263–288.

Nsoh, Christopher Ndikum. 2008. *The European Union Internal Exclusion and Extra-Territorialisation of Asylum Seekers and Migrants into Camps: Case Studies, Ukraine, Libya and Germany.* PhD Thesis. Freie Universität Berlin.

Nyers, Peter. 2010. 'Abject Cosmopolitanism: The Politics of Protection in the Anti-Deportation Movement.' In De Genova, N., and Peutz, N. (eds.) *The Deportation Regime: Sovereignty, Space and the Freedom of Movement.* Durham, NC: Duke University Press: 413–441.

Odugbesan, Abimbola, and Helge Schwiertz. 2018. '"We Are Here to Stay": Refugee Struggles in Germany Between Unity and Division.' In Rosenberger, S., Stern, V., and Merhaut, N. (eds.) *Protest Movements in Asylum and Deportation.* Cham, Switzerland: Springer Open.

Olusoga, David, and Casper Erichsen. 2010. *The Kaiser's Holocaust: Germany's Forgotten Genocide and the Colonial Roots of Nazism.* London: Faber & Faber.

Ortner, Sherry. B. 2005. 'Subjectivity and Cultural Critique.' *Anthropological Theory* 5(1): 31–52.

Pantazakos, Themistoklis. 2020. 'Erdogan e l'ipocrisia greca.' *DinamoPress.* Online.

Papadopoulos, Apostolos. 2007. 'Migration and Human Security in the Balkans (Editorial).' *Migration Letters* 4(2): 95–100.

Papadopoulos, Dimitrios, Niamh Stephenson, and Vassilis Tsianos. 2008. *Escape Routes: Control and Subversion in the Twenty-First Century.* London and Ann Arbor: Pluto Press.

Picozza, Fiorenza. 2017a. '"Dubliners": Unthinking Displacement, Illegality, and Refugeeness Within Europe's Geographies of Asylum.' In De Genova, N. (ed.) *The Borders of 'Europe': Autonomy of Migration, Tactics of Bordering.* Durham, NC: Duke University Press: 233–253.

———. 2017b. 'Dublin on the Move: Transit and Mobility Across Europe's Geographies of Asylum.' *Movements. Journal for Critical Migration and Border Regime Studies* 3(1): 71–88.

———. 2020. 'Fragilidad, blanquitud y libertad: pensar la pandemia a través de las migraciones ilegalizadas.' *Contranarrativas.* Online.

Pierre, Jemima. 2013. 'Race in Africa Today: A Commentary.' *Cultural Anthropology* 28(3): 547–551.

Post, D., and A. Niemann. 2007. 'The Europeanisation of German Asylum Policy and the "Germanisation" of European Asylum Policy: The Case of the "Safe Third Country" Concept.' Paper prepared for conference of the European Union Studies Association (EUSA), Montréal, May 2007.

Preciado, Paul. 2020. 'Learning from the Virus.' *Artforum.* Online.

Quijano, Anibal. 2000. 'Coloniality of Power, Eurocentrism, and Latin America.' *Nepantla: Views from the South* 1(3): 533–579.

Rankin, Melinda. 2019. 'The "Responsibility to Prosecute" Core International Crimes? The Case of German Universal Jurisdiction and the Syrian Government.' *Global Responsibility to Protect* II(4): 394–410.

Reath, Anne. 2004. 'Language Analysis in the Context of the Asylum Process: Procedures, Validity, and Consequences.' *Language Assessment Quarterly* 1(4): 209–233.

Reinisch, Jessica. 2015. '"Forever Temporary": Migrants in Calais, Then and Now.' *Political Quarterly* 86(4): 515–522.

Riedner, Lisa, Soledad Álvarez-Velasco, Nicholas De Genova, Martina Tazzioli, and Huub van Baar. 2016. 'Mobility.' In *New Keywords Collective. Europe/Crisis: New Keywords of "the Crisis" in and of "Europe".* Near Futures Online.

Riewe, Nina. 2017. 'Dwelling—Living—Waiting: Transformations of a Refugee Reception Camp in Germany.' *Metropolitics.* Online.

Rigo, Enrica. 2005. 'Citizenship at Europe's Borders: Some Reflections on the Post-Colonial Condition of Europe in the Context of EU Enlargement.' *Citizenship Studies* 9(1): 3–22.

Rivera Cusicanqui, Silvia. 2020. *Ch'ixinakax utxiwa: On Practices and Discourses of Decolonisation.* Cambridge, UK and Medfor, MA: Polity Press.

Roy, Sara. 2007. *Failing Peace: Gaza and the Palestinian-Israeli Conflict.* London and Ann Arbor, MI: Pluto Press.

Rubio Bertran, Pat. 2020. 'For Refugees at Sea, Covid-19 Is Another Border to Safety and Asylum.' *Refugee Rights Europe*. Online.

Santer, Kiri, and Vera Wriedt. 2017. '(De-)Constructing Borders. Contestations In and Around the Balkan Corridor in 2015/16.' *Movements. Journal for Critical Migration and Border Regime Studies* 3(1).

Sauer, Pieter J. J., Alf Nicholson, and David Neubauer. 2015. 'Age Determination in Asylum Seekers: Physicians Should Not Be Implicated.' *European Journal of Pediatrics* 175: 299–303.

Sayad, Abdelmalek. 2004. *The Suffering of the Immigrant*. Cambridge, UK and Malden, MA: Polity Press.

Scarvaglieri, C., A. Redder, R. Pappenhagen, and B. Brehmer. 2013. 'Capturing Diversity: Linguistic Land and Soundscaping in Urban Areas.' In Duarte, J., and Gogolin, I. (eds.) *Linguistic Superdiversity in Urban Areas: Research approaches*. Hamburg Studies on Linguistic Diversity 2: 45–74.

Scheel, Stephan. 2013. 'Studying Embodied Encounters: Autonomy of Migration Beyond Its Romanticization.' *Postcolonial Studies* 16(3): 279–288.

Schiffauer, Werner. 2008. 'Suspect Subjects: Muslim Migrants and Security Agencies in Germany.' In Eckert, J. M. (eds.) *The Social Life of Anti-Terrorism Laws: The War on Terror and the Classifications of the "Dangerous Other"*. Bielefeld: Transcript Verlag.

Schilling, Britta. 2015. 'German Postcolonialism in Four Dimensions: A Historical Perspective.' *Postcolonial Studies* 18(4): 427–439.

Schlembach, Raphael. 2010. 'Towards a Critique of Anti-German "Communism".' *Interface: A Journal For and About Social Movements* 2(2): 199–219.

Schmidt, Garbi. 2017. 'Going Beyond Methodological Presentism: Examples from a Copenhagen Neighbourhood 1885–2010.' *Immigrants & Minorities* 35(1): 40–58.

Schulz, Kathryn. 2016. 'The Perilous Lure of the Underground Railroad.' *The New Yorker*. Online.

Schuster, Liza. 2011. 'Dublin II and Eurodac: Examining the (Un)intended(?) Consequences.' *Gender, Place & Culture: A Journal of Feminist Geography* 18(3): 401–416.

Schwarz, Inga. 2016. 'Racializing Freedom of Movement in Europe. Experiences of Racial Profiling at European Borders and Beyond.' *Movements. Journal for Critical Migration and Border Regime Studies* 2(1).

Scott, James C. 1998. *Seeing Like a State: How Certain Schemes to Improve the Human Condition Have Failed*. New Haven and London: Yale University Press.

Scott, Joan. W. 2007. 'History-Writing as Critique.' In Jenkins, K., Morgan, S., and Munslow, A. (eds.) *Manifestos for History*. London: Routledge: 19–38.

Šeruga, Kaja. 2018. 'Timeline of the Refugee and Migrant Crisis 2015–2016.' In Žagar, I. Ž., Kogovšek Šalamon, N., and Lukšič Hacin, M. (eds.) *The Disaster of European Refugee Policy: Perspectives from the "Balkan Route"*. Newcastle upon Tyne: Cambridge Scholars Publishing.

Sontag, Susan. 2003. *Regarding the Pain of Others*. New York: Picador.

Spathopoulou, Aila. 2016. 'The Ferry as a Mobile Hotspot: Migrants at the Uneasy Borderlands of Greece.' *Society+Space*. Online.

Spivak, Gayatri Chakravorty. 1988. 'Can the Subaltern Speak?' In Grossberg, L., and Nelson, C. (eds.) *Marxism and the Interpretation of Culture*. Urbana: University of Illinois: 271–313.

Stanley, Flavia. 2015. *On Belonging, Difference and Whiteness: Italy's Problem with Immigration*. PhD Thesis. University of Massachussetts, Amherst.

Steiger, Tina. 2016. 'Beyond Squatting: An Autonomous Culture Center for Refugees in Copenhagen.' In Mudu, P., and Chattopadhyay, S. (eds.) *Migration, Squatting and Radical Autonomy*. London and New York: Routledge: 255–230.

Stierl, Maurice. 2015. 'The WachTheMed Alarm Phone. A Disobedient Border-Intervention.' *Movements. Journal for Critical Migration and Border Regime Studies* 1(2).

Tanriverdi, Abdullah. 2020. 'Refugees Share Ordeal of Torture by Greek Border Forces.' *TRT World*. Online.

Taparata, Evan, and Kuang Keng Kuek Ser. 2016. 'During WWII, European Refugees Fled to Syria.' *Pri.org*. Online.

Tazzioli, Martina. 2015a. 'Migrants' Uneven Geographies and Counter-Mapping at the Limits of Representation.' *Movements. Journal for Critical Migration and Border Regime Studies* 1(2).

———. 2015b. 'Border Interruptions and Spatial Disobediences Beyond the Scene of the Political.' *Darkmatter Journal: Border Struggles* 12.

———. 2016. 'Border Displacements. Challenging the Politics of Rescue Between Mare Nostrum and Triton.' *Migration Studies* 4(1): 1–19.

———. 2017. 'Containment Through Mobility: Migrants' Spatial Disobediences and the Reshaping of Control Through the Hotspot System.' *Journal of Ethnic and Migration Studies* 1–16.

———. 2018a. 'Book Review: Alexander Betts and Paul Collier, Refuge: Transforming a Broken Refugee System.' *Sociology* 52(3): 632–635.

———. 2018b. 'Crimes of Solidarity. Migration and Containment Through Rescue.' *Radical Philosophy* 2.01. Online.

———. 2018c. 'Between Visible and Undetectable Violence.' *Radical Philosophy* 2.02. Online.

Tazzioli, Martina, and William Walters. 2019. 'Migration, Solidarity and the Limits of Europe.' *Global Discourse* 9(1): 175–190.

Thiel, Markus. 2017. *European Civil Society and Human Rights Advocacy*. Philadelphia: University of Pennsylvania Press.

Translators Without Borders. 2017. 'Putting Language on the Map in the European Refugee Response.' *Translators Without Borders*. Online.

Triulzi, Alessandro. 2006. 'Displacing the Colonial Event.' *Interventions* 8(3): 430–443.

Trouillot, Michel-Rolph. 1995. *Silencing the Past: Power and the Production of History*. Boston, MA: Beacon Press.

Tsianos, Vassilis, Sabine Hess, and Serhat Karakayali. 2009. 'Transnational Migration Theory and Method of an Ethnographic Analysis of Border Regimes.' Working Paper 55, Sussex Centre for Migration Research.

Tuck, Eve, and K. Wayne Yang. 2012. 'Decolonization Is Not a Metaphor.' *Decolonization: Indigeneity, Education & Society* 1(1): 1–40.

Tuitt, Patricia. 2013. 'The Modern Refugee in the Post-Modern Europe.' In Juss, S. S. (ed.) *The Ashgate Research Companion to Migration Law, Theory and Policy.* Farnham, UK: Ashgate: 25–42.

UNHCR. 2018. 'Country of Origin Information on the Situation in the Gaza Strip, Including on Restrictions on Exit and Return.' *Refworld.* Online.

United Nations Economic Commission for Europe. 2006. 'Conference of European Statisticians. Recommendations for the 2010 Censuses of Population and Housing.' Online.

Ünsal, Nadiye. 2015. 'Challenging 'Refugees' and 'Supporters': Intersectional Power Structures in the Refugee Movement in Berlin.' *Movements. Journal for Critical Migration and Border Regime Studies* 1(2).

Vacchiano, Francesco. 2011. 'Discipline della Scarsità e del Sospetto: Rifugiati e Accoglienza nel Regime di Frontiera.' *Lares* 77(1): 181–198.

Vickers, Tom. 2012. 'Developing an Independent Anti-Racist Model for Asylum Rights Organizing in England.' *Journal of Ethnic and Racial Studies* 37(8): 427–1447.

Volpp, Leti. 2018. 'Refugees Welcome?' *Berkeley La Raza Law Journal* 28(4): 71–102.

von Oppen, Karoline. 2006. 'Imagining the Balkans, Imagining Germany: Intellectual Journeys to Former Yugoslavia in the 1990s.' *The German Quarterly* 79(2): 192–210.

Wagstyl, Stefan. 2016. 'Germany Plans 5-Year Benefit Ban for Jobless Migrants.' *Financial Times.* Online.

Walia, Harsha. 2013. *Undoing Border Imperialism*, Vol. 6. Oakland, CA: AK Press.

Walters, William. 2002. 'Deportation, Expulsion and the International Police of Aliens.' *Citizenship Studies* 6(3): 265–292.

———. 2010. 'Foucault and Frontiers: Notes on the Birth of the Humanitarian Border.' In Bröckling, U., Krasmann, S., and Lemke, T. (eds.) *Governmentality: Current Issues and Future Challenges.* London: Routledge: 138–164.

———. 2015. 'Reflections on Migration and Governmentality.' *Movements: Journal for Critical Migration and Border Studies* 1(1): 1–30.

Wari, Shahd. 2015. *Palestinian Berlin: Perception and Use of Public Space.* Zürich: Lit.

Webber, Frances. 2017. 'Europe's Unknown War.' *Race & Class* 9(1): 36–53.

Weizman, Eyal. 2007. *Hollow Land: Israel's Architecture of Occupation.* London and New York: Verso.

Wekker, Gloria. 2016. *White Innocence: Paradoxes of Colonialism and Race.* Durham, NC: Duke University Press.

Welch, Michael, and Liza Schuster. 2005. 'Detention of Asylum Seekers in the US, UK, France, Germany, and Italy: A Critical View of the Globalizing Culture of Control.' *Criminal Justice* 5(4): 331–355.

Welcome to Europe Network. 2010. 'From Abolitionism to Freedom of Movement? History and Visions of Antiracist Struggles.' Paper presented at the conference *Noborder Lasts Forever.*

White, Allen. 1999. 'Refugees, Asylum Seekers and Human Geography. Some Theoretical Perspectives.' *Critical Geography Forum Online.*

Whyte, Zachary. 2015. 'In Doubt: Documents as Fetishes in the Danish Asylum System.' In Berti, D., Good A., and Tarabout, G. (eds.) *Of Doubt and Proof: Ritual and Legal Practices of Judgment.* Farnham and Burlington: Ashgate.

Williams, Raymond. 1977. *Marxism and Literature.* Oxford and New York: Oxford University Press.

Wischmann, Anke. 2018. 'The Absence of "Race" in German Discourses on *Bildung*. Rethinking *Bildung* with Critical Race Theory.' *Race Ethnicity and Education* 21(4): 471–485.

Wittgenstein, Ludwig. 1958. *Philosophical Investigations.* Oxford: Basil Blackwell.

Wolfe, Patrick. 2016. *Traces of History: Elementary Structures of Race.* London and New York: Verso.

Wynter, Sylvia. 2003. 'Unsettling the Coloniality of Being/Power/Truth/Freedom: Towards the Human, After Man, Its Overrepresentation. An Argument.' *CR: The New Centennial Review* 3(3): 257–337.

Yarris, Kristin, and Hilde Castañeda. 2015. 'Discourses of Displacement and Deservingness: Interrogating Distinctions Between "Economic" and "Forced" Migration.' *International Migration* 53(3): 64–69.

Yildiz, Can, and Nicholas De Genova. 2017. 'Un/Free Mobility: Roma Migrants in the European Union.' *Social Identities* 24(4): 425–441.

Zeveleva, Olga. 2017. 'Biopolitics, Borders, and Refugee Camps: Exercising Sovereign Power Over Nonmembers of the State.' *Nationalities Papers* 45(1): 41–60.

Index

About the Author

Fiorenza Picozza is a researcher and activist who has been involved in refugee solidarity for over a decade. She has an interdisciplinary background, holding a PhD in Geography from King's College London (2019), an MA in Migration and Diaspora Studies from SOAS University of London (2014), and a BA in Philosophy from the University of Rome La Sapienza (2009). Her research interests concern borders, asylum, migration, race, coloniality, humanitarianism, and solidarity. Currently, she is a postdoctoral fellow at the Institute of Geography of the UNAM in Mexico City, where she is working on a project on asylum, racialization and humanitarian borders in Mexico. She is the author of the chapter 'Dubliners: Unthinking Displacement, Illegality, and Refugeeness within Europe's Geographies of Asylum', published in *The Borders of 'Europe': Autonomy of Migration, Tactics of Bordering*, edited by Nicholas De Genova (2017), and of the article 'Dublin on the Move: Transit and Mobility across Europe's Geographies of Asylum', published in *movements. Journal for Critical Migration and Border Regime Studies* (2017). She has also coauthored the paper 'Europe/Crisis: New Keywords of "the Crisis" in and of "Europe"' together with the New Keywords Collective, published on the online journal *Near Features* (2016).

CPSIA information can be obtained
at www.ICGtesting.com
Printed in the USA
LVHW101915290822
726885LV00003B/130